Charles Ives
Reconsidered

MUSIC IN AMERICAN LIFE

Charles Ives
Reconsidered

GAYLE SHERWOOD MAGEE

UNIVERSITY OF ILLINOIS PRESS

Urbana, Chicago, and Springfield

Frontispiece: Perhaps the most famous photo
of Charles Ives. Taken by *Life* photographer
Eugene Smith, ca. 1945. Courtesy Yale University
Irving S. Gilmore Music Library. © The Heirs of
W. Eugene Smith, courtesy of Black Star Inc.

The Library of Congress cataloged the cloth edition as follows:
Magee, Gayle Sherwood, 1965–
Charles Ives reconsidered / Gayle Sherwood Magee.
p.   cm. — (Music in American life)
Includes bibliographical references (p.   ) and index.
ISBN 978-0-252-03326-1 (cloth : alk. paper)
1. Ives, Charles, 1874-1954—Criticism and interpretation.
I. Title.
ML410.I94M34   2008
780.92—dc22   2007048091

PAPERBACK ISBN 978-0-252-07776-0

For Jeff,
with love and gratitude

"The fabric of existence weaves itself whole."

—Charles Ives

Contents

Acknowledgments

The writing and production of this book was supported by a Summer Fellowship Grant from the National Endowment for the Humanities; a grant from the Sinfonia Foundation for American Music; a summer grant from the University Research and Travel Fund from The University of Toledo; a publication subvention from the Otto Kinkeldey Publication Endowment fund of the American Musicological Society; a Special Funds Grant from the College of Fine and Applied Arts at the University of Illinois, Urbana–Champaign; and a Research Council Grant from the University of Illinois, Urbana–Champaign.

My heartfelt thanks go to the exceptional staff at the Irving S. Gilmore Music Library, Yale University, many of whom have assisted me since 1989 with unmatched professionalism, patient efficiency, and good humor. I am particularly indebted to the practical support of Kendall Crilly, Suzanne Eggleston Lovejoy, Karl Schrom, and Richard Boursy. Likewise, I am grateful to many individuals at the University of Illinois Press for editorial, production, and marketing assistance, including Judith McCulloh, Jennifer Clark, Michael Roux, and Joseph Peeples. My thanks as well to Terri Hudoba for a thorough copyediting of the manuscript.

Thanks to the anonymous reviewers who provided thoughtful and constructive feedback on the proposal. I am particularly grateful to Denise Von Glahn and Michael Hicks who reviewed the manuscript prior to publication, and whose informed critiques made this a better book than it might have been.

To those in both the Ives and the wider scholarly communities who have supported my work over the years I am very grateful: Geoffrey Block, Michael

Broyles, J. Peter Burkholder, Susan Cook, Kara Gardner, Felicia Miyakawa, Robert Morgan, David Nicholls, Thomas Owens, Vivian Perlis, and Judith Tick. I am thankful for the wisdom, guidance, kindness, generosity, and friendship of H. Wiley Hitchcock, who passed away on the morning that I completed reviewing the copyedited manuscript.

Special thanks go to three accomplished scholars who share a rare gift for discussing, debating, and encouraging new ideas in a truly collaborative and open environment. Clayton Henderson and Timothy Johnson each provided much needed opportunities to socialize this research through invited lectures in 2004–5 at St. Mary's College and the University of Buffalo. Jonathan Elkus, whose own painstaking and groundbreaking research on the Second Symphony inspired me to revisit my earlier ideas on the work, provided an astonishingly meticulous eleventh-hour review of the completed manuscript. I am indebted to him for his intellectual generosity, and he remains a model for scholarly collegiality.

I am grateful to the outstanding members of the faculty of the Musicology Division at the University of Illinois, Urbana–Champaign who have demonstrated that collegial relations, scholarly productivity at the highest level, and personal friendship need not be mutually exclusive. Sincere thanks to the many talented graduate students at the University of Illinois with whom I have had the great fortune to work. I am particularly grateful to L. Eduardo Herrera for his careful reading of this manuscript; and to my research assistants Ryan Ross and Aaron Ziegel, who invested both intellectual and practical energy during the completion of this project. Many thanks to the students in the two Ives seminars that I have been fortunate to teach, a decade apart: at the University of Michigan in spring 1996, and at the University of Illinois in fall 2005. Both groups congenially challenged my ideas and writings while inspiring my imagination and creativity.

No book is possible without the extensive personal support of a network of family and friends. Naomi André, Amy Beal, Laura Gray, Jacqueline Layng, Melinda Reichelt, Jennifer Stuart, and Marianne Williams Tobias, along with many others, have all sustained me and my work through good times and otherwise. Many thanks go to my two families, the Sherwoods and the Magees, who have provided me with encouragement and practical assistance during the research and writing of this work. I owe my understanding of much of Ives's source music to my father, Douglas Sherwood, whose powerful baritone voice introduced me to many of the hymn tunes that I later heard in Ives's compositions. He passed away while this book was in production, and I will miss the opportunity to engage in yet another spirited debate about Ives's music.

Finally, this book could not have been completed without the relentless encouragement, exceptional writing and editing skills, and unmatched generosity—intellectual, musical, and personal—of Jeffrey Magee. To paraphrase Ives, what my husband has done for this book I can't put into writing—not because he won't let me, but because to do so would fill any number of additional volumes. Along with our children, Ellen and Miles, he has convinced me that Ives was right: the fabric of existence does weave itself whole. He has earned the dedication of this book with my gratitude and love.

Charles Ives
Reconsidered

Introduction

Even before his death in 1954, Charles Ives commanded an unusual, almost cultlike following. Celebrated since the late 1920s as a great American innovator, Ives has been credited with anticipating, if not inventing, most of the experimental techniques of twentieth-century music well in advance of his European and American colleagues. The unique circumstances of Ives's career spawned a pre- and posthumous reputation that approaches beatification, and inspired an astonishingly loyal following among scholars, performers, and listeners alike. But is Ives's story more hagiography than fact?

That story reads something like this.[1] Born in Danbury, Connecticut, in 1874, Ives received a brilliant and unconventional education from his father, George Ives, an amateur bandleader and musical visionary. Charles proceeded to Yale where his forward-looking compositions outstripped the limited vision of his instructor, Horatio Parker, an academician and one of the leading conservative composers. But after Yale, Ives realized that his compositions were too far ahead of their time to appeal to his narrow-minded contemporaries or to be published by conservative musical presses. So, in his own words, he "gave up music" and chose to work in insurance by day while continuing to write daring music in his spare time. After more than a decade of this double life, Ives had a heart attack in 1918 that ended his compositional career. From then until the end of his life, Ives cleaned up his works and introduced them to and through a growing group of young American and European American modernists such as Henry Cowell, Bernard Herrmann, and Nicolas Slonimsky. With their support, Ives emerged from his self-imposed but necessary exile, gaining wider admiration that peaked with the awarding of the Pulitzer Prize in 1947 for his Third Symphony. Having proven the value of his work decades after it was first conceived, Ives's reputation as the ancestor of modern American music was secured, and his years of isolation and neglect vindicated.

This version of Ives's life, with its trajectory of rejection, struggle, acceptance, and redemption, remains incredibly attractive, perhaps especially to those of us who feel embattled on behalf of modern American music. The problem with this story is that, as with all narratives, it is only partially true. Conflicting information has been omitted or downplayed, and other perspectives overemphasized in the process. Gaps—of which there are many—have been filled in using problematic evidence and in keeping with the advocacy role that shapes most scholarship and biography. Frank Rossiter sounded a warning against the seductive pull of the "Ives Legend" in 1975, particularly the tendency to emphasize Ives's isolation, his American (and specifically New England) pedigree, the lack of recognition of his works during his life, and the thoroughly original and experimental nature of his music that predated similar works by European composers.[2] Indeed, Rossiter's admonition proved a significant early step in a slow but steady stream of revisions to these tropes.

Beginning in the mid-1970s, several commentators redefined Ives's connections to the European tradition, through parallels with contemporaries like Varèse and Mahler, and through his use of European compositions as sources and models.[3] Extending this approach resulted in a new appreciation of Ives's training at Yale under Parker as well as his conservative works and compositional style.[4] Rossiter and later scholars reassessed the influence of contemporary society, particularly intellectual and musical trends, on his compositions and prose writings.[5] Recently, the medical nature of Ives's "heart attack" in 1918 has been called into question.[6]

As the details of the myth have changed, however, its broad outlines have been maintained. George Ives is still regarded as a remarkably insightful musician whose deep knowledge of the European repertoire shaped his son's compositions. Charles Ives's decision to turn his back on his composing career in 1902, and to pursue a career in business, is still seen as a mark of integrity, an endorsement of his already experimental bent, and a criticism of the limitations of the existing musical establishment of composers, critics, and publishers. Ives's dedication to his music, isolation from other musicians, and triumphant reemergence in the 1920s and 1930s continues to strike a chord with American composers and musicians more than a century after his first major works were composed.[7]

In the midst of these fundamental reconsiderations, a controversy over the chronology of Ives's works has opened up the most far-reaching challenge to the legend. The most highly publicized challenge to the Ives myth began with an article that did not embrace a blatant, "pro-Ives" bias of advocacy—in this sense, the first significant publication of its type in a half-century, since the last dismissively negative reviews of Ives's work appeared in the 1930s. In his article "Charles Ives: Some Questions of Veracity," published in the *Journal of the American Musicological Society* in 1987, Maynard Solomon suggested that Ives could have falsified the dates of his compositions to appear more modern than he really was. This was easily done because of the delay between the composition of those works, and their introduction to a larger audience. Using source studies that demonstrate a disparity between the accepted dates of Ives's compositions and conflicting marginalia, as well as eyewitness testimony by Elliott Carter to Ives's later revisions, Solomon suggested that Ives could be guilty of "a systematic pattern of falsification."[8] In this scenario, Ives could have incorporated later ideas into works that were dated much earlier, thus creating the illusion that he was a greater innovator than was really the case.

Solomon's proposal threw into question the very core of the myth. Ives's life and works—in its original incarnation—has become a powerful symbol of American ingenuity and independence. Despite immediate responses from scholars within the Ives community—most notably J. Peter Burkholder, J. Philip Lambert, and Carol Baron—the questioning of Ives's integrity alongside his newly doubtable experimental compositional style filtered into the mainstream media on an unprecedented scale, especially for an American modernist composer who had died more than three decades earlier. Articles in the *New York Times* as well as mention in the *Atlantic Monthly* brought what had been an academic issue into the public arena.[9] The coverage underscored that a threat to our view of Ives was, in a sense, a threat to the foundation of American music in the twentieth century.

The problem with suggesting that Charles Ives falsified his musical scores to appear more sophisticated than he really was depends on two assumptions: that Ives carefully placed "incriminating evidence" such as return addresses and dates on his sources, and that he revised his scores. There are two serious problems with the first assumption. The whole scenario implies that Ives anticipated that his score marginalia would be carefully interpreted and analyzed by musicologists who would look at his manuscripts long after he was dead. In itself, this is rather hard to believe. But more incongruous is the hypothesis that Ives had knowledge of the processes and techniques of historical musicology. By leaving an apparently false address reference, Ives would have had to know that a musicologist would meticulously reconstruct when Ives had lived at each address using the Trow's directory (a precursor to the modern phone book) and Ives's unpublished writings such as letters and memoirs.

Did Ives really think like a musicologist, anticipating their research techniques? The prospect places far too much emphasis on the posthumous observers of Ives's archives. To see Ives clearly, we must take ourselves out of the picture as much as possible, at least in theory. If, as seems likely, Ives did not enter these marginalia for the sake of later analysts, what is their purpose? As I have suggested elsewhere, Ives's marginalia are scattered all over his manuscripts in a chaotic visual potpourri, creating a hodgepodge of associations and memories that mirror the aural collages in his music.[10] In effect, most of Ives's marginalia represent a complex network of memories that informed and shaped the musical compositions they surround.

Ultimately, Solomon's first hypothesis that Ives may have intentionally redated his works in order to mislead us does not hold up. However, Solomon's second suggestion—that Ives revised his manuscripts and incorporated later ideas into earlier compositions—remains to be fully considered. And because of Carter's eyewitness testimony and all that it implies, a further reassessment of the extent of Ives's compositional and revisional activities in the 1920s and later is necessary. This study offers the first step in that process while recontextualizing Ives's life and work.

In itself Solomon's questioning what we know about Ives, and how we know it, has been remarkably useful. It also represents part of a larger coming-of-age in Ives scholarship: a shedding of the previous, almost two-dimensional view of Ives as an independent experimenter that has hindered a clearer understanding of his identity and significance.[11] Likewise, Solomon's questioning of the sources and interpretation of the original chronology of Ives's work—which had been essentially accepted by those within the Ives community—represents a crucial step in the transformation of the Ives Legend.

As a result of Solomon's challenge, I have suggested new dates and date ranges for the extant manuscript sources of Ives's compositions based on extensive paper-type and handwriting analysis. In collaboration with J. Peter Burkholder and James B. Sinclair, executive editor of the Charles Ives Society and compiler of *A Descriptive Catalogue of the Works of Charles E. Ives,* these source dates have been combined with other documentation to produce a new chronology of Ives's works.[12]

Wherever possible, I have used those dates that are well established primarily through paper dates, and secondarily through other supporting evidence—connections to Ives's employment, his assignments for Horatio Parker's classes at Yale, publications of texts and scores, documented performances, eyewitness testimony, mentions in correspondence, for example—since the results of handwriting analysis will always be more subjective and impossible to prove. Even given these limits, it is possible to trace a portrait of Ives's music that is very different from previous evaluations, yet remains thorough.

Thus, this study is the first full-length reconsideration of Ives's life and work using the completed new chronology, and offers a new perspective. In sum, this book can be seen as a reconsideration of the foundation of Ives scholarship, or what Frank Rossiter termed the Ives Legend, which has emphasized Ives's musical experimentation, precedence over European contemporaries, isolation, and American identity above all else.[13] In conjunction with rethinking the dates, this book focuses on redefining Ives's relationship to his American origins, particularly the malleable meaning of his Euro-American education, from his earliest works through evaluations of his music through the end of the twentieth century. Later chapters discuss his activities and interactions with other musicians throughout his life, including his considerable and successful efforts later in life to establish himself as the pioneer of American modernism, and the impact of this incomplete image on musicians and audiences to the present.

Along the way, Ives's compositional activities in the 1920s and beyond—when he may have been revising earlier works, and composing new ones, in a self-consciously modernist vein—are scrutinized. It may be impossible to fully resolve the issue of exactly when and why Ives revised some works. However, I have suggested both why Ives rewrote parts of works such as the Fourth Symphony (in chapter 6) and the Second Symphony (in chapter 3 and the epilogue), and why these revisions are still problematic given the standard narrative of Ives's biography. What emerges from this study is a clearer sense of Ives as a composer, not just a reviser, during the latter decades of his life—that is, from 1918 into at least the 1930s. This shift requires acknowledging that Ives continued to grow and change as a composer well after 1918, during a time when he was exposed to other musical influences. If we accept this more fluid understanding of his work and output, and that many of Ives's works legitimately date from a span of several decades, then his later compositional activities can be seen as genuinely creative, rather than intentionally deceptive.

Discussions of Ives's works are included as appropriate, with a desire to communicate to nonspecialist readers as well as trained musicians. There has been no attempt at comprehensiveness. I have engaged with the work of other scholars whenever possible, although detailed responses are embedded in endnotes in order to keep the narrative uncluttered.

In this book, I have expressed long-developing ideas, interpretations, and opinions that may seem unconventional, perhaps heretical, to some of Ives's advocates. I ask such readers to keep the same ideal in mind that is apparent in Ives's own life, writings, and compositions: the ideal to value all points of view equally and on their own terms even, or perhaps especially, in the face of criticism and dissent. It is an ideal with which we all struggle—and Ives himself struggled, as will be apparent in this book—but it is an ideal that remains crucial for valid scholarly discourse. As Ives wrote in a different context, this work aims to spark productive dialogue among interested parties in the sincere desire to "converse, discuss, argue, . . . fight, shake hands, shut up—and walk up the mountain side to view the firmament!"[14]

1

The Discovery

In the sweet by and by,
We shall meet on that beautiful shore.
—from "In the Sweet By and By"

Outside, the thick August air clung to the thousands of visitors crowding the Chicago Midway. Excited chatter revolved around the newly displayed inventions, among them elevators, moving sidewalks, gas engines, and Edison's Kinetograph, a prototype of the "talkie." The din of barkers and brass bands competed with indigenous musical ensembles from around the world. Later, after the sweltering sun had set, the first large-scale use of electric lighting illuminated the Midway and flickered on the placid surface of Lake Michigan. The Columbian Exposition overwhelmed every sense, leaving awestruck fairgoers dazzled and exhausted. As one magazine described it, the Chicago World's Fair overflowed with "achievements and products of the mind and hand of man such as has never before been presented to mortal vision."[1]

Luminous in the summer sun, the white stucco Choral Hall echoed its sibling buildings within the enclave of the White City. The building's majestic neo-Baroque architecture loomed like a temple over the shore of Lake Michigan. Inside, the air was stuffy, and the folding seats were hard, cool wood. The hushed, respectful audience was eager to show its concert-hall manners in this newly sacred space, dedicated to "only the highest class of music," "to be used by musical talent and connoisseurs of the art rather than by the mass of people."[2] As the ritualized worship of European music unfolded, an ambitious, naive teenager from New England discovered a new world.

Professor Geo. E. Ives

The Columbian Exposition of 1893 entranced millions of Americans from rural areas and small cities like Danbury, Connecticut. By the end of the nineteenth century, Danbury was a New England industrial center known for its paper and hat factories. Family farms that grew everything from tobacco to fruit surrounded its developing commercial district.[3] In its cultural life, Danbury was considered above average. Just three years earlier in 1890, the *New York Herald* described the lively Danbury musical scene in an article entitled "Danbury's Delight is All for Music." At first glance this passage seems a simple portrait of the Danbury community in which Charles Ives grew up, with an appealing profile of his father, George Ives. But a careful reading of the article, and knowledge of nineteenth-century musical values, reveals much about the relationship between music and class in this small New England city, and George's awkward status within it.

Musically and otherwise, Danbury was typical of its time and region. Most music was provided by distinct secular organizations (orchestras, bands, and choruses). Pedagogical institutions such as the School of Music regulated instruction, while individuals (organists, cornetists) provided music for sacred

Exterior of the Choral Hall, Columbian Exposition, Chicago, 1893. From William Henry Jackson, *The White City* (Chicago: White City Art Co., 1894). (Jackson is listed as photographer.)

DANBURY'S DELIGHT IS ALL FOR MUSIC.

In No Town in the State Are More Distinguished Performers and Music Lovers.

CHORUS AND ORCHESTRA.

Concerts by Local Talent that Have Proved Noteworthy Events—Then There Is the Great School of Music—Church Choirs of Particular Merit—Children Taught Singing.

CONNE

POLI

STAMFORD'S PRESIDENT MARRI.

MARK FESSENDEN COMES HONESTLY BY HIS POLITICAL FORMULATION.

purposes. These clear divisions contained inherent social ranks, often determined by gender. Men directed the ensembles; women taught. Orchestras maintained a higher degree of respect and visibility than bands, judging from the emphasis and order of the discussion in the *Herald* report, and its nearly apologetic tone in describing the new brass band in the Virtuoso Club.[4]

Within this circumscribed orbit, George E. Ives maintained an erratic presence. While orchestras led by others had a "great reputation" or were considered "excellent," George was praised for his hard work rather than his results. Even the concession that the Danbury Band is "one of the best in Connecticut" seems qualified and unimpressive compared with the accolades given to the other associations, especially the national status of the school. George's seemingly random teaching activities, his lack of a "handsomely furnished suite" or "a costly suite of rooms," and the haphazard contributions of his students as performers and producers pale in comparison with the celebrated status of Isabel Fayerweather and the school. Indeed, students traveled *to* Danbury to study with Fayerweather; George Ives traveled *away* from Danbury to lead organizations of such little status that their names are not even mentioned. The writer is, in fact, referring to George's ensembles— the Salvation Army band and drum corps that he led—when he writes of "those who delight in noise," and who "make life miserable for those who really love music." The distinction between loving music and delighting in noise reinforces a division based on musical training, ability, and class that was hotly debated in America at this time.

This crucial snapshot of Danbury at the end of the nineteenth century reveals a population, indeed a nation, in transition. The school's emphasis on regimented instruction and a trained faculty, as well as the ranking of orchestras above bands, reflect a tidal change late in the nineteenth century. Until the Civil War, most musical instructors were male and advertised themselves as "Professor" and "Doctor of Music." Danbury maintained this quaint tradition by referring to almost all of the male leaders (including George Ives) as "Professor" regardless of their training and experience. Given the absence of standardized academic institutions, advertising oneself as "Professor" or "Doctor of Music" provided an aura of authority. For example, "dime museums," which featured both variety and freak shows, usually included a lecture by a "Professor" before audiences viewed the show. By the late century, these nonacademic titles had gained notoriety within professional circles. As one prominent musician declared, such titles were "a joke . . . sought for or desired only by the greater or lesser frauds who would fain climb by means of it."[5] Professor George Ives, then, had a token title, one that was quaint, old-fashioned, and potentially embarrassing outside of the narrow world of Danbury.

Taken as a whole, the portrait of George that surfaces from this article demonstrates a man willingly—even aggressively—bucking the prevailing trends of his time and context especially in regard to social and economic status. In his life and work, George seems to have made choices that went against those of his family and immediate community. Descended from a prominent family that proudly dated its American ancestry back to 1638, George's father and brothers were successful businessmen and community leaders.[6] His one sister, Amelia Ives, had married exceedingly well: her husband Lyman Brewster was a Yale-educated lawyer, judge, and politician. George had loved music since his childhood and chose it as a profession, first as a band leader in the Union Army during the Civil War and then as Danbury's most undervalued, poorly remunerated, but nonetheless "indefatigable worker." In keeping with his conspicuously unpretentious lifestyle, he had married appropriately. Molly Parmalee Ives came from a comparatively humble, economically modest background: her acceptance of George's unassuming ambitions made for what was by all accounts a cheerful marriage.

George Ives's musical training and background reflect a midcentury profile. He studied the basic theory and history of music with a German instructor, Charles A. Foepple, in New York City, between 1860 and 1867. As was typical, this individual rather than institutional instruction provided George with a foundational understanding of music history, instrumentation, and theory. George painstakingly copied his notes from the lessons into a few small notebooks, with brief musical examples hand-drawn among the text. The text's formal, rigid language shows that the notes did not record extemporaneous conversation. Rather, George would copy the tedious, dry text into his notebook, and Foepple would explain or answer questions as necessary. As such, George's education from Foepple provided a rudimentary introduction to the topics, but lacked a broad, experiential component in both the subjects and repertoire covered.

George supplemented his visits to New York with a few trips to hear the New York Philharmonic Society Orchestra, which at the time was not a full-time professional orchestra but rather a loosely organized, underrehearsed body of sixty part-time players.[7] The players themselves were not completely reliable, and due to economic necessity might skip a rehearsal in favor of a paying gig. As a result, "a clarinet or oboe part would be played on a violin, or a bassoon part on the cello, etc." New repertoire was not attempted, and audiences were known to talk through performances. Thus, even George's most extensive exposure to the European classical tradition preserved the amateur, flexible, informal, and eclectic attitude toward musical performance prevalent at that time in the United States.

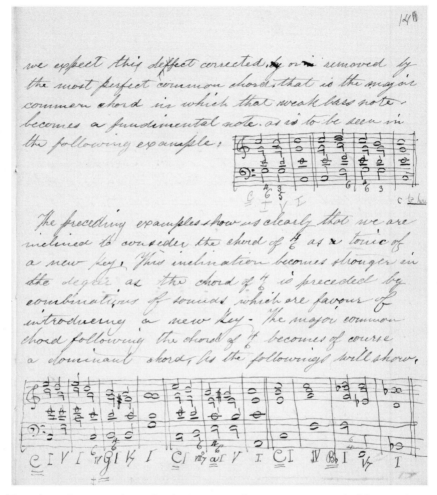

Page from George Ives's copybook. Courtesy Yale University Irving S. Gilmore Music Library.

   Instead of a structured or extensive period of study, the core of George's musical training grew out of leading a Union army band during the Civil War.[8] Here, he balanced experiential learning and instruction. Although there are no records of George studying the cornet, or learning how to teach and conduct a band, these were in fact his main activities during his enlistment. In the years following the Civil War, George pieced together a meager living conducting and arranging for ad hoc amateur bands, many of whose members were recent immigrants streaming to Danbury for factory jobs.[9] He performed as well in potpourri concerts that mixed popular classics with English, Scottish, and Irish folk songs. And George played for minstrel shows, the most popular entertainment of the time. Given the genre's penchant for opera parodies, it is possible that his amateur productions of Italian opera in English borrowed from minstrel tradition, and may have been performed at least partially in blackface.

Through his connection to Danbury's Methodist Church, George occasionally performed at services, but more often directed the hymn singing at outdoor revivals, or camp meetings. What was known as the "Second Great Awakening" (the first having occurred in the early eighteenth century) mobilized Methodists and some progressive Baptist sects across the country during the 1860s and early 1870s.[10] Camp meetings drew large, ethnically and racially diverse crowds primarily from the middle, lower, and working classes. Participants included former slaves and new immigrants. Characterized by a fervent, emotional evangelicalism, the revivals' sermons and hymn texts projected a simple religious, social, and economic formula: that the self-conscious humility of the lowly was rewarded with divine stability and security; that today's deprivations and losses would be surpassed by tomorrow's rewards; and that heaven's riches awaited the earthly pauper.

A typical example is the text of the first and fourth verses of "Just As I Am," written by the British hymn composer Charlotte Elliott in 1835, and sung to the tune "Woodworth," composed by the American William B. Bradbury in 1849. The text's structure makes it ideal for rote and oral musical performances. Each verse begins and ends the same way so that even a novice would be able to join in on the refrain after two or three verses. The first-person narration uses easily pronounceable, mostly one-syllable words. The hymn tune itself is strophic and moves mostly by steps, making it easier to sing. These were important factors in the performance and retention of the tune and text by singers relying on oral transmission, many of whom had limited English comprehension.

While "Just As I Am" had a strophic form, other popular hymn tunes matched a verse that changed text with an easily learned repetitive chorus, as in "In the Sweet By and By" (words by Sanford F. Bennett, music by Joseph P. Webster), which was written in Wisconsin in 1868. The chorus invokes a longing for reunion with lost loved ones—a recurring theme in all types of American songs after the bloodletting of the Civil War. Immigrants responded to the idea of returning to a distant, now unreachable shore. A call-and-response in the chorus, in which each phrase was echoed by another singing group, facilitates dialogue and connection among the hundreds of gathered participants, many of whom were moved to tears by the music alone.

Thus, in George's world, the value of music making lay in its participatory nature, not the authoritative score: in other words, context trumped text. George's music—in its ethnically heterogeneous ensembles, its outdoor and nonspecialized venues, and free blending of genres (popular, classical, and religious)—represents a distinctly midcentury slice of American culture. This lateral mix of what are now regarded as diverse cultural strata—folk, popular, classical, or elite—reflects what historian Lawrence Levine observed in the nineteenth-century American perceptions of both Shakespeare and opera. Throughout the country, average people knew large portions of Shakespeare's plays by heart, and audiences often participated in performances of familiar works like *Hamlet* and *Romeo and Juliet*. Levine attributes Shakespeare's appeal to an interpretation of the plays that "articulated a belief that was central to the pervasive success ethos of the nineteenth century and that confirmed the developing American worldview. . . . [Shakespeare's] plays had meaning

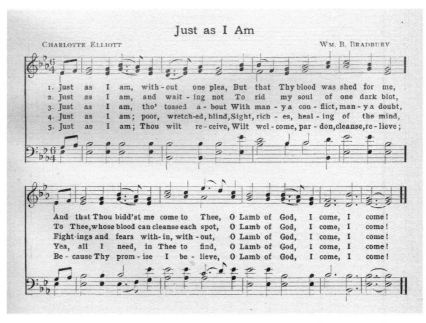

"Just As I Am." Text by Charlotte Elliott, tune (*Woodworth*) by William B. Bradbury. Reprinted from *Heart Songs*, ed. George W. Chadwick and Victor Herbert. Boston: Chapple Publishing Company, 1909.

"In the Sweet By and By." Text by Sanford F. Bennett, tune by Joseph P. Webster. Reprinted from *Heart Songs*, ed. George W. Chadwick and Victor Herbert. Boston: Chapple Publishing Company, 1909.

to a nation that placed the individual at the center of the universe and personalized the large questions of the day."[11] Opera enjoyed a similar status, and like Shakespeare's plays, operatic masterpieces were considered malleable: "Opera in America, like Shakespeare in America, was not presented as a sacred text; it was performed by artists who felt free to embellish and alter, add and subtract."[12] Engaging with a performed text, regardless of its origins or status elsewhere, typified the artistic democracy of George Ives's world, and of nineteenth-century America.

For a person of George's era, meaning came through direct, individual engagement with the material. George displayed the same democratic spirit as did his countrymen in treating the repertoire and rules of European concert music. He approached the theoretical basis of music, which he had studied with Foepple, as merely the starting point for his own understanding of musical processes. Applying the rules of democracy and individuality, George felt free to question the European system that he had been taught, modifying the rules when they impinged on musical practice as well as vice versa.[13] In fact, George was fascinated with the validity of musical practice and its disjuncture with conventional music theory. Ives's later recollections describe George trying to analyze and reproduce the microtonal clusters and the effect of a moving train whistle (also known as the Doppler effect), or of church bells ringing in the distance. This attempt to reconcile two different worlds—those of American musical life and European composers and theorists—convey a typical midcentury view that parallels similar interactions with literature and opera texts.

George's education and activities took place within the context of a highly public debate about American musical identity that had simmered since the 1850s.[14] On one side, the composer and journalist William Henry Fry (1813?–64) argued for a nationalist American style of composition that was independent from European precedents. Fry fervently hoped that a new nationalist school would be based on the model of Italian opera, but use English texts that would engage the majority of the population. He endorsed programmatic music as well, particularly in invoking the American landscape: "The emotions which might be felt in standing on an eminence of the Katskill [sic] Mountains and surveying an expanse of country beneath of nearly one hundred miles; with the landscape, the cottages, the barns, the crops, the sunlight, the Hudson all sublimely eloquent yet silent, may successfully be assumed as the right ones with which the musical artist should paint Peace."[15] Fry wanted American composers to represent more specifically the uniqueness of their cultural and physical environment. But as a member of the educated elite, Fry had an enormous advantage over potential "nativist" composers who faced exactly the same limitations seen in George's musical education and practical experience: lack of standardized, high-quality education; lack of adequately trained and rehearsed performers and full-time venues; the absence of noncommercial patronage and income sources; and limited access to musical scores. Fry continued to battle for a nationalist composition school until his death, with little success.

The opposing viewpoint came from John Sullivan Dwight (1813–93), a former minister, Transcendentalist, and powerful music critic who published his own journal from 1852 to 1881. Dwight urged American composers to emulate the works of the great German composers (especially Beethoven's Ninth) and ignore popular music such as Stephen Foster's minstrel tunes. Only then could "an American new era of musical Art . . . be distinguished not by narrow nationalities but by the universality, the generous humanity, the broad and glorious inspiration that shall make it the language of a brighter period of a whole human family redeemed and reconciled."[16]

In the decades following the Civil War, after Fry's death, prominent musicians such as Theodore Thomas joined Dwight in pressing for a more standardized and institutionalized pedagogical system, more full-time professional musicians, and more emphasis on European masterworks, especially those in the Austro-German tradition. Lawrence Levine argues that such efforts represented a reaction against increased immigration. The new emphasis on written Western European texts, in conjunction with elitist pedagogical traditions unavailable to new immigrants, demanded a more specialized class of musicians and audiences. The "sacralization" of musical spaces further enveloped the emerging elitist class, and strict boundaries between so-called "popular" and "art" musics became entrenched.

George Ives did not participate in the transition. His exposure to European music was limited to Italian opera and operetta hits, and a booklet of exercises in four-part harmony from his lessons with Foepple. The vast majority of printed notices of George's activities as soloist, church musician, entrepreneur, and band director mention vernacular, not classical repertoire. George's notebooks, copybook, and surviving scores indicate that he had a limited repertoire of classical pieces—a few Bach chorale arrangements, some fugue torsos (written to illustrate the entrance of voices), a few bits of opera (the sextet from Mozart's *Don Giovanni* and choruses from Gluck) and a smattering of Baroque choral music standards.[17] Many of these are notated in such a way that they could not have been performed by George's ensembles, and several have his harmonic analyses carefully penciled in beneath each chord, supporting their use as pedagogical, not performance, materials. His handcopied notes on music history appear to be directly copied from a textbook, indicating merely a secondhand connection with the material. Because the notes are not illustrated by actual excerpts, George's instruction in this area may well have been limited to reading about the music, but never hearing or performing it.[18]

In his training and later in his amateur activities, George valued the musical experience above all, in oral and aural traditions more than written scores, and in the peculiarities of real-life sound production. To George, the personal and social roles of music making—the *process* of creating music with one's colleagues and friends for civic and religious events—far outweighed the actual sound of the results. To him, the music was valuable not in spite of the performers' lack of formal training or rehearsal, but because of it. The volunteer band members, the singers at the revivals, like their leader, were amateurs in the truest sense of the word: they sang and played not for applause, or for money (except to cover their expenses), or even for art, but for love of the music.

One recorded story of George's sound world is particularly telling. According to Charles's later accounts, and confirmed by Philip Sunderland, a friend and neighbor of the Ives family, George would march his bands from opposite sides of the park while he stood in the middle—another example of his exploration of amateur musical practice outside of the European theoretical system. According to Sunderland, "the two would clash—that interested him very much, but people in Danbury didn't think it was very interesting to see the two bands blending and playing different tunes. They didn't take George Ives very seriously. He was only the bandleader."[19]

George's lesser position within Danbury musical circles is evident in the *New York Herald* profile. His work was acknowledged in the most basic terms, but not celebrated or particularly admired. In the opinion of the journalist and George's peers, the scattered activities of teaching, band directing, and playing the cornet in church added up to fewer contributions than any of the other named musicians, most of whom were participating in the Europeanization of American music. As a bandleader amidst teachers and orchestra leaders, George's earnings were commensurate with the respect given him—in other words, both were minimal.

George maintained and taught the tradition with which he had grown up—that of a mid-nineteenth-century village musician—even as the world around him changed. He bequeathed to his son that paradigm of musicianship, along with his preliminary attempts to integrate American practice into European theory. Charles's handling of that legacy, from admiration to abhorrence to public celebration, reflects a conflict resulting from a century of cultural transformation.

The Inheritance

From his birth on October 20, 1874, Charles Ives heard band marches, hymn tunes, patriotic songs, dance music, and, from a uniquely midcentury viewpoint, European "classical" music, mostly in the form of band arrangements of popular opera excerpts. Like his father, Charles followed an informal plan of instruction that emphasized musical experience over formal training with hired teachers. By the age of twelve or thirteen, he had learned basic music reading, notation, and four-part harmony from his father's two-decade-old notebooks. Three of his first compositions from 1886, *Schoolboy March: D & F* Op. 1, *Hymn* Op. 2 No. 1, and *Chant* Op. 2, No. 2, are simple four-part compositions that appear to be written exercises rather than music to be performed.

Charles's understanding of the "rules" of standard harmony came straight from George, and was limited to a reading of the copied lessons with Foepple in the 1860s. More important to Ives, as to his father, were the three-dimensional aspects of musical sound and performance. Not surprisingly, Charles had a pragmatic approach to performance and wrote for the ad hoc performing forces that were available to him: namely, whatever musicians George could pull together from his marching band or within the church. Charles's first extended work, *Holiday Quickstep* from 1887–88, was performed by assorted instruments that included cornets, violins, piccolo, and piano.[20]

Ives at 3. Detail from a larger photograph. Courtesy Yale University Irving S. Gilmore Music Library.

Charles's training and early experience were very much in tune with his father's, and his early works stemmed from a midcentury outlook, in comparison with musical activities and values in larger and more current urban areas. The *Holiday Quickstep* uses an opening section with a contrasting trio, capped off with a da capo return to the first section. This single-trio da capo form of the quickstep had been popular since the 1830s, but during the 1880s, John Philip Sousa and others had enlarged this form in marches featuring three or more contrasting sections, with the da capo omitted. Indeed, by the 1880s the term "quickstep" itself had fallen into disuse. Charles Ives, unaware of these changes, followed his father's lead and wrote in the earlier form.

Moreover, as the *Herald* article implies, the amateur band had ceded popularity to "orchestras" and professional bands like Sousa's. With more emphasis on professional training, instruction, and rehearsal; changes in expectations for "correct" harmonic usage; and the emphasis on written text over performance traditions, Ives's early works such as *Holiday Quickstep* maintain earlier musical and performance values. In their written sources, these works express the youthful exuberance and confidence of a talented young teenager. The opening fanfare communicates a certain pride of accomplishment, yet the melodic lines lack direction, limited harmonies remain static or lurch forward, all accompanied by a repetitive, conventional patter in the piano—evidence that despite what he later celebrated as George's thorough and demanding instruction, Ives had a limited compositional technique at the time.[21] What *Holiday Quickstep* really sounded like cannot be clearly ascertained, because a performance may well have included additional instruments, instrument substitutions (a flute playing the violin part, for example), improvisation, or other modifications. But what the score preserves is hardly evidence of an impeccable musical instruction at the hands of George Ives, whatever standard might be applied. What is known is that the entire concept and realization of this piece, whether heard from the perspective of the emerging musical elite or from the viewpoint of Sousa's disciplined and polished concert band, was an amateur anachronism.

Soon after the premiere of *Holiday Quickstep* in January 1888, Ives began studying the organ in earnest with local teachers, J. R. Hall and later Alexander Gibson of the Danbury School of Music. In the course of what may have been under- or unrehearsed, amateur-level public performances, did Ives sense the limitations of his father's musical world and seek more qualified instruction? Or did the success of the work inspire Ives to greater accomplishments?

Excerpts from the piano and violin parts of *Holiday Quickstep*. Courtesy Yale University Irving S. Gilmore Music Library. Rights held by the Theodore Presser Company/Carl Fischer. Used by permission.

Ives's very first original compositions—the *Schoolboy March: D & F* Op. 1, *Hymn* Op. 2 No. 1, and *Chant* Op. 2, No. 2—hold a valuable clue. On the manuscript for these works, Ives took the ambitious step of assigning opus numbers, borrowing a badge of legitimacy, authority, and seriousness from the hallowed European tradition. What kind of compositional career did this adolescent imagine for himself by identifying his first works with opus numbers? Perhaps while scrutinizing the brief harmony exercises in George's copybooks, Ives realized that "real" composers use opus numbers. Equally likely, the son may have been enacting his father's participatory, democratic attitude toward the European tradition, a tradition that midcentury Americans recognized as flexible and personal. In any case, Charles made it clear that his sights were set on a level of achievement above that of a midcentury amateur musician, and he moved ahead quickly to achieve his goals, henceforth without the validating aura of opus numbers.

An American Organist

The organist-composer offered the only model of an economically successful musician in late-nineteenth-century America. Instead of poorly paying, socially marginal band-leading positions and sporadic performances with makeshift amateur ensembles, a professional organist had steady employment and, under optimal conditions, access to a well-maintained instrument with regular performance schedules and expectations. By embracing the role of trained organist, Charles quickly ascended the musical hierarchy of Danbury and had obtained a permanent post at Danbury's Baptist Church by the time he was fifteen.[22] He would spend almost fifteen years working as a full-time organist.

By joining the ranks of American organists, Ives was building on a recognized and well-established tradition of public performance, private pedagogy, and church employment that had solidified by midcentury.[23] In the 1850s and '60s, the organ became a recital instrument in addition to its continuing role in accompanying solo and choral music. According to organ historian Barbara Owen, by 1863 "an average program by a good player would consist of roughly one-third older organ music (Bach, Rinck, Mendelssohn, etc.), one-third orchestral or choral transcriptions of various periods, and one-third contemporary works, often including some by the performer." Transcriptions were included for three main reasons: to make up for what Owen terms the "dearth of contemporary organ literature"; to introduce popular orchestral, choral, and operatic repertoire to a public that would otherwise have no opportunity to hear it; and, in the case of transcribed overtures and other "light" classical selections, to lure otherwise reluctant listeners into a setting where their musical tastes could be expanded.[24]

Thus, the American organ recital occupied a middle ground in the Fry-Dwight continuum. On the one hand, recitals most often took place in churches—spaces that were otherwise used for sacred worship and not associated with secular activities. Organists sought to educate and elevate the tastes of their audiences by including high-quality older compositions by Bach and Mendelssohn, and sometimes demanding new works as well. But the most popular European organ composers in America were not German, to Dwight's dismay, but French and Belgian. Dense, demanding, grandiose, and often colorful works by Lemmens, Batiste, and their contemporaries formed the mainstay of contemporary "serious" organ music introduced in this milieu.[25]

On the other hand, organists were aware of the need to entertain through virtuosity and familiarity as well as lighter repertoire. Audiences heard technically demanding transcriptions as well as new American works in the most popular organ compositional form of the time: variation form. A theme with variations exploited the full timbral range of the organ, and provided an irresistible opportunity for showmanship in the final variation, which tended "always to be loud, flashy, and with a certain amount of fancy pedal work." Moreover, the most common themes used by American organists were familiar folk tunes, patriotic songs, and hymns, in another accommodation to the average audience member.[26]

Perhaps the best-known church organist, composer, and teacher of this era was Dudley Buck, a key figure in Ives's early career whose publications and compositions reflect the practical side of this career path. Trained in Germany, Buck established a studio in Hartford in the 1860s before moving to Chicago where his home, studio, and library were destroyed in the great fire of 1871. After relocating to Boston, then permanently to New York in 1875, Buck composed and taught prolifically, and his published writings provide a clear view of the standards and goals of the American organ school. In 1869, Buck defended the playing of overture arrangements for their broader purpose: "Even the playing of light overtures may find a certain justification in this land, where so much musical missionary work has yet to be done. . . . It is certain that from a true art standpoint an organist should throw his influence towards works originally composed for his instrument. Yet this matter of overture playing not unfrequently [sic] serves as a stepping-stone to the church."[27] Buck's own works reflect similar goals—elevation with accommodation—as in his *Variations on "The Star Spangled Banner,"* *Variations on "Home, Sweet Home,"* and the *Grand Sonata in E-flat,* which includes a theme based on "Hail! Columbia." The same impulse lies behind his collaboration with Theodore Thomas, the German-born conductor and violinist who tirelessly promoted symphonic music in the United States, and who would eventually become the founding conductor of the Chicago Symphony Orchestra. Thomas and Buck joined forces to "make good music popular," by accommodating the broader public taste in efforts such as the Central Park Garden Concerts of 1875.[28] The express purpose of this concert series was to educate and elevate the public beyond the offerings of the New York Philharmonic Society Orchestra, which George had heard in the previous decade. The 1875 concerts introduced European classical music alongside "lighter" music (waltzes and polkas) in an outdoor, informal atmosphere.[29] This approach, of mediating between popular taste and artistic values, places Buck's music as a bridge between George Ives's midcentury musical world and the advance of the late-century "highbrow" elite. As music historian John Tasker Howard put it, "Buck wrote for his market, and his work as a whole represents a compromise between the public taste and the composer's own ideals. Yet he constantly worked to raise standards, and he succeeded."[30]

In addition to their public role as recitalists, organists chose and performed appropriate solo music (voluntaries, preludes, and postludes) within the church service. J. P. Morgan, a well-known New York organist and teacher, shunned the performance of virtuosic music within the service and advocated instead Bach's fugues, if the player had the technique, or chorale preludes, if the player's ability was lacking.[31] Added to this, organists accompanied congregational hymn singing, accompanied (and possibly directed) choirs, and worked with any vocal or instrumental soloists, particularly during the musically demanding holy seasons of Easter and Christmas. Organists played every Sunday throughout the year, usually at morning and evening services, with extra services during the holidays: any vacation time had to be arranged well in advance, and an equally trustworthy substitute had to be engaged. No wonder, then, that being a full-time organist meant achieving a certain musical, social, and economic status that connoted education, ability, and responsibility.

Having achieved a foothold in this more valued, economically secure career before the tender age of fifteen, Ives was determined to prove himself a full-fledged member of the rather conservative organ world. His practice and performance repertoire no longer reflected the eclectic, populist approach of his father. Indeed, by choosing to specialize on the organ, Ives withdrew musically from the context of the outdoor camp meeting. As part of his professional duties for Danbury's Congregationalist and Baptist churches, Ives learned to play a much wider range of the hymn repertoire that reached far beyond the gospel hymns associated with his father.[32] Many of these were older hymn tunes in standard poetic meters for which alternate texts could be used. There was only one text and tune combination for songlike gospel gems such as "In the Sweet By and By," "Just As I Am," "What A Friend We Have in Jesus," and "Are You Washed in the Blood of the Lamb?" But the older, venerable, and unusually named hymn tunes such as *Nettleton, Toplady,* and *Azmon* could be used for numerous texts. In fact, these three tunes all shared a similar genealogy. Each originated as a newly written or arranged American tune in the early nineteenth century for an imported English text from the eighteenth century: *Nettleton* from 1813 for the text "Come, Thou Font of Every Blessing"; 1830's *Toplady* for the august text "Rock of Ages"; and *Azmon,* arranged and published in 1839, for "O For a Thousand Tongues to Sing." Compared to later, upstart gospel tunes by writers such as Ira David Sankey, all were far more dependent on the written tradition in their more wordy texts, and less repetitive and rhythmically varied, which along with their longer heritage represented a type of authority.[33] Here, as elsewhere, Ives must have noticed how his new musical life stood some distance from George's world.

In addition to the expanded hymn repertoire, Ives studied the most proven solo works and arrangements of the time. In fact, Ives's sheet music collection and recital programs march in lockstep with other contemporary American organists, reflecting a strong alliance with the acceptable and standardized activities of his peers. The European organ composers that Ives studied and performed were, of course, Mendelssohn, Bach, and the contemporary Belgian and French organists.

Yet, original compositions by Europeans formed only a small portion of Ives's repertoire at this time. The vast majority of the surviving organ scores from this period are original American compositions, or transcriptions of European overtures and orchestral works prepared by American organists, particularly by Dudley Buck and his student Harry Rowe Shelley, a successful organist in his own right.[34] His earliest public recitals reflect exactly Owen's recipe for programs decades earlier: older works by Bach and Mendelssohn; transcriptions; and popular variations. In June 1890, for example, Ives performed Buck's 1868 arrangement of the *William Tell Overture,* Bach's "Dorian" Toccata and Fugue in D Minor, BWV 538; Mendelssohn's Organ Sonata in F Minor, Op. 65, No. 1; and concluded with Buck's *Variations on "Home Sweet Home."*[35] While these works were technically demanding, and

Ives seems to have played very well in his recitals, the repertoire itself was utterly safe, even predictable.

In keeping with tradition, Ives added his own set of popular variations to the program in later recitals, namely the *Variations on "America,"* complete with the expected flashy pedal work in the concluding passages. Buck's *Variations on "Home Sweet Home"* served as the prototype for Ives's *Variations on "America"* of 1892. Moreover, in works such as *The Star Spangled Banner Overture,* Buck blended Romantic orchestral traditions with American sources; this potent combination would resurface years later in works like Ives's Second Symphony. Ives's work draws more generally on the popular variation tradition that other organist-composers in the United States had already established. But more importantly, Ives could have easily chosen a tune associated with George's amateur marching bands or camp meetings— something like the hymn tune "In the Sweet By and By," or the rousing patriotic march "Columbia, the Gem of the Ocean." Instead, Ives chose a patriotic tune of imported origin (it was originally "God Save the King"), with a distinguished history, a poetic text, and a tune that, through its rhythm, range, and difficulty, was neither martial nor particularly participatory in character. Here, again, Ives distinguished his own career from that of his father.

Between 1889 and 1891 Ives played transcriptions of operatic passages by Wagner, Verdi, Weber, and Rossini. While continuing the American fondness for operatic transcriptions, the inclusion of the nearly contemporary Germans Wagner and Liszt, and the Frenchmen Guilmant and Gounod, reflects a new awareness of contemporary European trends typical of the American organ school of the era. At the same time, performances of transcriptions were falling out of fashion. In 1898, only a few years after Ives's last public recital, Harry Rowe Shelley earned a reviewer's scorn for including such artistically inappropriate selections.[36]

Merely performing these works was not enough, however; Ives needed a model for integrating composition with the practical realities of employment by the average church congregation. He found that model once again in Buck. Drawing on his church experience, Buck wrote numerous anthems and cantatas that became extremely popular with church choirs, including Ives's own. During 1891, for example, the Baptist choir performed three anthems with Ives accompanying; during 1892, the choir performed Buck's cantata *Light of Asia,* once again with Ives at the keyboard.[37]

Of course, Ives used Buck's anthems as compositional models for his own initial forays into this repertory, particularly in his anthems for the quartet choir. The quartet choir was a uniquely American ensemble consisting of an amateur chorus and a paid, professional quartet that alternately reinforced the chorus, sang separately within larger works, or performed independently as soloists. Buck's anthems for quartet choir showed that peculiar division of labor. Simpler, homophonic passages for the untrained chorus contrasted with more demanding quartet sections, while anthems for the quartet soloists displayed their individual abilities and provided a much-needed break for the amateur choir. Both anthems and solo works showcased the barbershop-style harmonies popular at the time. In his own early sacred works, such as *Rock of Ages* for soprano soloist, Ives imitates Buck's own composition of the same name. Both aimed for a tasteful balance of Victorian modesty and virtuosity appropriate to a paid professional.[38]

By early 1893, Ives was actively forging his own identity as a professional American organist-composer, basing his musical style and activities on the career of a nationally known model, and getting his organ, choral, and vocal works performed wherever possible. He had left behind George's amateur-focused musical voice in favor of a contemporary "middlebrow" style and repertoire that guaranteed competent performances and satisfied, uncritical audiences.

While Ives seemed set on pursuing a stable and respectable career in music, his family pushed him to attend Yale, like his more successful uncles. In February, Ives relocated to New Haven to attend Hopkins Grammar School, a preparatory school to which he was sent with the specific purpose of preparing him for Yale. He spent most of the next eighteen months cramming academically and starring on the school's baseball and football teams—the latter a particularly appropriate pastime for a future Ivy Leaguer of his generation. With this move came a new position at St. Thomas's Episcopal Church, a more demanding and socially higher post than he had at the musically uncritical Baptist church, and Ives tackled it with discipline and energy.[39]

The year 1893 represents a turning point as Ives moved out of his family home and into the great world. For all of his accomplishments in his young life, there was much that Danbury could not provide for an aspiring composer. Access to reliable scores of European music was limited; instead of reading Beethoven symphonies in their original form, Ives relied on truncated organ arrangements. Like the vast majority of Americans, he had never seen a professional symphony orchestra, a string quartet, or a fully staged opera; he had never been inside a concert hall.

And, at the core, Ives lacked something even more basic, and more necessary, for success at his chosen level. Unlike Buck and the professors George Whitefield Chadwick (at the New England Conservatory), John Knowles

Paine (at Harvard), and others who had studied music in Germany, Ives did not have a disciplined, thorough training in harmony and counterpoint. Although a professional organist, Ives's exposure to music theory and history was limited to George's secondhand notes copied from a text a quarter century earlier. Later in life, Ives would vigorously defend George's instruction, insisting that his father had let him write "the wrong way" only after he had learned the correct usage.[40] In fact, not a single source survives to show Ives following the standard rules of harmony and counterpoint. In the absence of a thorough command of conventional European theory, Ives freely borrowed ideas from the keyboard and choral literature that he encountered through his organist position. On the other hand, Ives did occasionally explore his father's interest in the gap between American practice and European theory in rare works that were not made public. One cautious questioning is the "Credo" from Ives's *Communion Service* in which he struggled to produce coherent bi-tonal counterpoint as well as a barbershop-inspired, wedge-shaped, fully chromatic cadence. While the remaining movements of the service were recopied in good form (and probably performed at St. Thomas's in 1894), the "Credo" remained in an unfinished sketch, a private testament to Ives's unconvincing but intriguing early experiments.[41]

What Charles learned from George would eventually prove far more important than the nuts and bolts of standard harmony: the physical experience of music as more important than any written source; the fast-disappearing repertoire of mid-nineteenth century America; a flexibility of expression and technique that allowed any musical construction the right to exist, regardless of the written rules of harmony; and the unique performance practices of amateur bands and camp meetings. For the moment, George's legacy was hidden at best, and disregarded at worst. Instead, Ives chose to emulate as best he could the American organist school, by stitching together fragments and imitations of hymns, keyboard textures, and band trios in his earliest organ and choral works.

As he traveled to Chicago in August 1893 with his uncle Lyman Brewster, Ives could not have known that a new model—that of the university-employed composer of "highbrow," or "art" music—was growing in stature, and that he would be inescapably drawn into that tradition. What Ives witnessed at the Columbian Exposition was the powerful emergence of Euro-American musical culture in the form of professional ensembles, international performers and composers, and an expansive repertoire of classical music performed in consecrated spaces for elite, educated audiences: in sum, the impending annihilation of both George Ives's and Dudley Buck's musical worlds.

From Midway to White City

Dedicated in October 1892, the Columbian Exposition celebrated the four-hundredth anniversary of Columbus's so-called "discovery" of America. Over twenty-seven million visitors attended the Chicago World's Fair between its official opening in May 1893 and its closure in October of that year. Physically, the fair was divided between the Midway and the Court of Honor, or "White City." The Midway offered a hodge-podge of entertainment (including the massive new Ferris Wheel) mingling with supposedly educational "ethnographic" exhibits from around the world. European colonies from Africa and Asia figured most prominently, with indigenous displays from Canada and the United States as well.

For Americans, the World's Fair embodied a divided nation poised on the brink of social, economic, and cultural upheaval. With over one hundred thousand visitors per day at its peak, the Exposition provided the unprecedented opportunity for Americans to experience both the unity and diversity of their country in one location.[42] The fair idealized technology, consumerism, and urbanization all in the name of progress. No less than sixty-five thousand technological exhibits (many of them American in origin) celebrated new inventions alongside native cultures and Davy Crockett's cabin. Adjacent to the fair, Buffalo Bill's Wild West show dramatized Custer's battle at Little Big Horn. In so doing, the fair's organizers presented an evolutionary history of the country that culminated in the arrival of the United States as a technological and economic world power.

Musically, the Midway and its offsite surroundings offered the richest and most diverse environment ever heard on the continent to that time. The authentic performers in the ethnographic district offered a glimpse of the diversity of the world's music: from the unfamiliar scales of the Javanese gamelan to the complex rhythmic polyphony of Samoan drummers, these sounds had never been available to the average American, and would not be for decades to come. Only white musicians were allowed to perform outside of the ethnographic district except on prearranged dates, so African-American pianists such as Scott Joplin and Eubie Blake played ragtime in the restaurants and clubs around the city. Famous domestic and international bands, including John Philip Sousa's newly formed ensemble, offered daily concerts that mixed popular songs and patriotic tunes with arrangements from well-known operas and symphonies. Their free performances in bandshells along the Midway attracted large, appreciative audiences unused to seeing and hearing such professionalism and polish.

All of this musical experience was new to Ives. Even though he knew some of the repertoire of the band concerts, these would have been performed at a much more sophisticated level than the enthusiastic but ragtag bands that George directed at home. Perhaps Ives stood at the center of the fair enjoying and absorbing the mixture of competing melodies, timbres, rhythms, and instruments, all of a completely different scope and character than George's crossing marching bands. Yet, if Ives was introduced to what would be considered microtones and polyrhythms by the gamelan and drummers, to ragtime at a Joplin performance, or to large-scale simultaneity and spatial effects through the dense aural soup swirling around him, we have no record of it. Even though each of these elements would become a critical tool in Ives's compositional palette, there is no evidence that he first became acquainted with them in Chicago.

What excited Ives was not the interweaving of these diverse elements in what would later be dubbed a "global village" atmosphere. What intrigued

Interior of the Choral Hall, Columbian Exposition, Chicago, 1893. From Jackson, *White City,* Chicago 1894.

Ives most were the monumental offerings of the White City, where he encountered the familiar and the new, all within an imposing environment. First, the top organists of the day played in the Choral Hall (also called "Festival Hall") throughout the week that he and his uncle attended, culminating in an organ recital by Alexandre Guilmant.[43] Second, Ives had many opportunities to attend free orchestral concerts, many performed by members of Theodore Thomas's Chicago Symphony Orchestra, in both the Choral Hall and the Music Hall. All classical music performances took place in the ethereal, alabaster Roman-style temples that stood, architecturally and physically, separate from the Midway's pandemonium.

The Choral Hall was particularly intriguing. While other buildings boasted statues representing gods, muses, and proper civic values, the statues surrounding the entrance to the Choral Hall were of Bach and Handel, the twin gods of Anglo-European musical enlightenment. The names of the great, primarily Austro-German composers (Gluck, Berlioz, Wagner, Schumann, Mozart, Mendelssohn, Bach, Handel, and Beethoven) "representing the progress of music" surrounded the doors to the hall.[44]

The "progress" of these composers and their musical milieu was underscored by the layout of the fair. Some commentators have even suggested that the fair's physical organization encouraged visitors to view a new world order based on the still-radical theory of evolution and class by "progressing" through the Midway's entertainment and ethnological exhibits (which included "low" European musics such as military and gypsy bands) to the White City's "high" culture offerings. In such a model, Ives's conscious choice of "high" culture over the everyday popular music clearly indicates his preferences at the time.[45]

While the rest of the fair emphasized the advancement of human endeavors (usually American), or at least an international freak-show entertainment environment, the musical components enclosed in the White City emphasized distinctly German products. The indefatigable Theodore Thomas organized an ambitious musical program throughout the fair that included a large segment of older German classics. Thomas's "campaign of education" programs were extremely unpopular with the public. An editorial in one Chicago paper complained that "Mr. Thomas is unable to discover any melody in a piece of music unless it emanates from a German composer." The commentator warned that if Thomas persisted "in giving the patrons of the fair nothing but German music," out of "sheer bullheadedness," Thomas would face "a revolt."[46] Notwithstanding young enthusiasts like Ives, attendance at the classical music concerts was abysmal: much to the dismay of the board of directors, the orchestra of 114 members sometimes outnumbered its audience. In addition to issues of repertoire, the series' popularity suffered from its high-priced tickets (yet another signifier of its elitist dimensions), the one dollar admission price being twice the cost of a ride on the Ferris wheel. Thomas's programs also suffered from competition with free bandshell performances. Keenly aware of his audience's preferences, Sousa featured orchestral transcriptions and popular selections including the ever accommodating overture and operatic excerpt—genres banned from Thomas's stage.

Thomas was forced to resign in mid-August, a few weeks before Ives's visit, and the esoteric programs were scratched in favor of free concerts. Now under the leadership of Thomas's concertmaster Max Bendix, the programs featured a more audience-friendly lineup. It was this repertoire that Ives heard on August 22, 1893, the first day of the "largely popular" new series.[47] The orchestra was still excellent, having been drawn from the ranks of Thomas's Chicago Symphony Orchestra, by now considered the best in the country. This orchestra, founded just two years earlier, introduced Ives to a previously unknown ideal: a polished, full-time, professional ensemble, adequately rehearsed and performing written scores as directed by the composer. On September 2, at the noon concert, Ives may have heard marches and overtures, arias, waltzes, plus Mendelssohn's *Spring Song* and Dvořák's Slavonic Rhapsody No. 3.[48]

On the same day, September 2, that the orchestral concerts offered Ives a new sound ideal, he also experienced the high point of his visit to the fair in Guilmant's recital. According to his uncle's letter of September 1, 1893, "Charley . . . is rejoicing in the prospect of hearing the famous French organist, Guilmant tomorrow. . . . Charley says he is the best organist in the world and the papers seem of the same opinion."[49] Lyman was referring to an article that appeared in the *Chicago Tribune* that day, stating that "Guilmant possesses a superb technique and absolute mastery of the organ. These great qualities he uses as a means, not an end. He is always the artist, absolutely true to that which he portrays, disdaining tawdry effects, and subjugating his own identity to that of the composer. Dignity, breadth, and nobility of treatment distinguish his work, and above all there is that human sympathy that elevates the artist so immeasureably [sic] above the virtuose [sic]."[50] The article contains the seeds of highbrow values: a clear hierarchy stretching from empty virtuosity to "true" artistry, which is subservient to the will of the composer; class-imbued descriptors such as "tawdry" versus "dignity, breadth, and nobility"; and the specific metaphor of this European artist being elevated, or raised above the mere virtuoso.

More than a fine organist, Guilmant had achieved international fame as a composer. In his third solo recital at the fair, which Ives and Lyman attended,

Guilmant performed compositions well known to Ives: the Mendelssohn Sonata No. 1 and Bach's Toccata and Fugue in D minor, as well as his own Caprice in B flat, Elevation in A flat, and Nuptial March. Ives's own recital program consisted of only the Mendelssohn, Bach, an overture arrangement by Buck and the popular variation (either his own or Buck's). But Guilmant went on to include a second entire sonata, this one by the little-known organ composer Salomé, Buxtehude's Ciacona in E minor, Liszt's Adagio in D flat, Wagner's Pilgrim's Chorus (arranged by Liszt), and Lemmens's Finale in D. Guilmant's recital was gargantuan in comparison to Ives's program, which had seemed extremely demanding at the time. Here, in the sixty-five-hundred-seat Festival Hall, in the sanctified aura conjured by engraved names and statues, Guilmant assumed a certain authority as a composer. To Ives, the program not only introduced an exclusively European lineup, but one in which a living composer could be interpolated into the predominantly Austro-German historical panoply.

In fact, Guilmant's Exposition appearances proved extremely influential for organists nationally. In her study of French and Belgian organists, Orpha Ochse states that these three recitals were a crucial step in the education of American organists, as "no European of his stature had come to the United States before, and the self-conscious, insecure American organ profession needed confidence as much as it needed guidance"—a remarkably apt description of Ives in 1893.[51]

For Ives, Guilmant's performances at the fair introduced a vivid hybrid image, that of the elite, cosmopolitan organist-composer of art music (unlike the compromised commercialism of Buck), alongside a greatly expanded, more contemporary, and more challenging European repertoire. Yet, how could Ives integrate this seemingly unreachable model with what he already knew—namely, the American and European synthesis of George's democratic adaptability to music making and Buck's more structured though wholly functional approach? Guilmant himself offered an intriguing solution at each of his three recitals, and it may be this solution that caused Ives the greatest excitement. The *Chicago Tribune* recounts how, at the end of each of his first two recitals, Guilmant improvised on a theme provided by the audience. In the first recital on August 31, the theme was "the 'Star-Spangled Banner,' a particularly happy choice. . . . the ingenuity, the modulations, and the contrapuntal ability displayed made it a delightful performance." The September 1 program included an improvisation on Foster's "Old Folks at Home."

As Ives sat in the great Festival Hall, breathing the rarified air of European art, a common citizen suggested a short tune for Guilmant's improvisation.[52] Although the name of the tune was not recorded, the venerated French organist affected a rapprochement with the average American in the audience, seeming to elevate an everyday tune through the medium of late Romantic musical form, harmonies, and techniques. By the end of his visit to the Exposition, Ives had glimpsed a future in which he, as an American composer, could achieve the same nobility, dignity, and breadth, even while connecting with the average, untrained amateur in the audience.

"That Beautiful Shore"

Ives left the exposition in September 1893 with a mission, and he quickly moved to implement it through the next year. First, Ives began to write more prolifically, producing a *Canzonetta* for organ and a few attempts at songs such as "Far from my heav'nly home" and "Song for Harvest Season." Ives even attempted some liturgical settings for St. Thomas's, including a *Gloria,* a *Benedictus,* and the *Communion Service* (minus the tentatively experimental "Credo" movement). Since performing parts exist for some of this music, Ives was obviously pushing for public performances of his music that year.

Second, he sought out publishers for his music, beginning with *Variations on "America."* Now conspicuously validated by Guilmant's patriotic organ improvisations, Ives must have felt that the time continued to be ripe for an American publisher to issue such a composition, and so, with George's help, he mailed the work off. Making his own compositions publicly known, and announcing his arrival as a serious composer, amounted to a major step for Ives. Although *Variations on "America"* was rejected for publication, Ives persisted, and saw several easily realized, uncomplicated part-songs (or glees) published over the next ten years.

Next, he needed to find a higher level of teacher, a mentor of sufficient status who could coach him not only as an organist, but as a professional composer, and someone well-connected enough to open professional doors that, to his father and Danbury teachers, remained locked. He planned to study with the most accomplished organist/composer within reach. Ives had met Harry Rowe Shelley in Danbury the previous January, when Shelley directed his chorus in Mendelssohn's *Elijah* at the Baptist church where Ives was organist. Ives's "scheme" to use his lessons with either the regionally famous Shelley or even with Shelley's teacher, Dudley Buck, to advance his career, is obvious in this letter to his father from December 1893: "Don't you think that after I have the pieces, that I could play at recitals, worked up sufficiently, it would be a good scheme to write Mr. Shelley, and see what arrangements I could make with him for a few lessons, in which I could play them, over to him. . . . Do you think it would be best to get him or Dudley Buck. I think I can pay for the lessons myself."[53] Here, Ives uses economic autonomy, gained through his organist position, to take control of his own career. The letter is less about asking George for anything—approval, advice, or money—than Ives working out his plans on paper. The next year, Ives would refer to taking lessons with Buck in unabashedly careerist terms: "If I don't get any other good from it, just being a pupil of Buck's would be very helpful."[54]

Lastly, Ives aggressively sought out performances of increasingly elitist repertoire in newly restricted performance spaces. He wanted to see famed singer Adelina Patti in concert; he attended string quartet concerts, a performance of the New Haven Symphony, and an organ recital by a new professor at Yale, Horatio Parker, whose instruction would have a far-reaching impact on Ives's music.[55] In the spring of 1894, Ives saw his first professional opera, Wagner's *Götterdammerung,* at New York's Metropolitan Opera. After its opening season in 1883, the Met had enforced the cultural legitimacy of German opera over Italian "popular" opera, with special emphasis on Wagner. The switch from Italian to German works was due in part to the personal intercession of the German-born conductor Leopold Damrosch and his son Walter, who succeeded him as musical director. According to Levine, from 1884 to 1891 "the Metropolitan Opera Company presented German-language operas exclusively, performing all operas, including French and Italian, in German. In the first twenty years after its opening season of 1893–94, more than a third of its presentations were Wagner operas. During its first fifty years, the company continued to perform Wagner more frequently than any of the Italian masters."[56] The opera arrangements played by the bands, and the amateur opera productions in Danbury in which George participated, were culturally and musically as far from a professional performance of Wagner as could be imagined.

What may be most surprising is that, after hearing Guilmant's recital, Ives stopped giving recitals of his own. Part of this may be due to his new focus on his studies, as well as participation in precollegiate sports like baseball and football. But perhaps it was the spectacle of Guilmant tossing off the hardest selections from Ives's recital program alongside several other virtuosic works that forced Ives to realize his own limitations. He could not reach Guilmant's level of virtuosity as a performer at this point in his life, especially given his economic and time constraints. But, he could use his post and performing abilities to build a career as a church performer and composer.

By his nineteenth birthday on October 20, 1893, Ives knew that the world held many things of value beyond Danbury's boundaries, and he wanted to

LIEUT. JESSE D. STEVENS.   CAPT. JAMES E. MOORE.   LIEUT. FRED'K STARR.
LIEUT.-COL. HENRY M. STONE.   SERGT. JOHN MARSH.
GEORGE E. IVES.
COL. NELSON L. WHITE.   MAJOR WILLIAM MOEGLING.

Portrait of George Ives with cornet, ca. 1892 (lower, center). This collage groups a much later picture of George with Civil War-era pictures of other Danbury veterans, most of whom died during the war. It was published in *A History of Danbury* in 1896, only two years after George's death, in a chapter on the Civil War. James Bailey, *A History of Danbury* (Danbury, Conn.: Burr Printing House, 1896), photo insert between 382 and 383.

experience them. He had visited a great city in a moment of national triumph, yet sensed that even greater rewards lay in the discovery of the arts of another continent. In order to reach that beautiful shore, he would have to leave Danbury, and George, behind. His family had planned on his attending Yale: his successful uncle Lyman Brewster had done the same, as would Ives's only sibling, his younger brother, Moss, who followed in Lyman's footsteps. But now Ives saw the usefulness of such an education for his own ends, and studiously worked to gain admittance.

While he expected his new authority and knowledge to separate him from the musical world of Danbury, Ives could not have known that his departure for Yale would coincide with a permanent separation from George. Shortly after the beginning of the 1894 fall term, just as Ives was discovering the stimulating social and intellectual world of college, George died suddenly of a stroke. Throughout Ives's young life, George had remained just as he was: a midcentury amateur musician who valued human participation, interaction, and social context over standardized education, virtuosity, and professionalism in all of its meanings. His concept of the malleability of European theory and repertoires must have seemed particularly naive to Ives in light of the Columbian Exposition performances that embraced precise performances and the authority of the musical score. Ives had already surpassed his father educationally, socially, and economically, and he was poised to surpass him musically as well. Meanwhile, George stubbornly preserved dying traditions in the face of the hierarchical progress and advancement embraced by his own son, sacrificing his amateur musical activities only for the sake of earning money to pay Ives's college expenses.[57]

Having left George musically and physically, Ives continued along his chosen path with more determination than ever, eager to succeed as a composer in the European mold. Like his idol Guilmant, Ives would see his music celebrated internationally; in surpassing his idol, Ives's music would be regularly performed in the best concert halls by the finest musicians for large, appreciative audiences. Little did he know, however, that the key to his most renowned accomplishments lay in the humble, discarded musical world of George's America.

2

Classes

Forward, when in childhood
Buds the infant mind.
All through youth and manhood,
Not a thought behind.
—from *The Celestial Country*

The professor made time to meet with the student to review his work, despite his pressing duties as Dean, the demands of his six classes, independent studies with the graduate students, and many other professional engagements, most of which were out of town. He would have preferred to use the time to compose—something he was rarely able to do during the school term, only a few precious hours here and there, late at night or while commuting on the trains. But the student earnestly wanted to take the free composition class even though he lacked the required prerequisite.

The professor looked over the manuscripts. At the end of one song, the final pitch hung unresolved in an odd way, which he pointed out to the budding composer. Perhaps he wondered if the student had enough of an understanding of the standard rules of harmony to handle the class. Still, the manuscripts showed skill, and the student's grades in the previous courses had been quite good, with obvious improvement in the counterpoint class through the year. The professor remembered hearing the student perform as organist while accompanying a lecture a few years before. He must have some talent, the professor thought, since he held the same organist position that one of the professor's own colleagues had held before. The student was quiet, polite, and hardworking. To hold down a professional organist job while attending school full-time was not easy, as the professor well knew. Perhaps the student needed to work to help pay his way through Yale, unlike most students, for whom money was never an issue.

Yet another set of assignments to review, more exams to grade, more record-keeping—this is not what he needed. But he gave the kid a break, and signed him into the free composition class. One would think that the student, Charles Ives, would long remember this personal favor from his professor, Horatio Parker, with gratitude. Such an assumption would be wrong.

Professor Horatio Parker

Born into a well-to-do family in Massachusetts in 1865, Horatio Parker had received the finest musical training available both at home and abroad. After private lessons with George Chadwick in Boston, Parker studied in Munich, honing his skills with Chadwick's own teacher, Joseph Rheinberger. Accessing the German tradition at its source, Parker immersed himself in the technicalities of composition. His later works were marked by the complex counterpoint and sophisticated harmonic and formal structures of a true German pedigree.

Professor Horatio Parker (1863–1919). Courtesy Yale University Irving S. Gilmore Music Library.

On returning to the United States with his German fiancée, Parker established himself as a composer, teacher, and church organist in the urban centers of Boston and New York. On May 3, 1893, the Church Choral Society of New York premiered Parker's oratorio *Hora Novissima*: it was the only work on the program. Parker once stated that he wrote the cantata with an expectation of a performance at the Chicago World's Fair, but the work was not produced there, perhaps because of its length and unfamiliar text. An eleven-movement work written on a medieval Latin text, *Hora Novissima* describes a heavenly city of ethereal beauty that, had it been heard in Chicago, may have evoked the White City itself.

The work is challenging to perform for both chorus and soloists. The complicated part writing in the a capella penultimate movement "Urbs Syon unica" was acknowledged at the time by critic Louis Elson, who wrote, "That an American can write such music is something that we should be proud of; that the Handel and Haydn Chorus could sing it (unaccompanied) is something to congratulate them upon." Parker's demanding score incorporates a wide variety of polyphonic techniques, most often extended fugues or fugatos. A full orchestra plus organ accompanies the singers, performing independent instrumental parts rather than just doubling the sung lines.[1]

The work's premiere was, according to Parker's biographer William Kearns, "the most important performance in [Parker's] career" due to the high profile of the performing ensemble, the growing reputation of the composer, and the expectations of New York critics that *Hora Novissima* would be "the major effort in the field of American oratorio up to that time." Part of the anticipation involved the high quality of the Church Choral Society, a formally trained ensemble that counted among its patrons wealthy Manhattanites such as J. Pierpont Morgan and the Vanderbilts. Founded in 1888, the society was organized "for the purpose of holding musical services in the larger churches where the sacred compositions of the great musicians could be properly rendered": to this end, programs included works by Dvořák, Mozart, Liszt, Mendelssohn, and Wagner.[2]

According to Parker, *Hora Novissima* was written for this socially and musically significant ensemble that presented concerts "of a very high order."[3] But despite its excellent credentials, the Church Choral Society did not adequately perform *Hora Novissima*. Critic William J. Henderson lamented the "inadequacy of the chorus," and stated that "the work ought to be given by a chorus of 300 or 400 voices to get full justice." This obstacle was overcome with the February 4, 1894, performance by the Handel and Haydn Society in Symphony Hall, Boston. In this much-anticipated concert by an even more venerated ensemble, the choir consisted of 383 voices accompanied by an orchestra of fifty-seven.[4]

Hora Novissima was composed on a grand scale, merging the Romantic orchestra with a powerful choral component. Despite the work's austere religious text and disciplined, Germanically transmitted counterpoint, Hora Novissima is surprisingly luxuriant. Critic Philip Hale felt compelled to defend the work's controlled Romanticism by stating that Parker's "sensuousness is not eroticism." Hale went on to say that

> [t]he conception of this impressive work is of noble proportions; the execution of which is an honor to our national art. Nor is it perhaps foolish to predict that the future historian of music in America will point back to Hora Novissima as a proof that, when there were croakers concerning the ability of Americans to produce any musical compositions save imitations of German models, a young man appeared with a choral work of long breath that showed not only a mastery of the technique of composition, but spontaneous, flowing, and warmly colored melody, a keen sense of values in rhythm and in instrumentation, and the imagination of the born, inspired poet.[5]

Hale endorsed Parker's "great talent" as approaching genius, "if it is not absolute genius." Louis Elson went further, predicting that Parker could become "the greatest composer that America has produced," while another reviewer claimed that "a work of such magnitude . . . must take a high stand among compositions of its class."[6]

With Hora Novissima's glowing reviews and a growing national reputation, Parker was offered Yale's Battell Professorship of Music the following year. Until Parker's arrival in 1894, Yale's music department was run single-handedly by Gustave Stoeckel. As in many American educational institutions, music at Yale had entered the curriculum through the back door. Although Stoeckel began teaching music courses at Yale in 1855, he was only recognized as an official professor thirty-five years later, in 1890. Faced with Stoeckel's retirement in spring 1894, and the competition of John Knowles Paine's music program at Harvard, Timothy Dwight, the president of Yale, hired Parker and provided him with the institutional authority to create a competitive music program.

Parker dove into his new appointment with unrestrained energy. He organized the program into six academic courses plus one practical (performance) course, based on the model of German music schools. Each course lasted a full academic year. Parker's curriculum from 1894 on looked like this:

I. *Harmony*—Monday and Thursday, 2 P.M. A study of chords, their construction, relations, and progressions. This course covers the following subjects: Intervals; triads of M & m scales and their inversions & resolutions; Modulations; Chromatically altered notes; Harmonization of a given melody; Harmony in two, three, and five parts; Simple instrumental accompaniments. The work is principally the writing of exercises from figured basses. The exercises will be corrected in the class-room with explanations & illustrations. Jadassohn's Harmony (B & H, N.Y. & Leipzig) is used as text book.

II. *Counterpoint*—Mon. & Thurs., 3 P.M. The work will be harmonizing and supplying melodious additional voices to choral [sic] and other melodies used as Canti Firmi. The different orders of Counterpoint in two, three, and four voices, also double counterpoint, and more or less free imitative writing. Students taking this course are encouraged to try the simpler forms of free composition. No text book is used.

III. [*Strict Composition*] Monday and Thursday, 4 P.M. [prerequisites listed from later catalogue: Courses I and II.] The more severe kinds of composition will form the basis of the work in this course. Harmony in Five and more parts; Triple and Quadruple Counterpoint; Four and three part Fugues for voices or for instruments; Canons of various kinds, with or without accompaniment of free voices; free treatment of different kinds of thematic materials. This course is preparatory to Course VI. No text book is used.

IV. *The History of Music.* [No time given, but later catalogues list the time as Wednesday at 5 P.M.] Lectures on the development of music from its earliest stages. History of Church music from the time of Gregory; History of Opera and Oratorio; Biographical sketches of famous composers, with descriptions and analyses of their principal works; History of purely instrumental music showing the growth and development of musical forms up to their culmination in Beethoven. Practical illustrations of the lectures on musical form will be given in the classroom.

V. *Instrumentation.* Tuesday and Friday, 3 P.M. prerequisites: Courses I & II with a recommendation that Course III precede it also. Lectures are given on the nature, compass, tone-color, and other characteristics of all the instruments of the modern orchestra, with written illustrations of their use by great composers. Exercises in the practical Orchestration of short pieces from the works of classic and modern composers, in the Analysis of scores, etc.

VI. *Free Composition.* Tuesday and Friday, 2 P.M. prerequisites: Courses I, II, III, V and "an unmistakable talent for original composition." Several of the smaller forms of free instrumental and vocal music will be composed by the students, such as part-songs, glees for male and mixed voices, and pieces of different sorts for the piano and other instruments. At the close of the year, the student will be required to produce an extended work, probably in sonata form.[7]

Of these, Parker detested giving the public lecture in music history, in part because he lacked formal training in the subject, and because of the students' apathetic reaction. According to his daughter, Parker would occasionally request, "Will those of you in the last row try *not* to rustle your newspapers?"[8]

In his revision of Yale's music program, Parker reserved the final and most desirable course—free composition—for a highly select population. Only those with "an unmistakable talent for original composition" would be allowed to take it. The wording suggests that Parker's direct approval was necessary: not just anyone could sign up for this class. According to William Kearns, the free composition class "was the crowning achievement of the music curriculum and the one [Parker] took the most delight in teaching. Students took it after a careful disciplining in harmony, contrapuntal techniques, orchestration, and creativity in the smaller forms."[9] In addition to this screening mechanism, Parker built in a second obstacle to signing into the free composition class. The structuring of the prerequisites throughout the program made it almost impossible for most undergraduates to qualify for the course. Because Yale's required core curriculum during the first two years emphasized difficult subjects including Latin, Greek, mathematics, and foreign languages, undergraduates were not allowed to register for any elective courses (including music) until their junior year. While freshmen and sophomores could audit some of the early music courses, most would not have time in their schedules to include more than one full-year music course during their first two years.

But in order to complete all four prerequisites in time to take the free composition class in their final year, a student would need to have completed the harmony, counterpoint, instrumentation, and strict composition courses by the end of his junior year. Just to be sure, Parker installed another fail-safe: students could be denied admission to the instrumentation course if they had not already completed the strict composition class. By structuring the curriculum and prerequisites in this way, Parker guaranteed that the only students registered in the free composition class would be those who had received his specific approval.

For the first few years, Parker taught all six courses, in addition to serving in his role as Dean of the Music School. In itself, Parker's academic position would have been a time-consuming job. But he also directed several community groups and had a demanding church position in Boston, and later New York, which required him to travel by train regularly for rehearsals and services. As any experienced church musician knows, leading a large music program is immensely demanding even without having to travel more than an hour to the site, especially during holiday seasons. David Stanley Smith, Parker's successor at Yale who was a student there during Ives's time, recounted a typical week in Parker's life as follows:

> It may be of interest to follow Parker through a week, typical of the weeks through which he passed for many years. Late Saturday afternoon, choir rehearsal in New York; Sunday, service morning and evening; Monday afternoon and evening in Philadelphia for rehearsals of the Eurydice and Orpheus Clubs; night train to New York, thence to New Haven for two classes on Tuesday; Tuesday evening by trolley to Derby for a rehearsal of the Derby Choral Club, arriving in New Haven at midnight; Wednesday, a lecture on the History of Music and a class in composition; Thursday, again two classes; Thursday evening, rehearsal of the New Haven Symphony Orchestra; Saturday, off again for New York. Naturally these rehearsals culminated in frequent concerts. Then there was the inevitable grind of the Dean's office, with conferences and letter-writing.[10]

Why did Parker take on so many extra commitments? In part, he needed the money. In other cases, Parker took on commitments because of his belief in their nonfinancial value. For example, he conducted the New Haven Symphony Orchestra for twenty-five years to achieve community enrichment and education, create a town-and-gown bond, and provide his students with a venue for premiering their orchestral works.[11]

In addition to his unrelenting work schedule, Parker, with his family, worked to create a sense of community among the professional musicians who passed through New Haven. They hosted late-night dinners for the working musicians—particularly the members of the Kneisel quartet—and housed John Philip Sousa's family for several weeks while the famous bandleader recuperated from malaria in a local hospital.[12] A frequent guest later recalled the Parker family house as follows: "We were often at their house (especially after a concert by the Kneisels or some other musical occasion). Mr. Parker was altogether delightful in his functions as host, husband and father. Mrs. Parker—the perfect wife for him—played up to him with charming banter. Sometimes Yale undergraduates joined the group and Mr. Parker was always amused by their cublike cavortings around his three attractive daughters."[13] Behind this lively domestic scene, Parker's private correspondence was filled with worries about financial issues, particularly the cost of maintaining his household and providing for his wife and three daughters. For three decades he scrambled to find paying jobs over three states to stretch his modest income, but at a terrible cost. Most of his works were finished on summer vacations when he composed rather than relaxed. After twenty-five years of this brutal schedule, Parker suffered a complete health breakdown, and died at the age of fifty-six, in 1919.

If Parker had bent to the tastes of the day, and modeled his own career on the prevailing trend, he could have spent much more time composing, less time traveling, and secured a more substantial income. Parker would have earned more by establishing a booming private teaching studio like Dudley Buck, instead of being worked to death teaching courses and doing administrative work for a set salary at Yale. But Parker believed in education as a means of elevating the level of music making in his home country, and he sacrificed for this belief. As an educator, Parker worked so that one day, in his words, "the great American composer will be found and trained among us here in New England."[14]

Meanwhile, more commercial composers like Buck enjoyed considerable economic success writing approachable music for paying performers. Beyond the quartet choir anthems, Buck's secular and sacred cantatas, operas, glees, organ works, and teaching manuals sold very well, and publishers commissioned works from him.[15] Parker wrote his own music regardless of its commercial value and success, and without concern for its popularity among performers or audiences. Amateur choirs could not perform the complex polyphony of *Hora Novissima* for the Sunday service, most congregations would not appreciate—or understand—a Medieval Latin text, and his instrumental works were written beyond the reach of the average American performer.

In what has proven a continuing paradox, Parker's musical world belonged to the upper class: from the many wealthy Yale students to the well-heeled, class-conscious audiences of the *Hora Novissima* premiere. Yet Parker's meager compensation left him struggling to remain in the middle class. When Parker did receive a decent paycheck, the circumstances were fraught with the unique challenges of public institutional patronage. In 1909, the Metropolitan Opera in New York announced a competition to premiere an original American opera in its 1912 season. Parker entered and won the contest, which included an astonishingly large cash prize of ten thousand dollars—a fact noted prominently by the media—with his first opera, *Mona*.[16] But the New York press attacked the choice immediately after its announcement in 1911, claiming that the judges—all Parker's personal friends—had rigged the contest, and that America's great oratorio composer lacked the dramatic and melodic talent to write a successful opera. By its premiere in 1912, Parker had spent more time promoting, defending, and assisting in the production of the work in every detail than he had spent composing it. After much public criticism and unfavorable reviews, *Mona* disappeared after only four performances and has not been performed in its entirety since. Parker often said, "If my work is any good, it will last, if not, it had better die with me—the sooner the better in fact." In the case of *Mona*, and most of the rest of his compositions, the latter has been the case.[17]

Ives in his dorm room at Yale. Detail from a larger photograph. Courtesy Yale University Irving S. Gilmore Music Library.

Ives's Classes

Parker and Ives started at Yale in the same year, 1894, so Ives was one of the first graduates of Parker's program. Although his official college record does not record every class, a close analysis of the program and Ives's surviving scores and recollections indicates that he took all six courses with Parker, culminating in the free composition class. In *Memos,* Ives stated that he took "the music courses at Yale (four years with Parker) in connection with the regular college courses."[18] Because Ives couldn't register for music courses until his junior year, he attended Parker's public lectures in music history and audited the harmony course during his first two years, based on surviving exercises and the requirements of his later courses.[19] Ives's scholastic record lists grades for four music courses taken during his junior and senior years—counterpoint and instrumentation during his third year, and strict composition and instrumentation again in his fourth year.

Ives received his best grades in these four music courses, raising an otherwise dismal average into the high D range, or, according to an Ivy League euphemism, a "Gentlemen's C."[20] In fact, the Gentlemen's C was the norm at fin-de-siècle Yale where sports and social ability were valued far more highly than academics. Again, Ives proved remarkably adept at fitting himself into the prevailing mold. His social skills gained him acceptance into both the fraternity Delta Kappa Epsilon (DKE) and one of three extremely elite secret societies, Wolf's Head, in his senior year. The senior societies chose Yale men on the basis of athleticism, social standing, and extracurricular activities— and specifically *not* because of intellectual achievement. Ives was admitted to this group based on two of these three criteria, as the combination of athletic prowess and musical talent, in conjunction with a decidedly middling scholarly career, compensated for the absence of a high social status. In retrospect, it wouldn't be surprising if Ives intentionally underachieved academically since his preferred peers—the Yalies deemed most likely to succeed after graduation, and who acted as gatekeepers within the school as well—viewed "the man who attends strictly to study ('the grind') . . . as peculiar or even contemptible."[21]

Concerning his coursework, Ives's two semesters of instrumentation appear inconsistent with the curriculum. No sequel to the instrumentation class is listed in the catalogue, and it seems unlikely that Ives would retake a course in which he had received an honors standing the previous year. A clue can be found in the career of David Stanley Smith. Like Ives, Smith took instrumentation twice in his third and fourth years, suggesting that there was a consistent reason for advanced students to enroll in this course twice in their final years.[22] Like most other Yale undergraduates, Ives and Smith both lacked one prerequisite needed to take Parker's free composition course in their senior year. Apparently, Parker enrolled both students in the free composition class, but recorded their grades under the instrumentation course number. In other words, Parker, whom Ives later claimed was "governed too much by the German rule," deliberately *broke* the rules to advance Ives's musical training, and to include Ives among the highly select population of Parker's favorite course.

To "pass" students into the free composition class, which was the most demanding course in the curriculum, Parker would have wanted to review some of the compositions of the aspiring composer. Ives brought in what he had been working on. In Ives's works, Parker recognized what was needed for the class—"an unmistakable talent for original composition"—and allowed Ives to take the free composition class.[23] With a demanding, "hard-boiled" (Ives's term again), no-nonsense teacher like Parker, the importance of such a favor cannot be overestimated. Without this final, cumulative course, Ives would not have had the technical ability to pursue his later compositional vocation.

Moreover, Ives produced a stack of independent compositions in his classes with Parker, especially the strict and free composition courses. By the end of his senior year, Ives had amassed a substantial portfolio of work under Parker's tutelage: numerous resettings of German Lieder and French chansons, almost all of which he resurrected two decades later for *114 Songs;* possibly the men's chorus *The Bells of Yale,* published in 1903; a string quartet fugue used in his First String Quartet, then transferred to the third movement of the Fourth Symphony; and the opening movement of what would become his First Symphony, which Walter Damrosch performed in a rehearsal in 1910. Not only did Ives absorb everything that Parker taught him in the composition classes, but Ives continued to mine the assignments themselves, as a partial foundation of his compositional voice, through the ensuing decades.[24]

In his courses with Parker, Ives acquired what he had been lacking: an understanding of music history, and a thorough instruction in standard harmonic practice, counterpoint, instrumentation, and compositional approaches. Of course, Ives was involved with many types of music outside of the classroom during his Yale years. Even here, however, Parker's influence is apparent in the new harmonic sophistication and ease of Ives's nonacademic compositions, particularly the choral anthems written for his ongoing organist position, and part-songs for his contemporaries at Yale.

After leaving the difficult post at St. Thomas's, Ives took up a prestigious position at Congregationalist Center Church on the Green in fall 1894. Harry B. Jepson, organ teacher at Yale, had preceded Ives on the bench, while Ives's own replacement, David Stanley Smith, succeeded Parker as head of the Yale School of Music.[25] Here Ives found a surrogate father in the choir director, John Cornelius Griggs. Griggs was a musical scholar in his own right, having earned his Ph.D. in musicology from the University of Leipzig in 1893 with the dissertation "Studien über Musik in Amerika."[26] Griggs championed the quartet choir in this document, stating that it "represents the people and in no manner represents the priesthood or any other specially ordained class."[27] Griggs included an endorsement of the quartet choir in one of a series of lectures at the Yale Divinity School on October 25, 1895, that included musical examples performed by the Center Church Choir with Ives on the organ. Later lectures included musical excerpts performed by Ives and Professor Parker himself.[28] In his lecture, Griggs discussed both the "Limitations and Advantages" of the quartet choir based on his own experiences and understanding of the democratic nature of the ensemble. Under Griggs's direction, and with Ives accompanying, the Center Church choir regularly performed Buck's anthems for quartet choir as shown in surviving calendars.[29]

With a friend and supporter in charge of the choir, Ives produced many anthems in the Buck style for the Center Church ensemble. An anthem such as *Crossing the Bar* of 1894–95 answered both Ives's desire to compose for his newly available performing ensemble, and to express some very personal feelings about the sudden loss of his father. The text, a hymnized version of Tennyson's poem, mourns the loss of a beloved leader. Ives's sensitive setting builds to an aching emotional climax in the final phrase "I hope to see my pilot face to face / When I have crossed the bar" that surpasses the orderly part writing and quaint Victorian-style harmonies. Ives continually refined his command over the process of composition so that, by the end of his Center Church tenure, he was producing polished, publishable, effective anthems and solos for the quartet singers on a professional level.

Ives put Parker's teachings into practice in his part-songs as well. Part-songs were popularized by a cappella singing groups (usually all male) nationwide including the Apollo Club.[30] Musically, these part-songs combined barbershop and gospel elements with the Americanized sound of the German male chorus, or Mannerchör. At Yale, the Whiffenpoofs, Yale Glee Club, and fraternity ensembles all performed choruses, and the ambitious Ives was not shy in offering his commercial works to these groups and to publishers. In fact, Ives had a number of glees published and performed during his Yale career. *For You and Me* was published in 1895, *Scotch Lullaby* in 1896, and *Song of Mory's* in 1897. *Bells of Yale* was performed by the Yale Glee Club and later published in 1903: its unprecedented length and difficult, Lied-like accompaniment mimic Parker's own extended male choruses. And Ives's publications were not limited to vocal works either, since his *March "Intercollegiate"* was published in 1896.[31] In all of these works, plus another half-dozen glees, the conventional part writing, predictable harmonic language, sophisticated text setting, and carefully constructed accompaniment bear witness to the fruit of Ives's studies.[32]

"The Greater Man"

Parker's courses, particularly the free composition class, gave Ives the tools to become an accomplished composer. Parker's instruction filled in the many technical gaps remaining from George's open-minded but incomplete education, and the equally partial on-the-job education Ives cobbled together as a working organist. In these courses Ives encountered the type of musical experience that he eagerly sought. Under the circumstances, Ives was fortunate to be in Parker's class at all, even apart from the special accommodations: if he had entered Yale two years earlier, in 1892 at the age of eighteen instead of in 1894 when Parker started, Ives would have missed fully half of the curriculum. Parker's character and personal style did not meet Ives's need for an uncritical father figure; yet, Ives's memories of Parker in the classroom often portray his former professor as smiling during their interactions. For example, when Ives handed in an unconventional fugue that used four keys, Parker "took it as a joke" and handed it back "with a smile, or joke about 'hogging all the keys at one meal.'" Similarly, Ives disagreed with Parker concerning what would become the first movement of the First Symphony: "It (that is, the symphony) was supposed to be in D minor, but the first subject went through six or eight different keys, so Parker made me write another first movement. But it seemed no good to me, so I told him that I would much prefer to use the first draft. He smiled and let me do it, saying 'But you must promise to end in D minor.'"[33] Here, the smiling Parker accommodates his headstrong student, allowing him to follow his own muse. Parker's smile may have been one of indulgent teasing, patronizing amusement, or simple collegiality, since, as Ives remembers, Parker was "seldom mean." Parker's indulgence of Ives as well as his in-class countenance were surely intentional revisions of the severe training Parker himself had received from Rheinberger in Munich, and more in keeping with an informal (if not actually democratic)

American pedagogical climate.[34] Given his inclusion of Ives in the elite free composition course, Ives's high grades in his music classes, and the long-term effects of Parker's instruction, it would come as no surprise that Ives would acknowledge his mentor with gratitude.

Instead, Ives's reminiscences of Parker, including those that concern an anonymous professor of music, range from somewhat critical to devastating, in part because Parker voiced opinions that were difficult for Ives to hear. In Parker's opinion, the amateur quartet choir was the scourge of American church music. In a lecture titled "Church Music" that Parker delivered in 1897—while Ives was attending his class—he directs strong criticism at Buck's amateur style:[35]

> It seems strange . . . that the only characteristic American Institute in Church Music should be that *abomination of desolation*—the quartet choir. . . . There is only one other American musical product which approaches it in possibilities of horror, and that is the Moody and Sankey tune. . . . The Quartet Choir is a labor-saving device I admit. They do not require much training; in fact some of them are not susceptible to training, but I do not feel at liberty to commend them for that. . . . Individually I love the quartet singer. Many of the Sopranos and Altos are of great personal beauty, and many of the Basses and some of the Tenors are good fellows; but as quartet singers I loathe and abhor them, and trust the time may never come when I shall be at their mercy. Hunger alone shall drive me to it, after a fair trial of begging. . . . I am not in favour of the Quartet Choir, so-called. It is a bad Chorus indeed that is not better than one of these. . . . I sincerely hope we shall all live to see the last of the quartet choirs sing its final Nunc Dimittis.[36]

Parker's harsh criticisms extended to the following biting comparison: "People ask for bread and we give them sponge cake; for fish, and they are lucky if they get eels—sometimes real snakes, loathsome, wriggling, slimy moody and snakey [Moody and Sankey] snakes—vulgar with the vulgarity of the streets and the music hall."[37] One of Parker's favorite targets was "In the Sweet By and By," a hymn beloved by Ives throughout his childhood and recalled in many of his later works. In discussing Mendelssohn's *Elijah*, Parker stated that "the thematic material is often dull and sometimes vulgar. [For instance,] 'Be not afraid.' This is, as music, but little less vulgar thematically than the 'Sweet Bye and Bye' [sic], although the intense offensiveness of the words in Moody and Sankey's production gives it a flavour stronger than anything so commonplace as the combination of Mendelssohn and the Bible could produce."[38] In the surviving 1904 lecture notes, Parker combined his scathing criticism of

"In the Sweet By and By" (written by Sanford Fillmore Bennett and Joseph Philbrick Webster, not by Moody and Sankey) with his disparagement of the quartet choir in a passage that reflects what Ives later described as Parker's "hard-boiled" approach: "The two contributions which America has made to the church music of the world are the Quartet Choir and the Moody and Sankey hymn tunes. Can you imagine our great grandchildren boasting of the good old days when our churches, through the medium of a committee composed of a merchant, a banker, a lawyer, and a mechanic engaged quartet singers, or can you picture their reviving 'The Sweet Bye and Bye' [sic] for other than humorous purposes? . . . I believe no lower level can be found than that of the quartet choir and sickly sentimental hymn tune."[39]

In his lectures and no doubt in his contemporary classes, Parker ridiculed two of the central experiences in Ives's musical life to that point: the camp-meeting hymns of his father that he remembered from childhood, and the quartet choir of Dudley Buck that was his compositional model through his youth and Yale years.[40] Both were considered lowbrow by musicians like Parker who preferred trained boy choirs over quartet choirs, and traditional Episcopalian hymns over gospel tunes. For Ives, Parker's comments must have dug particularly deep in the aftermath of George's sudden death.

Parker also objected to the prevailing trends in American music on theological grounds. Parker's views clearly endorse the Oxford movement that opposed liberal evangelical Protestantism; supported a wholesale revival of the theology and philosophy of the Middle Ages, closer ties with the Roman Catholic Church, and a generally more formal approach to worship; and advocated the reinstatement of unaccompanied male choirs in place of mixed choruses, quartets, and organ.[41] Although these musical and theological ideals spread to the United States in the 1850s and '60s, they had difficulty competing with the far more popular quartet choir and the secular liberalism and evangelical Protestantism of Moody and Sankey.[42]

Parker's unrestrained, public loathing of the standard musical experiences of many ordinary Americans, including Ives, seems to be in uncharacteristically bad taste. Why would a professor, an educator, a musician at a major school attack the activities of everyday musicians working outside of the academy? Parker's vitriolic comments may be better understood as salvos from the front line of the Euro-American cultural advancement in the face of what seemed to be overwhelming opposition, apathy, and a lack of resources. These are the words of a man who fought to elevate American music his entire life, and in Parker's eyes the quartet choir and gospel hymn were the enemies.

In fact, Parker made no distinction between revivalist hymn tunes and quartet choir anthems. The middle-class professional organist-composer model that Ives had emulated while moving beyond George's training and sporadic employment was irrelevant to his new instructor. Both musical worlds, in his opinion, were infinitely inferior to what Parker considered real music. While Parker's snide attacks on gospel hymns went far beyond what Ives himself would have acknowledged, Ives had abandoned George's sound world during his Yale years all the same. In a sense, Parker's public rejection of gospel hymns magnified Ives's own rejection of George's repertoire and values. The crucial difference was that Parker rejected Buck's music as well, which Ives had valued up to that time without question.

In *Memos,* over thirty years later, Ives recounted the condemnation of gospel hymns by an unnamed "professor." The first quotation involves Moody and Sankey hymns in which Ives can be heard countering Parker's attacks on the patriotic band tunes of the Civil War and gospel hymns by emphasizing the experiential, nonnotational, participatory, amateur, and interactive performance qualities of George's music:

> Exception has been taken by some . . . to my using, as bases for themes, suggestions of old hymns, occasional tunes of past generations, etc. As one routine-minded professor told me, "In music they should have no place. Imagine, in a symphony, hearing suggestions of street tunes like *Marching Through Georgia* or a Moody and Sankey hymn!"—etc. Well, I'll say two things here: (1) That nice professor of music is a musical lily-pad. . . . He never took a chance at himself, or took one coming or going. (2) His opinion is based on something he'd probably never heard, seen, or experienced. He knows little of how these things sounded when they came "blam" off a real man's chest. It was the *way* this music was sung that made them big or little.[43]

The second statement concerns the last movement of the *Second Orchestral Set (From Hanover Square North At the End of a Tragic Day),* in which Ives recreated a moment when strangers in New York were moved to sing a gospel hymn:

> Now what was the tune? . . . It was (only) the refrain of an old Gospel Hymn that had stirred many people of past generations. It was nothing but—"In the Sweet Bye and Bye" [*sic*]. It wasn't a tune written to be sold, or written by a professor of music—but by a man who was but giving out an experience. . . . [This] remnant of American folk art . . . has been so long belittled and despised by too many nice, respectable, well-intentioned but unimaginative Americans with arrested muscles above the neck, especially those who have

too much to say in musical and other circles today—and who say, think, deride, or approve only what some business-man-musician-European (with a bigger reputation than anything else) has carefully told them to say, think, deride or approve.[44]

Although Ives avoided mentioning Parker by name in these more strident passages, his defense against his professor's stinging criticisms remained passionate. Some thirty-five years after the fact, Ives defended the experiential, participatory value of George's music, its democratic profile—although not the quality of the hymn tune itself.

As Feder contends in his psychoanalytic biography of Ives and his father, Ives's later criticisms of Parker reflected filial loyalty, exacerbated by his earlier shame about George's status, and guilt about his own rejection of George's musical world.[45] Interestingly, Ives offers two telling comparisons between his father and his professor, including this recollection of their first meeting, which Ives misdated to the beginning of his freshman year:

> In the beginning of Freshman year, and getting assigned to classes, Parker asked me [to] bring him whatever manuscripts I had written (pieces, etc.). Among them a song "At Parting"—in it, some unresolved dissonances, one ending on a E-flat (key [of] G major), and stops there unresolved. Parker said, "There's no excuse for that—an E-flat way up there and stopping, and the nearest D way down two octaves,"—etc. I told Father what Parker said, and Father said, "Tell Parker that every dissonance doesn't have to resolve, if it doesn't happen to feel like it, any more than every horse should have to have its tail bobbed just because it's the prevailing fashion."[46]

In Ives's fantastical recreation of his audition for the free composition class—the course which Parker generously allowed Ives to take, and which helped shape his compositional voice and repertoire for decades to come—he portrays Parker as arrogant, cold, and unimaginative. But his grumbling over Parker's criticism of nonstandard part writing decades later is not enough. Ives resurrects his father, who had died three years before this encounter, to defend him in colorful, folksy language. This vignette in which Ives supplied both parts of the dialogue gave George a belated opportunity to defend his instruction and musical viewpoints—values that Ives had rejected at the time, but later vociferously championed. Ives's need to pit Parker against George turns up in another, more direct comparison that voices what was apparently a shared idolization of George by both Ives and his mother Molly: "Parker was a composer and widely known, and Father was not a composer and little known—but from every other standpoint I should say that Father was by far the greater man."[47]

The staged battle between the elitist Yale professor and the amateur band-leader distracts from what Ives may not have realized at the time: that despite their considerable differences, Horatio and George had much in common. Both his professor and father set aside the goal of economic success to promote the music in which they believed. Although their respective musics engaged participants and listeners at opposite ends of the social scale, both willingly embraced music that had little or no economic value. Neither George nor Horatio earned enough from their musical activities to comfortably support their families. At least Parker received respect for his efforts, but the end result was the same. Both Professors George Ives and Horatio Parker died prematurely, exhausted from fighting for noncommercial music within an increasingly commercialized society.

"Ta ta for money"

Of the three, it was Charles Ives who most actively participated in commercially lucrative genres. He composed easily learned, publishable glees, songs, and anthems for the American mainstream: that is, amateur middle-class choristers and the professional working musicians—organists and paid soloists—of the church quartet choir. Ives later claimed that he turned his back on the professional music world in an act of integrity, so as not to weaken or dilute his music, and in compliance with his father's beliefs:

> Father felt that a man could keep his music-interest stronger, cleaner, bigger, and freer, if he didn't try to make a living out of it. Assuming a man lived by himself and with no dependents, no one to feed but himself, and willing to live as simply as Thoreau—[he] might write music that no one would play, publish, listen to, or buy. *But*—if he has a nice wife and some nice children, how can he let the children starve on his dissonances—answer that, Eddy! So he has to weaken (and as a man he should weaken for his children), but his music (some of it) more than weakens—it goes "ta ta" for money—bad for him, bad for music, but good for his boys!![48]

On the surface, Ives is justifying his decision to be a successful businessman like the vast majority of his Yale colleagues instead of a professional musician. But his description could equally be applied to his childhood. Although George's family didn't exactly starve on his dissonances, they certainly didn't thrive either. Without a sense of financial security from his father, Ives made career decisions controlled by the need to succeed: he would not recreate the instability and problematic social status of his birth family.[49] Through his Yale activities and compositions, Ives moved always forward, away from the model of his childhood and, in some ways, against the model of his college years. By aggressively seeking secure employment in the business arena, and acceptance by his peers and colleagues, Ives steered a middle path between the ideals of both George and Horatio, taking what he liked from each while conspicuously rejecting the hardships endured by each.

Ives's later use of George as a foil for Parker found little expression in the actual music that he composed between 1894 and 1902. After the dissonant but unformed "Credo" of 1894, Ives seems to have abandoned the personal approaches of his father in favor of the rule-based language of Parker. After his Yale period, Ives infrequently, privately, and tentatively revived some of the experimental approaches he developed under his father in works like *Psalm 67* and *Psalm 150*. Each of these choral settings expands the rulebook of European harmony, in conjunction with the transference of dense keyboard textures to voices, all fitted into the conventional form of a quartet-choir anthem. The inspiration for *Psalm 67* may have its roots in another one of George's ideas—that of transcribing amateur, nontraditional sounds—in its use of a choir in two distinct but conjoined keys. Ives's new interest in experimenting with the choral sound is understandable in that his post-Yale positions involved more direct control over the choir. Yet despite the fertile ground of the psalm settings, Ives's public output continued to be dominated by publishable, performable anthems and sacred songs.

This middle path, which guaranteed audiences, performers, and social status, illuminates Ives's musical activities in and out of the classroom. Beyond the glees, the most significant popular music style that Ives encountered at Yale was ragtime. Following its introduction to mainstream white audiences at Chicago's Exposition, ragtime and its imitators spread through performance and written traditions over the next decade. Between 1894 and 1898, Ives regularly heard and played ragtime at New Haven bars and at Poli's, a vaudeville theatre.

But what exactly did Ives hear? During the 1890s "ragtime" identified many different types of music, not simply the piano style known today. In fact, the word "rag" only first appeared in published music in 1896.[50] Even after Joplin's huge hits like *Maple Leaf Rag* (1899), ragtime songs constituted the most commonly performed style. In the 1890s, vaudeville hits imitated ragtime rhythms and accompaniments but contained texts brimming with every possible negative African-American stereotype, including dialect. Singers, often women known as "coon shouters," usually performed these songs in blackface, and the lyrics were intentionally irreverent and risqué—in other words, the polar opposite of the sentimental song or glee. Songs like *May*

Irwin's Bully Song (1896) and *At A Georgia Campmeeting* (1897) formed the kind of repertoire heard in vaudeville theatres like Poli's.

Ives equated these staged dialect songs with ragtime in *Memos*. He described hearing "black-faced comedians then, ragging their songs" at Poli's, and goes on to quote one of the songs he heard in 1893 or 1894: "I'm a-livin' easy on pork chops greasy / I'm always a-pickin' on a spring chickin [sic]."[51] As in others of the genres, this text maintains the dialect and stereotypes that dominated minstrelsy, now transferred to a new musical and theatrical genre. Later, Ives quoted from at least one ragtime song, "Hello Ma Baby" (1899), in his orchestral work *Central Park in the Dark*. Like its contemporaries, the song combined dialect lyrics with two new fashions, ragtime and the telephone.

Ives had more contact with ragtime after his move to New York in 1898. In fact, his first residence in the city was merely a few city blocks from the original Tin Pan Alley on West 28th Street. Ives would have heard nascent ragtime songs mingling with the other sounds by merely walking through his neighborhood. He may have encountered written instrumental ragtime here as well, as works by Joplin became much more accessible. Although he may have heard instrumental ragtime performed in New Haven, it is impossible to gauge the repertoire or style.[52] Publications lagged behind performance traditions, and even as ragtime publications grew in popularity, performers departed from printed versions as a rule. Ragtime improvisers combined "barbaric harmonies" with "audacious resolutions" that were not written into the score.[53] Professional ragtime musicians were trained to perform not only improvisations on published music and oral traditions, but to "rag" patriotic tunes, popular songs, and classics. Occasionally, composers mixed several "ragged" tunes into one piece, as in *Ragtime Jimmie's Jamboree* (1899), which combines syncopated versions of "The Star-Spangled Banner," "On the Banks of the Wabash," and Mendelssohn's *Wedding March*.[54] Ives's later rag transformations of borrowed material such as hymn tunes or Civil War songs—that is, George's music—may have been inspired in part by these models.

Ives's excitement over this popular, contemporary style of music was that of a white university student from a well-respected, socially powerful family (excepting his father, of course) attending an Ivy League school. His encounters with ragtime continued what was by then the foundation of American popular music: the fascination with and imitation of African-American culture. In this way, Ives's cultural appropriation of ragtime was typical of this period (and others, from jazz and rock and roll to hip hop). Such subversive music was popular on the Yale campus, and Ives likely drew on this model (along with male part-songs) when performing and composing music for staged musical entertainments at his fraternity, DKE. As in vaudeville, black-face comedy would have been included in the DKE shows as well.

Within the highly select Yale student body, the fraternities and secret societies proved almost completely homogeneous in terms of race, ethnicity, class, and religion.[55] If Yale itself was a bastion of white male privilege, DKE and Wolf's Head—Ives's two associations—formed part of the core of that privilege. Ives spent four years in this environment, and as a senior proved an insider even among insiders. In such a homogeneous society, the racial allure of ragtime must have proven particularly potent.

Donning the mask of ragtime allowed Ives a rare opportunity to assert a socially beneficial identity that had a tangential but nonspecific connection with George. Ragtime drew heavily on the march tradition, and in some ways vaudeville songs and shouters succeeded the minstrel shows of George's day. But both the form and context of Ives's ragtime indulgence marked his musical, personal, and social independence. Nor was this rebellious idiom subject to the compositional finesse and ideals learned in Horatio Parker's classes.

Ragtime, then, emerges as the first vernacular music that Ives learned on his own, a music with which he could impress his peers and achieve his ambitions of social status, and even economic security. Ives mentions the "freedom" of ragtime while comparing his ragtime-influenced works with those based on hymn-tunes and other quotations associated with his father: "The early ragtime pieces and marches . . . seemed to get going 'good and free'—and the hymn-tune sonatas and symphonies less so."[56]

By the turn of the century, Ives was able to perform, and possibly compose, in the most popular musical genre of his day. These skills helped him succeed socially at Yale, and provided him with a performance approach—the ability to rag—that could come in handy in pursuing a musical career. As ragtime publications reached the mainstream American market, Ives continued to embrace the most commercially successful music to date.

In addition to learning ragtime, Ives adapted his noncommercial compositions to reach a larger market, once again in opposition to his teacher's values. One such compositional hybrid occurred right under Parker's nose: a fugue for string quartet, later used as the opening movement of the First String Quartet. This movement was probably written as the assignment for the end of the first term of the strict composition class, during the winter of 1897–98.[57] As a subject for the fugue, Ives chose the first phrase of Lowell Mason's stately "Missionary Hymn." Ives's choice of an American hymn tune could be seen as an allegiance to his father, in opposition to Parker's stated

Manuscript source for Ives's String Quartet Fugue for Parker. Courtesy Yale University Irving S. Gilmore Music Library. String Quartet No. 1 by Charles Ives © 1988 by Peer International Corporation. Copyright renewed. International copyright secured. Used by permission. All rights reserved.

views. But in fact, "Missionary Hymn" could not be further from George's gospel hymns. The text is wordy, highly poetic rather than personal, and, unlike the easily repeated texts and choruses of the gospel hymns, would have been difficult to transmit orally. While camp-meeting hymns concerned the future well-being of the participants in both spiritual and economic terms, Mason's work presents a model of religious noblesse oblige in which an insular and homogeneous American church—implicitly white, whose roots precede the waves of immigration that changed the country in the later nineteenth century—are called to work on behalf of the less fortunate (and less Christian) abroad.

Faced with such a compositional assignment, Ives could have looked back to the music of his childhood, and written a fugue on a phrase from "In the Sweet By and By." Instead, he avoided what Parker termed the "sickly sentimental hymn tune." At the same time, Ives could have written a fugue on a newly composed subject of his own, thus breaking his ties to potentially provincial American hymnody, and fully embracing the European, post-Beethovenian emphasis on original genius. Yet, such a work might seem off-putting to potential performers and wider audiences. He compromised by using a hymn tune that rose above the lower classes in practice, text, and context. The result blends an ensemble associated with European noncommercial music with an obviously American, hymn-based work that reasserts the potency of models like Buck's *Star-Spangled Banner Overture,* and Ives's own *Variations on "America."* But more importantly, the string quartet movement is a model of contrapuntal discipline with sensuous, luxurious, controlled Romanticism. In other words, despite its hymnic origins, the work is the very progeny of Horatio Parker.

After his graduation from Yale and move to New York, Ives attempted two large-scale works, each of which willingly continued his connection to Parker. Around 1902, he completed the First Symphony, continuing the Parker-esque voice of the first movement in the remaining three movements. As in his earlier classroom compositions, here Ives obediently follows contemporary European models, and the work unfolds in unapologetic order. By continuing to write in Parker's voice after his graduation, Ives showed his preferred connections to the Euro-American tradition of his teacher.

Moreover, Ives's first completed symphony uses direct and indirect quotations from historical and contemporary representatives of the idiom, from Beethoven (the Ninth) and Schubert (the Eighth, or "Unfinished") to more recent examples from Tchaikovsky (the Sixth, or "Pathétique") and Dvořák (the Ninth, "From the New World").[58] Burkholder suggests that, in the First Symphony, "Ives is doing more than his homework; he is both demonstrating and announcing his command of the European symphonic tradition, his strong affiliation with composers like Dvořák and Tchaikovsky, and his ability to say something new and individual."[59]

Beyond this, however, Ives's choice of models is particularly illuminating because Dvořák and Tchaikovsky subordinated nationalist styles to the dominant symphonic idiom, as represented by the German tradition. Both are singled out by Richard Taruskin as examples of composers whose perceived subordination to the German tradition affected evaluations of their work even during their lifetime.[60] Labeling their efforts as "tourist" and "colonialist" nationalism, Taruskin claims that both composers faced "the dilemma that all 'peripheral' composers have had to face since the establishment of Germanic musical hegemony (that is, the discourse of 'classical music')": that such peripheral composers could only express an identity with the intervention of a collective folkloristic or oriental mask. To Taruskin, Dvořák in particular was "the master of the unmarked mother tongue" (i.e., the Austro-German tradition), and the "'tourist nationalism' that Dvořák practiced (and preached to his American pupils) was a matter of superficially marking received techniques, forms and media with regionalisms as one might don a native holiday costume." If, as Burkholder states, Ives is announcing "his strong affiliation" with Dvořák and Tchaikovsky in the First Symphony, then this affiliation extends to the works of composers who, in Taruskin's terms, "deliberately adulterated" regional musical resources to suit the dominant model.

How much the borrowing owes to the instructional material in Parker's classroom cannot be known. What is intriguing, however, is that Ives imitates the processes of his two "colonialist" models, Dvořák and Tchaikovsky, by adapting American hymn tunes to suit the needs of the Austro-German symphonic model. Ives truncates passages from "Beulah Land" and *The Shining Shore* to make them rhythmically regularized and melodically smoothened so as to better function in two- and four-bar thematic segments. Perhaps Ives intuitively recognized the appropriateness of choosing these adulterated hymn tunes as his own American mask. Both original hymn texts express a desire to reach "my heav'n, my home forevermore," and refer longingly to "the shining [glory] shore" that waits to be discovered "across the sea"—in effect and practice, locating artistic heaven on the shores of Western Europe.[61]

In his seven-movement cantata *The Celestial Country*, Ives attempted a slightly different but equally ambitious synthesis by merging specific borrowings from Parker's *Hora Novissima* with a quartet-choir structure. Ives wrote *The Celestial Country* with the limitations of congregational choirs in mind, much like Buck's quartet-choir cantatas published during the 1890s. Buck's five cantatas had been commissioned by publisher Rudolph Schirmer "to fill the current need for works of about an hour's duration and of moderate difficulty to be performed at evening musical services." Historian John Tasker Howard described these Buck cantatas as "not difficult to perform, and any one of them may be performed in connection with a Christmas or Easter service."[62]

Concert

And Presentation of a New Cantata,

"The Celestial Country!"

WORDS BY HENRY ALFORD.
(*Latin Text from St. Bernard.*)

MUSIC BY CHARLES E. IVES.

For Solo, Quartet, Octet, Chorus, Organ and String Orchestra.

MISS ANNIE WILSON	Soprano
MISS EMMA WILLIAMS	Contralto
MR. E. ELLSWORTH GILES	Tenor
MR. GEORGE A. FLEMING	Baritone

The Kaltenborn String Quartet:

MR. FRANZ KALTENBORN	First Violin
MR. WILLIAM ROWELL	Second Violin
MR. GUSTAVE BACH	Viola
MR. LOUIS HEINE	'Cello

MR. CHARLES E. IVES	Organist

Assisted By

MRS. SPRINGER,
MRS. DULANY,
MISS CAROLINE ANDRESEN,
MISS MARTHA SNEAD,
MISS CHARLOTTE SNELL,
[Soprano.]

MISS MARY GROUT,
MISS MANSFIELD,
[Mezzo-Soprano.]
MISS SARAH EDWARDS,
MISS MINA ANDRESEN,
MISS DOLORES REEDY,
[Contralto.]

MR. JOHN W. CATCHPOLE,   MR. A. C. EADIE,
MR. HARRY B. MOOK.
[Tenor.]

MR. EDWIN F. FULTON,   MR. HERMAN TROST,
MR. FREDERICK BALLANTYNE,   MR. THOMAS.
[Basso.]

Horns: { In B flat (Euphonium)   .   .   MR. W. S. PHASEY
{ In A   .   .   .   .   .   (Player to be Announced)

Central Presbyterian Church,

New York

Friday,

April 18, 1902.

Program of the premiere of *The Celestial Country,* April 18, 1902. Courtesy Yale University Irving S. Gilmore Music Library.

The Celestial Country fits these specifications precisely. It premiered on April 18, 1902, by a small amateur chorus of seventeen, plus solo quartet, that Ives directed in his current position at Central Presbyterian Church in Manhattan. The moderately difficult work lasts under an hour, and constituted only half of the evening's program at its premiere that took place in the church at Easter.[63] Although Ives's work typically has been seen as an imitation of Parker's oratorio, its connections to Buck's cantatas are numerous and remarkable. Both Ives and Buck have featured the quartet soloists extensively in ensemble and against the amateur chorus. Ives drew his English text from a hymn, like Buck, but unlike Parker who preferred the demanding Latin of *Hora Novissima*. Ives and Buck rely heavily on organ accompaniment in their cantatas (often doubling the amateur chorus's lines) with a few other instruments added for effect; once again, a world away from Parker's full orchestra and complex choral polyphony.[64]

Ives consciously blended two opposites in his attempt to infuse the populist anthem style of Buck's cantata with specific quotations from Parker's *Hora Novissima*: commercial and noncommercial; middle-class accessibility and upper-class elitism; small quartet choir with large, trained chorus. Once again, Ives wanted the best of both worlds. Despite Parker's public condemnation of the quartet choir, Ives attempted to make the styles compatible in a work that could be easily published and performed by mainstream church musicians.

With the cantata's premiere, Ives introduced himself to the New York public as a professional composer in the Parker mold.[65] Ives may have hoped to establish his career in the same way that Parker had with *Hora Novissima*, which had led to the Yale position. In doing so, Ives did not hesitate to identify himself as "a Yale graduate and pupil in music of Professor Parker" to the reviewers attending the premiere.[66] Perhaps Ives even harbored a fantasy of receiving approval from Parker himself. If Ives hoped for recognition by his teacher however, he was sorely disappointed. Just as Ives publicly lobbied to be recognized as a Parker protégé, another of Parker's students received his teacher's blessing. William Edward Haesche (1867–1929) studied with Parker at Yale at the same time as Ives but as a graduate student; he was the first candidate to receive a Bachelor of Music (at that time, Yale's only graduate degree in music) in 1897.[67] On April 17, 1902—the day before the premiere of *The Celestial Country*—Haesche's appointment as Acting Battell Professor of Music was announced in the *Yale Daily News*, under the title "Mr. Haesche's Appointment," which read: "Mr. William E. Haesche, Mus. B. of Yale, has been appointed to take charge of Professor Horatio W. Parker's classes in Theoretical Music until the latter's return in October. Mr. Haesche is well known in New England as a musician and is the leader of several musical organizations in the city, among which is the Choral Union. One of his symphonies was given at the fourth concert of the New Haven Symphony Orchestra this winter."[68] This announcement appeared elsewhere, according to Parker's correspondence, including "the next issue of the University Bulletin, repeated in the Yale Daily News and posted on the Bulletin Board of the Music Department [and] in the New Haven papers."[69] According to a score memo, Ives had had contact with Haesche himself as recently as the previous December (1901), and must have heard of this appointment within days of *The Celestial Country*'s premiere. The event that should have marked Ives's arrival as a professional composer, the end of his youthful training and the beginning of his musical manhood, instead was punctuated by what Ives perceived as a public failure to match his teacher's accomplishments.

"Damn rot and worse"

In his vitriolic reminiscences, Ives expresses his disillusionment over not just Parker and his views, but with Ives's own infatuation with Parker's world, and over his willingness to embrace an inauthentic musical and class identity. Having decided to pursue the European tradition, Ives found himself composing in musical genres to which he had no personal connection. He had performed very little of this music as an organist. The few original Bach and Mendelssohn compositions that he knew were part and parcel of an inherited American tradition. The remainder of the repertoire had to be partially recreated from a score, or rarely, and passively, heard in a live performance. Having traveled as far as possible from the amateur performance traditions of his father, Ives discovered that even his hard-won status as a professional church musician was inadequate, since he accompanied and composed for the much-derided quartet choir.

Did Ives truly aspire to be like Parker, to fully embrace the European tradition? If he did, Ives must have known that, even after his "four years with Parker," he was still lacking an essential component for a successful career: European, preferably German, postgraduate musical polish. There is no indication that Ives's family—now headed by his Uncle Lyman and Aunt Amelia—had any intention of funding such a tour. In fact, his family arranged an entry-level position in the insurance industry soon after his graduation from Yale, through the intervention of two well-placed relatives.[70] The message from the family was clear: Charles was going into business. Without independent resources, Ives could not gain admission to Parker's world in

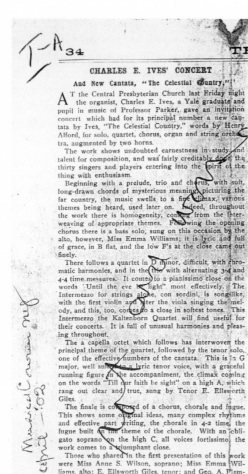

T-A 34

TH

CHARLES E. IVES' CONCERT

And New Cantata, "The Celestial Country,"

AT the Central Presbyterian Church last Friday night the organist, Charles E. Ives, a Yale graduate and pupil in music of Professor Parker, gave an invitation concert which had for its principal number a new cantata by Ives, "The Celestial Country," words by Henry Alford, for solo, quartet, chorus, organ and string orchestra, augmented by two horns.

The work shows undoubted earnestness in study and talent for composition, and was fairly creditably done, the thirty singers and players entering into the spirit of the thing with enthusiasm.

Beginning with a prelude, trio and chorus, with soft, long-drawn chords of mysterious meaning, picturing the far country, the music swells to a fine climax, various themes being heard, used later on. Indeed, throughout the work there is homogeneity, coming from the interweaving of appropriate themes. Following the opening chorus there is a bass solo, sung on this occasion by the alto, however, Miss Emma Williams; it is lyric and full of grace, in B flat, and the low F's at the close came out finely.

There follows a quartet in D minor, difficult, with chromatic harmonies, and in the trio with alternating 3-4 and 4-4 time measures. It comes to a pianissimo close on the words "Until the eve be light" most effectively. The Intermezzo for strings alone, con sordini, is song-like, with the first violin and after the viola singing the melody, and this, too, comes to a close in softest tones. This Intermezzo the Kaltenborn Quartet will find useful for their concerts. It is full of unusual harmonies and pleasing throughout.

The a capella octet which follows has interwoven the principal theme of the quartet, followed by the tenor solo, one of the effective numbers of the cantata. This is in G major, well suited to a lyric tenor voice, with a graceful running figure in the accompaniment, the climax coming on the words "Till our faith be sight" on a high A, which rang out clear and true, sung by Tenor E. Ellsworth Giles.

The finale is composed of a chorus, chorale and fugue. This shows some original ideas, many complex rhythms and effective part writing, the chorale in 4-2 time, the fugue built on the theme of the chorale. With an obligato soprano on the high C, all voices fortissimo, the work comes to a triumphant close.

Those who shared in the first presentation of this work were Miss Anne S. Wilson, soprano; Miss Emma Williams, alto; E. Ellsworth Giles, tenor; and Geo. A. Phem-

Musical Courier, April 1902

Review of the premiere of *The Celestial Country* with Ives's handwritten commentary. Courtesy Yale University Irving S. Gilmore Music Library.

the same way as William Haesche or David Stanley Smith, who joined Parker in Munich in March 1902 and enjoyed the personal introductions that his teacher offered.[71]

As an independent composer, Ives relied on the mainstream market to support himself despite the knowledge, gained in Parker's classroom, that reaching the masses entailed musical compromises like those made by Buck. Faced with a choice between upholding Parker's upper-class ideals and continuing as a professional composer for the middle class, Ives attempted an impossible reconciliation. He rehearsed the ensemble, had the programs printed, brought in extra instrumentalists and choir members (including some of his own roommates), and naively hoped for the professional payoff that Parker had had nine years earlier with *Hora Novissima*.

Ives's efforts included notifying the media, and as a result two reviews of the work were published in the *New York Times* and *Musical Courier*. Both clearly recognized that *The Celestial Country* belonged to a different class from *Hora Novissima*. The *Musical Courier*, which identified Ives as a student of Parker's, implied that the composer was still a student by praising its "undoubted earnestness in study." The *New York Times* review was strikingly less positive, pointing out that the text was "not particularly felicitous," and that the work "obviously suffered from the want of the chorus . . . the choral climaxes thus failing of their intended effect." The review commented again that the work "has the elementary merit of being scholarly and well made," another reference to this being a student work and not the masterly tour de force of *Hora Novissima*. Ives later scrawled "Damn rot and worse" across one of the reviews, a statement that could refer either to the critics' words, or the cantata's ineffectual concessions.

The Celestial Country's failure to achieve its intended goals of publication, position, and recognition sealed Ives's fate. He resigned almost immediately, walking away from the successful fourteen-year public career that he had been building since his childhood. Between 1898 and his death in 1919, Parker achieved international success, reaching a career high in 1911–12 with his opera *Mona*. He was hailed as a major American composer, particularly in the musical circles of New York where Ives lived. In 1902, neither could have predicted that by the end of the century Horatio Parker would be primarily remembered not for his own compositions, or his significant contributions to American musical education, but as the mossback professor of the brilliant iconoclastic composer Charles Ives. Instead of his music, only the distorted echo of his words would be heard through the unforgiving recollections of his former student.

3

On the Verge

I went along the road that lonely lay,
The road I love to wander day by day.

—from "Longing"

Six weeks after *The Celestial Country*'s premiere, on June 1, 1902, Ives completed his final service as organist and choir director at Central Presbyterian Church in New York. At twenty-seven, Ives abandoned the only career he had ever known, the career in which he had worked for half his life—that of a professional church organist and composer. After nearly fourteen years of steady employment at increasingly prestigious and well-paying churches, culminating in a reviewed premiere of a significant work that he hoped would establish his reputation as a major composer, Ives, as he put it, "gave up music."[1]

Indeed, Ives's resignation signaled a nearly complete withdrawal from music. Over the next few years, Ives struggled to redefine himself in all spheres of his life: in his professional career, his personal relationships, and his temporarily ambiguous musical direction. The stress of these sweeping changes peaked in late 1906, when he faced the most significant crisis of his life to that time. In its aftermath, Ives forged a compositional coalescence that resolved, at least temporarily, the conflicts that drove him away from music that Sunday in 1902.

Poverty Flat

After graduating from Yale, Ives moved to New York in summer 1898. Rooming at the Yale Club on Madison Square placed him adjacent to the street that would soon be dubbed Tin Pan Alley, the new center for American popular song, on West 28th Street in lower midtown Manhattan. By fall of that year, he had moved into living quarters shared by a half dozen or so bachelors, most of them recent Yale graduates. Many of the residents studied at the New York College of Physicians, some were in law, and a small minority, like Ives, worked in business. Over the years, the residency changed as members finished their degrees and moved on to establish impressive careers and residences.

The communal apartment was nicknamed "Poverty Flat" in what appears to have been a popular nickname for the bachelor apartment of the early century. The term appeared in an article by journalist Deshler Welch, published in *Cosmopolitan* magazine in 1900 and titled "The Connoisseurs of Poverty Flat."[2] In fact, Welch had published the cookbook *The Bachelor and the Chafing Dish* in 1896 for young men like Ives and his friends: middle- and upper-class college graduates who delayed marriage, lived in a communal flat, and (perhaps) cooked their own meals in a chafing dish. Welch's publications thus highlighted the fashionable lifestyle of the new urban bachelor, a lifestyle that Ives and a growing number of his recently graduated peers conspicuously embraced.

For Ives and his cronies, "Poverty Flat" referenced not just their modern urban lifestyle but also social currency and generational identity. The term offered a tongue-in-cheek description of the temporary living standards of its educated white-collar worker residents, who would enjoy executive earning power in the near future. In this sense, "Poverty Flat" was a joke among privileged insiders, unlike the Lower East Side only a few miles away where real poverty, starvation, and filth reigned. In its Bohemian pretensions and loose-knit male collegiality, the residence acted as a way station between youthful freedom and the adult responsibility of earning an upper-class living. Ives, who lived in Poverty Flat for ten years, had the dubious distinction of being the Flat's longest permanent resident.[3]

During his early years in Poverty Flat, Ives seems to have drifted between a lingering desire to return to a professional career in music and an entry-level job in insurance. While his medically directed roommates looked forward to increasing professional and social authority in American society, Ives, through the intervention of distant family members, was working in a business that was widely—and rightly—suspected of fraudulent and unethical practices. In its capitalist form, insurance was never truly an altruistic business, the phrase being an oxymoron. At its worst, insurance could be seen as gambling on the one sure thing, human mortality. With the help of mortality charts that analyzed life span and risk factors, insurance companies minimized financial risk and guaranteed a profit, barring unforeseen disasters such as earthquakes, fires, and epidemics.

In the early 1900s, the unregulated insurance industry enjoyed an un-precedented boon. Profits soared thanks to population growth and the investment of policyholders' payments into risky ventures, many of which involved executive conflicts of interest with banks and railroad companies. Unlike stock companies, mutual insurances companies at least appeared to be democratically organized. They held elections in which policyholders could choose the companies' directors, and possibly executives. And mutuals were organized on the principal of profit sharing between the executives and the mostly middle- and lower-class policyholders. However, no legislation dictated how much wealth had to be distributed among policyholders, and only a tiny fraction of company profits were ever disbursed. Some executives and their high-ranking family members took home huge salaries, and some spent company money on lavish parties. For example, Richard A. McCurdy, the president of Mutual Life of New York (the parent company of Ives's employer, the Raymond Agency), and his son earned five times what the president of the United States made in a year, and more than the salaries of all state governors combined.[4]

Such extravagances outraged the public. Newspapers and magazines decried the gap between the lifestyles and salaries of the executives compared to the policyholders who were nominally "served" by the companies. Many suspected that the near-monopoly held by the largest businesses (including Mutual) kept premiums artificially high and competition at a minimum. To address these and other pressing issues, the New York legislature convened an intensive investigative committee headed by Senator William H. Armstrong. Unlike previous inquiries that industry executives had shaken off, the Armstrong Investigation would completely rewrite the business. According to one insurance historian, its probes revealed and addressed "rampant nepotism, almost complete directorial control of proxy votes, executives more interested in high finance than safe insurance, outrageously costly marketing methods that hurt existing policyholders, unrealistic sales illustrations, declining dividend scales, attempts to buy control of politicians, dubious accounting techniques, and outright fraud. NYLIC [New York Life Insurance Company], for instance, made fictitious sales of junk bonds at par so that it could list the dubious assets at unrealistically high prices on its annual statements."[5]

As the Armstrong Investigation proceeded through the fall and winter of 1905, the insurance field was rocked by looming regulations, the exposure of high-profile corruption, bad publicity, and organizational uncertainty. In this shifting climate, Ives lacked a mentor. Even if his father had lived, George could not have provided the experience or advice that Ives needed at this time, since he had thoroughly rejected a career in business himself.

Ives's uncle Lyman Brewster, a judge who might have offered some counsel despite not being a direct part of the business world, died early in 1904, after having guided Ives's younger brother Moss to a law career; Moss later became a respected judge.[6]

Under different circumstances, Ives could have looked to his cousin Robert Granniss for direction. Granniss was a vice president at Mutual who, along with another cousin, had arranged for Ives's original hiring in 1898. He had begun his long, distinguished career at Metropolitan, leaving that company in 1877 when it couldn't match the salary offered by Mutual. During fall 1905, Granniss was called as the first witness before the Armstrong committee. In light of the committee's grilling of Granniss, the investigators may have planned their attack to bring down one of the field's most prominent executives right off the bat.

Granniss was questioned about the procedure for involving policyholders in Mutual's elections. Although he initially answered that the directors were chosen by the nearly half million policyholders, further questioning revealed the uncomfortable facts. Only some two hundred policyholders, "nearly all officers or employees of the company," actually voted to install their own directors and officers. Granniss and McCurdy, the corrupt Mutual president, held the proxies of another twenty thousand policyholders. A later analyst claimed that "as no election had been contested the McCurdy-Granniss proxies had never been used." New York papers summarized Granniss's testimony in the most caustic, scandalous terms: "Mutualization Called a Farce, Elections a Sham," ran the *New York Herald* headline.[7]

With this embarrassing and very public testimony, Granniss's career was over. Indicted for "false entries" in spring 1906, he resigned under pressure as part of Mutual's post-Armstrong executive housecleaning, along with McCurdy, and McCurdy's son and son-in-law.

With a shadow over his cousin's career, Ives was alone and vulnerable, working in a field with an uncertain future. He had seen what happened to well-intentioned, successful, intelligent people in unfortunate circumstances through the model of Granniss. In the same way that he patched together his early music career as an organist and composer, he now had to feel his way through the complicated world of business on his own, starting at the bottom. Although Ives worked hard, was promoted to managing agents, and made important contacts—with one of whom, Julian "Mike" Myrick, Ives would eventually found his own business—the task ahead of him was still daunting. No wonder that Ives was "grumpy and morose" as close pal Keyes Winter prepared to marry and move out of Poverty Flat in spring 1907, leaving Ives more isolated than ever.[8]

Ives foundered in his personal life as well. While his Poverty Flat room-mates like Winter were building future marriages as well as profitable and respectable careers, Ives fell behind in this area too. Although he had met his future wife, Harmony Twichell, as early as 1896 through one of his Yale classmates, Ives showed no interest in developing the relationship for almost a decade; an understandable circumstance while he remained an undergradu-ate, but more curious as time went on. Perhaps his characteristic shyness was an obstacle. Equally likely, his lack of confidence and direction made it impossible for him to imagine a successful marriage to an educated, polished, and accomplished young lady from a nearly aristocratic family.

The Twichell family was highly respected in Hartford, the Reverend Joseph Twichell being a well-known Congregationalist minister and a close friend of Mark Twain. In his erudition, professional connections, and respectabil-ity, Joseph Twichell must have seemed an intimidating figure to the now-fatherless Ives, representing as he did the social opposite of George. Joseph's son David Twichell was in the Yale class right behind Ives, and moved into Poverty Flat in 1899 while completing medical studies at the New York Col-lege of Physicians. David went on to work at the Saranac Lake Sanitarium in upstate New York after graduating in 1903.

Through David, Ives met Harmony Twichell, an impressive young woman with an excellent education and splendid family connections. Her youth was filled with religion, finishing school, and singing and painting lessons, capped with such extravagances as a two-week tour of the Chicago Exposition in 1893, and even a personal visit with President McKinley. Harmony was among the thousands of middle- and upper-class women of her generation who chose nursing as both a vocation and a profession.[9] On the one hand, a nursing ca-reer maintained the accepted profile of the nurturing Victorian woman. The role of nurse was believed to foster feminine inclinations such as compassion, nurturing, and household management; thus, nurses were viewed as more marriageable than women in other careers, such as the Gibson Girl-type office worker. At the same time, a nurse could enjoy travel, income, relative autonomy, and authority. For a single woman, it offered an inviting alterna-tive to spinsterhood. For those who were socially inclined (with or without the spur of a religious impulse), a degree in nursing provided opportunities for direct intervention in the lives of those less fortunate.

Despite advantages, student nurses had to overcome severe obstacles. They worked grueling hours for little or no pay, often ten to twelve hours a day, followed by coursework at night. Institutional employment remained scarce, so those who graduated faced the likelihood of private service, where the pay was low and their status that of a servant. In 1900, when Harmony Twichell

Harmony Twichell, ca. 1902. Courtesy Yale University Irving
S. Gilmore Music Library.

completed her degree, the fastest-growing field was that of community or
public health nursing.

The role of public health nurse in New York had been founded by Lillian
Wald and Mary Brewster in 1883, when both women began treating impoverished immigrants in the Lower East Side.[10] Their efforts sprang from the
same impulse that inspired Jane Addams to cofound Hull House in Chicago
in the same era. As urban slums swelled during the ensuing decades, so did
the role of community health worker. In 1901 alone, Wald reported that the
seventeen nurses associated with their Henry Street Settlement had treated
almost forty-five hundred patients, and made over twenty-five thousand
nursing visits. The settlement served all needy residents, but first and fore-

most among these were the children. The nurses of the Henry Street Settlement, according to one nursing historian, were deeply affected by the health of their youngest patients: "Desperately poor immigrant families lived in crowded squalor within a maze of garbage-strewn streets. Victims of periodic economic depressions, periodic epidemics, and low-quality care during pregnancy and childbirth, children were among those most greatly afflicted. Often, mothering the family was left to a child of nine or ten years. Many children worked long hours for low wages and assumed family burdens far beyond their years."[11] Among the street waifs in this neighborhood lived an entire generation of future entertainment stars including Al Jolson, Eddie Cantor, Irving Berlin, and George Burns. In addition to treating hundreds of children for malnutrition, injuries, and disease, the settlement maintained a country vacation home in rural New York at Riverhold. Here, Wald and her nurses provided inner-city children with fresh air, clean play spaces, and a homelike atmosphere.

In her 1900 graduation essay, "The Nurse's Gain," Harmony anticipated the experience of caring for the poverty-stricken as a tremendous opportunity for personal growth: "The people of the slums become our acquaintances. We come near the grim affairs of living, poverty and pain—and what food for reflection is offered! See what an immense gain in the *furnishing of our minds!* We come into a sort of humble fellowship with some of the noblest women that ever lived. Florence Nightingale and Sister Dora and Alice Fisher, their lives and what they did and tried to do, have a much greater significance."[12] While exploring her social commitments, Harmony worked as a visiting nurse in Chicago and later New York. At the same time, Harmony took advantage of other opportunities that her new profession offered. She traveled to Europe both with her family and as a nurse-companion to a wealthy widow. Thanks to David's connection, she worked at Saranac Lake, a respected facility that serviced upper-class patients, thereby bypassing the drudgery of private duty or limited work at hospitals that nurses from the rural and lower classes endured. As for marriage, Harmony entered into an ill-considered engagement to a family friend in 1904, breaking the engagement almost as soon as it was formed. For the moment, Harmony seemed ambivalent about her future direction. Whether her restlessness conveys wanderlust, disenchantment, or uncertainty is anyone's guess.

For his part, Ives's behavior showed the same half-hearted disposition, and nowhere is this lack of direction more evident than in his musical activities. He undertook very few new compositions—only a handful of mostly conventional songs, as well as some abandoned sketches for string quartets. The sketch of the song "Longing" is typical of this period. In its listless thirteen measures, Ives returned to the Yale practice of resetting Lieder texts, this time drawing on a translation of von Lilencron's version of "Sehnsucht" originally set by Richard Strauss.[13] Ives floundered between an uninspired barbershop language and something more expressionistic and less conventional. Having no clear direction, the song sputtered out and Ives summarily abandoned it.

Apart from these meager attempts at new compositions, most of Ives's musical activity focused on recopying and completing works from his student years. After his retirement from music in 1902, Ives had his student works recopied to compile a professional dossier, thereby emphasizing even more his connection to Parker. His creativity temporarily stagnant, Ives reviewed his dossier and wistfully remembered an earlier period of musical immersion, ambition, and optimism.

"On the verge of a nervous collapse"

Ives's emotional fragility can be understood not only from circumstantial evidence, but also from the perspective of his medical history. According to Ives's family and his first biographers, Ives began experiencing heart palpitations and tachycardia (a rapid heart beat) late in 1906, just after Keyes Winter, one of his closest friends, moved out of Poverty Flat. On the advice of the doctors at Mutual Insurance, whose job it was to recognize any disabilities in potential policyholders, Ives took a vacation at Old Point Comfort in Virginia with his future business partner Mike Myrick. His later medical records confirm this crisis in late 1906 as the beginning of Ives's heart troubles.[14]

In fact, surviving correspondence from Ives's Aunt Amelia and Harmony before and after Harmony's marriage reveals that Ives was suffering from the most common affliction of the time, an illness that was defined culturally, nationally, and socially as much as by physical symptoms. A letter of 1907 expressed Amelia's concern about Ives's health problems as follows: "It is not strange that men in business circles break down—for many of them are working to the very *limit*—in ordinary times and then when additional strain comes . . . there is no reserve strength to meet the emergency." Two 1908 letters from Harmony are more specific: Aunt Amelia had ongoing fears that Ives "was on the verge of a nervous collapse," while Harmony herself believed that Ives was "bankrupt of nervous energy."[15]

In early twentieth-century America, the phrases "break down," "nervous collapse," and "bankrupt of nervous energy" had very specific, pre-Freudian connotations: a neurasthenic condition. And the connotations of the most commonly diagnosed illness in America during this period are no mere coincidence. Ives's lifestyle, education, family background, and current circumstances all predisposed him to become a classic neurasthenic.

Neurasthenia, or nervousness, was first recognized by George Beard in 1881. Beard, the acknowledged "father of neurasthenia," was a Yale graduate who completed his medical studies at the New York College of Physicians, a career path duplicated by Ives's medical student roommates at Poverty Flat. Although initially controversial, Beard's theories quickly became popular throughout the United States—though less so in Europe—so that by 1896 neurasthenia was described as "almost a household word."[16] Indeed, by 1907 the New York Times identified the condition as "our national malady," stating that "not without reason has nervous prostration been called the 'National disease.' Wherever Americans work and worry, and especially in New York, where the pressure is at its worst, thousands of men, women, and children throw down their tools or leave their desks prostrated, to go to hospitals and sanitariums."[17] Through the first decade of the twentieth century, descriptions of the disease appeared constantly in newspapers, magazines, popular fiction, and medical journals. During this period, Beard's assistant and protégé J. H. Kellogg continued his mentor's work and became a leading exponent for the value of nutrition in preventing and treating neurasthenia. His findings live on in Kellogg cereals. In 1914, Kellogg observed that over the past two decades, from 1894 to 1914, "the disease was as popular with the laity as with the [medical] profession. . . . A wave of neurasthenia, so to speak, swept over the whole civilized world and it became rather popular to be neurasthenic. . . . [I]ts prevalence has increased in modern times so that it has come to be, in this country at least, almost a national malady."[18]

But what were the origins of this national malady? Writers cited continuous overwork as a common cause, often employing two metaphors common to industrialized America, banking and machinery. Banking metaphors referred to nervous "reserves," "stores," "spending," "impoverishment," and "bankruptcy." Echoing Amelia and Harmony's words, a neurasthenic's "store of nerve energy is exhausted," mental work "exhausts their stores of energy."[19] For businessmen who overwork "there is no reserve, and [in] the emergencies which constantly arise . . . [they] come to us as nervous bankrupts."[20]

Regarded as a valid medical illness, the most widely diagnosed medical condition in America was introduced into medical textbooks by the mid-1890s. By 1907, Thomas D. Savill could write that "considerable space is devoted to the subject in all current textbooks."[21] Doctors and nurses were well acquainted with neurasthenia or nervousness in all its forms. Ives's doctor roommates and Harmony, a trained nurse, would have all had a thorough training in the recognition and treatment of this widespread sickness. Symptoms included a dizzying array of ailments, some of which are currently recognized as psychological or physiological in origin: chronic eye strain, supersensitive hearing, trembling in the hands and fingers, cold or sweating feet, and "fits of despondency" or depression.

Heart palpitations were considered "exceedingly common in neurasthenics."[22] Typically, these were specifically linked to emotional trauma or overexcitement rather than organic heart disease. In 1914, describing heart palpitations associated with neurasthenia, Paul Hartenberg explained that some patients "are seized at intervals associated with pain, simulating angina pectoris. They then fear that they are suffering from cardiac disease, and in relieving them it is important to convince them that these are purely functional phenomena and thus to reassure them. The general treatment, and above all the regime and rest, the special indications which are suitable for irritability—warm hydrotherapy, sedative drugs—have a favorable action upon these palpitations. . . . Emotions are particularly to be avoided." Hartenberg also noted that when examining the heart condition of a neurasthenic, "emotional tachycardia must be borne in mind," suggesting that an unusually rapid heart rate could be psychosomatically induced.[23] "Distressing attacks of nervousness" related to heart troubles were also common; specific physical symptoms, which caused real pain, were identified by J. Mitchell Clarke in 1905: "These come on quite suddenly and without cause, and may occur at a time when the patient is feeling fairly well. In these attacks the patient gets a feeling . . . of sinking or faintness, generally starting from the epigastrium, or in cases where the heart is especially affected, from the praecordial region. . . . the heart and vessels may throb violently." Neurasthenic heart conditions, as opposed to organic heart disease, involved several possible symptoms, the two most common being attacks of tachycardia, "often after excitement or mental overstrain," and a fast pulse accompanied by tremors in the limbs. Furthermore, Clarke detailed several different types of "heart-attacks of neurasthenia," including the common form where "the pain is accompanied by palpitation, and by tachycardia."[24]

In 1906, Ives suffered from exactly these two ailments: palpitation and tachycardia, the two ailments listed in his later medical records, which do not describe organic heart disease. For the doctors at Mutual Insurance, the diagnosis would have been clear: "cardio neurasthenia," or nervousness affecting the heart. They recommended the standard treatment, a rest cure.

"The Cure"

S. Weir Mitchell published his first treatise on rest cures in 1878, and his recommendations soon became the standard treatment for neurasthenia. Mitchell's cure included six to twelve weeks of full or partial bed rest in a warm climate, in "well-wooded districts where there are hills to protect from cold and irritating winds, and trees to lend their soothing influence."[25] Rest cures in the mountains or countryside, along with hydrotherapy (therapeutic baths), were recommended as "essential" for "severe cases of neurasthenia" including "cases with marked cardiac symptoms."[26] In 1905 Robert W. Taylor further recommended for such patients "that one or two compatible and companionable people should be with them. Bathing is of much benefit, particularly at the seashore. . . . Change of scene and or air is of the highest importance in these cases. Sea voyages, short or protracted, restful quiet in the mountains or in some pleasant country place, and camping out, offer sources of much relief, and often lead to marvelous improvement."[27] Rest cure treatments varied in form, incorporating everything from complete bed rest (generally prescribed for women) to moderate exercise such as hiking, swimming, and horseback riding (more often recommended for men).

In keeping with his condition, the Mutual Insurance doctors recommended a rest cure for Ives, at Old Point Comfort, Virginia, whose renowned rest cure featured natural warm baths deemed particularly necessary for cardio-neurasthenic visitors like Ives. A later advertisement for Old Point Comfort's Hotel Chamberlin, where Ives stayed, paints a portrait of an idealized medical institution and luxurious spa: "When advised by your Physician to take 'The Cure' . . . you picture visions of up-to-date Hotels, interesting surroundings, unusual and celebrated people, and agreeable out-of-doors activities. To take 'The Cure' means all these, and also, certain Baths and Treatments, the Drinking of Medicinal Waters and Systematic, Out-of-door Exercise. . . . There is just one place in America that combines all of these pleasurable features, together with the Treatments and Medicinal Waters. That place is Hotel Chamberlin." On the advice of his doctors, Ives spent several weeks at "one of the most scientifically administered, best-equipped Bath Establishments in America" with, as Taylor recommended, a "compatible and companionable" person, his colleague Mike Myrick.

In addition to the rest cure, many doctors recommended marriage for the treatment of the neurasthenia in young men. In his study *Sexual Neurasthenia,* Beard outlined a subcategory of the disease—"sexual exhaustion"—that was particularly prevalent in young unmarried men as a result of "evil habits," excessive worry, and other causes. For such cases, Beard recommended "that it would be well for them to make arrangements, if possible, to become married in a year or two, more or less. . . . Some cases are better for marrying promptly; but in a majority it is sufficient to look ahead to marriage in a definite or approximately definite time." Physicians commonly dispensed Beard's advice to unmarried young men; indeed, Beard noted that "marriage, like travel, is recommended for these cases by wholesale." He concluded that, while a combination of treatments was preferable, a minority of patients "are positively benefited—perhaps cured—by marriage, whether resorted to as an incident to treatment, or as the main and only dependence." Interestingly, eighteen months after his health crisis, Ives married Harmony Twichell—no doubt for reasons beyond achieving an immediate cure.

In fact, Ives's neurasthenic condition and its contemporary meanings illuminate other aspects of his post-1906 life: his role within the business of insurance, his relationship with Harmony, and the resumption of his creative activities. Ives's cure at the Hotel Chamberlin provided more than just the physical environment necessary to treat his illness. Ives's direct employer at the time, the Raymond Agency (which acted as a selling agent for Mutual) faced closure due to the Armstrong Investigation. Ives and Myrick used their vacation to plan the beginning of their own agency. Their planned company would replace the Raymond Agency while using a second Mutual-sponsored company, Washington Life, as a buffer between themselves and the parent company, which still faced fallout from the investigation. In their history of the life insurance industry, Robert Wright and George Smith go so far as to suggest that Ives and Myrick "led a movement to professionalize life insurance salesmanship. . . . Ives and Myrick made the best of the uncertain post-Investigation environment in 1907 by opening their own general agency for the Washington Life Insurance Company, a small insurer not implicated in any fraudulent activities."[28] Less than a week after their return, their new company was founded on January 1, 1907. After Washington reinsured with another company in 1908, and the impact of the Armstrong Investigation had died down somewhat, Ives and Myrick rejoined Mutual directly. Soon, they would become the company's most productive agency. By 1929, the company characterized by "honesty, professionalism, and extensive use of well-trained brokers" was the largest agency in the country.[29] Ives and Myrick were part of the generation that "cleaned up" the insurance industry. They belonged to the first wave of professional managers that reinvigorated the field, while extending the business trend of separating ownership and management to the insurance industry.[30]

His professional identity resolved, Ives now had the equilibrium necessary to pursue a personal relationship with an unusually qualified partner. As a member of the professional medical community educated in the 1890s, Harmony could not have escaped a close knowledge of nervousness and its treatment. In addition to her training, Harmony had extensive practical experience from caring for the identified neurasthenic members of her own family, beginning with her brother David, Ives's roommate at Poverty Flat. In March 1903, while finishing his medical degree, David was "completely used up with overwork," and went for a month-long rest cure in South Carolina. His companion and nurse was his younger sister Harmony. Later references in the Twichell family correspondence to David's "condition," and to his apparent breakdown and unsuccessful rest cure in Asheville, North Carolina, in 1924, confirm that he continued to suffer from nervous ailments for the remainder of his life. During David's first breakdown in 1903, Ives gained a close knowledge of his roommate's condition, his cure, and his caregiver.[31]

After receiving his medical degree, David Twichell spent much of his career as a doctor at the Saranac Lake Sanitarium. The facility treated both tubercular patients and recovering neurasthenics, including the close Twichell friend Mark Twain, who sought out a rest cure for his neurasthenic condition at the sanitarium after an exhausting 1901 world tour. A combination of a professional hospital (for tuberculosis) and a hotel-resort (for neurasthenia), Saranac Lake Sanitarium offered an "atmosphere more of a club" to its nervous patients. Harmony joined David at Saranac off and on between 1903 and 1907; the longest period was as a visiting nurse between September 1903 and November 1904. Just as Harmony's 1903 trip entailed caring for David after his collapse, so her extended later visits to Saranac Lake may have involved continuing to look after her unmarried, hardworking brother in addition to, or perhaps even instead of, the official patients at the institution.

Ives visited David and Harmony at the Saranac sanitarium in September 1905, and the couple later marked this moment as the beginning of their serious relationship. This visit may have been more than a fortunate social opportunity, however. Rather, Ives, who may have already suspected his "condition," was pursuing his own rest cure at a health-care facility that had both the natural and human resources to treat him in accordance with common knowledge and every published account of the disease. Perhaps it is no coincidence, then, that Ives fell in love with a nurse who had practical experience in treating his illness. The couple's courtship, however, proceeded at a glacial pace—Ives's reluctance perhaps owing to his continuing underconfidence as a capable breadwinner. It only gained momentum when Harmony moved to New York in summer 1907, ostensibly to continue her service at the Henry Street Settlement. In so doing, Harmony exercised her strongly held beliefs of service, especially to underprivileged children, while making it clear that she was available to date Ives.

The couple's surviving letters and later accounts of the marriage leave no doubt that Ives and Harmony loved each other deeply. For Harmony's part, marrying Ives offered more than just a romantic attachment, although this was significant in its own right. Their marriage represented an opportunity to abandon certain obligations, not the least of which involved caring for many members of her family. David was not the only neurasthenic member of the Twichell family, according to the family's correspondence. Harmony's brother Burton took a rest cure and extended treatments at Battle Creek, Michigan, the home of Kellogg's world-famous neurasthenic treatment center. Her sister Sally would spend much of her life in rest cure treatment facilities including Saranac Lake (where her brother and sister treated her) and Asheville. And Harmony's father Joseph Twichell spent a period in a sanitarium in Brattleboro, Vermont, in early 1913 due to what was later described as a mental breakdown.[32]

By 1907, Harmony had explored all possible avenues of employment and avocation open to a young woman of her generation, class, and training. After donating her skills and energy to the most abject urban populations, Harmony did not aspire to continue that exhausting, depressing, sometimes horrific work as had Nightingale and her peers. Given the increasing dependency of her family, what had begun as an independent career in professional caregiving could have become an inescapable role as the Twichell family nurse. In fact, such a situation was common among spinster nurses of Harmony's background.[33]

With both her matrimonial prospects and opportunities for outside employment limited, Harmony's future would be to care for every neurasthenic family member—that is, unless Charles Ives furnished her with an alternative life plan, one in which she could continue to exercise her nursing skills but limit their focus to one patient. Harmony's relocation to New York in summer 1907 seems to have pushed the situation along. At last, Ives and Harmony reached an understanding on October 22, 1907—two days after his thirty-third birthday—and they became officially engaged the next month.

Harmony relished devoting her talents to Ives's care, and their correspondence from fall 1907 onward teems with her concerns over his health. Her letter to Ives of February 6, 1908, contains a typical blend of matrimonial eagerness and maternal fussiness, combined with the explicit recognition of marriage as a chance for her to cure Ives of his sickness: "It makes me so *anxious* to have you not well—It seems as if I couldn't stand it to be away from you when you're not perfectly well—If you are going to be sick you've got to let me marry you and get you well. . . . Dear lamb, it makes me feel so badly. How I wish I had you evenings, to love you and hold you and . . . make your head feel better."[34] Through their courtship and later marriage, Harmony maintained her role as Ives's personal nurse, a description echoed by their family and friends who noted "the wonderful care" that she gave her husband.[35] Harmony arranged their married life to include vacation rest cures in the Adirondacks—Saranac Lake, Elk Lake, Keene Valley, and the Berkshires. Eventually they purchased a country property in Redding, Connecticut, where they spent summers after 1913. This yearly relocation met another condition for the treatment of neurasthenics, that to maintain optimum health "a country life would be preferable. . . . if the patient could change his residence and carry on his work in the country, this would be better than living in a dusty and smoky town."[36]

His engagement in 1907 ushered in a new era of stability for Ives as his condition came under the control of a professional caregiver. And, their marriage represented yet another social dimension of the disease. Beard and many later writers linked the nervous epidemic to the growing number of women in the work force who had exchanged their domestic obligations for a share of the almost exclusively male professional world.

This led to two outcomes. First, many more women became "nervous" because of the new demands on their time and skills in the public work-place. For such women, the rest cure involving infantilization of the patient, immobility, and seclusion served as a cultural restraint as well as a medi-cal treatment. Second, the removal of women from private domestic space, concomitant with their infiltration of the work force, made them less able to provide a "serenely calm oasis, a private interior realm for [the] physical and mental rehabilitation" of their overworked husbands. Without such an oasis, men became doubly susceptible to the nervous condition as well. In effect, neurasthenia in both men and women underscored the dislocation of white men at home and at work in American society.[37]

Between 1898 and his marriage in 1908, Ives lived in a nondomestic space with the transient bachelors of Poverty Flat. Considered within the cultural matrix of neurasthenia, Harmony restored Ives's domestic ideal, thereby re-instating traditional gender roles as part of his "cure." The abatement of Ives's illness and his transition from bachelorhood to marriage coincided with the establishment of a new domestic space and Harmony's withdrawal from the workplace: after their marriage, she did not practice nursing professionally again. Through Harmony's restoration to private life—in itself, a preservation of traditional values—Ives gained the stability that enabled him to return to composing.

"O sweetest day!"

Given Harmony's central role in revitalizing Ives's compositional career, it is not surprising that many of his first completed works in years were song settings of Harmony's poetry. Ives employed the conventional language that he had mastered at Yale with songs such as "Spring Song" and "The World's Highway," part of which reads:

> O sweetest day!
> I came to a garden small,
> A voice my heart knew called me in;
> I answered its blessed call.
> I left my wandering far and wide,
> The freedom and far away;
> But my garden blooms with sweet content
> That's not on the world's highway.

Charming, effortless, and lovely, Ives's music matches Harmony's religiously intoned, reservedly sensuous images with sweet harmonies and dramatic late romantic gestures (pounding octaves, for example), all wrapped up with a proper "Amen" cadence.

Indeed, Harmony brought new hope to Ives in both his personal and musical life. Setting her poetry helped bring Ives out of his slump and provided an opportunity for a new, more optimistic approach to his work. But Harmony offered another important impetus to composing: the chance for Ives to reshape his musical voice, to revise the impact of Horatio Parker on his music, and to resurrect his father George as his main musical influence. Early on in the relationship, George loomed as an idealized presence from Ives's early life, especially in the revised version of his education. Harmony, in a 1907 letter to Ives, conveyed the importance of George as a living presence among them in no uncertain terms: "In Church I thought all of a sudden of your father—so intensely that the tears came into my eyes and I thought how much I love him—actually as if I'd known him—I almost *felt* him and

I am sure he knows all about this and how dearly I love you and that your welfare is my happiness."[38]

George's resurrection as a musical mentor had three outgrowths. First, it allowed Ives to reshape his ideas about the "experimental" attitudes he had learned before Yale. While compositions such as the "Credo" operated outside of the norms of European conventions, and no doubt Ives had once viewed them as amateurish flailing, now these approaches appeared as viable compositional alternatives that would soon bear fruit. With Harmony's support, Ives now had permission to combine his thorough discipline in European conventions, gained from Parker, with the attitude of musical flexibility and democracy inherited from his father.

Second, in memorializing George, Ives could now return to those quotations associated with his father and the amateur, mostly lower-class contexts that they represented. Unlike the staunchly middle-class *Missionary Hymn* quotation of the string quartet movement, or the European quotations of the First Symphony, Ives now felt free to draw on all of the musical traditions endorsed by his father. Most appealing were the gospel hymns and minstrel tunes so vociferously decried by Parker. His professor's ban on these sources no doubt represented part of their appeal in addition to their associations with George. In practice, however, Ives's treatment of George's repertoire would reveal lingering mixed allegiances.

Lastly, by establishing George as his only significant teacher, Ives constructed a pre-Yale identity that minimized the impact of Parker and his ideas. Just as Ives would one day repackage his musical career for the public and his compositional peers, so he revised his early activities for his wife. Once again, Ives wanted the best of both worlds: the skills he had acquired from Parker, and validation by a mentor who was no longer alive, whose revisable presence could erase the problematic professor. With Harmony at his side and George reshaped into an ever-present influence, Ives found a new context for his musical expression, one that conformed again to his contemporary environment, and indeed to his identity as a neurasthenic.

"This distinguished malady"

Neurasthenics were believed to be "people of refined susceptibilities, sensitive about themselves and their feelings," and cases of the disease were "far more numerous among the educated and so-called refined classes." Indeed, its diagnosis became a badge of honor among the higher classes. Famous Americans such as Theodore Roosevelt and Mark Twain admitted to suf-

fering from, as Beard labeled it, "this distinguished malady." Writers including Edith Wharton and Henry James incorporated neurasthenic characters
into their works whose illness signified social, racial, economic, and ethical
distinction. Thus, neurasthenia was not only a socially acceptable condition,
but one that reflected well on the patient.[39]

As early as 1881, Beard suggested that nervousness was a direct result of
the transformation of American civilization. These changes were not only
societal—in the overwhelming technological and cultural upheavals that
America faced at the turn of the century—but also included specific personal
crises. According to Thomas Lutz, nervousness "in literary, academic, and
journalistic discourses was most often used in explaining change in gender
roles, change from one stage of life to another, change in financial circumstances, change in cultural values, change in marital status, change in social
status, change in an individual's relationship to institutions, or changes in the
institutions to which an individual is related."[40] Between 1902 and 1908, Ives
experienced so much upheaval in every area of his life as to satisfy almost
all of these criteria. From 1902 when he resigned as a church musician, he
faced a change of identity, not to mention a loss of secondary income. The
insurance industry in which Ives worked was under attack throughout this
period, as the federally sponsored Armstrong Investigation exposed corruption and nepotism. Having obtained his position at Mutual with the help of
his influential cousins, Ives must have been deeply shaken by the scandal. The
resolution of his professional identity with the founding of his own company
marks the end of this period of transition.

The class and racial implications of neurasthenia are also significant in reassessing Ives's contemporary musical voice. Many writers associated nervous
disorders not only with a fear of change in one's personal circumstances, but
with anxiety stemming from the redefinition of class and ethnicity in American society. In 1905 Clarke stated that the chief causes of neurasthenia were
"the great and rapid changes in the social conditions of the present day . . .
involving, as [they do], the breaking down of the old barriers between classes."
More specifically, medical studies, the media, and literature consistently associated the disease with those in the highest niche in the American social
order, who were reacting against widespread changes in class configurations
and ethnic demographics. Members of the upper class were identified not
only by social standing, education, economic security, and Anglo-Saxon
heritage, but also by their tendency toward neurasthenia. According to Lutz,
writers believed that neurasthenia affected "only the more 'advanced' races,
especially the Anglo-Saxon," and that the disease's "class and racial implica-

tions" were "closely allied to the discourses justifying dominant American culture, and Anglo-American high culture in particular."[41]

Simultaneously, as Lawrence Levine has shown, the alliance between elitist culture and European culture—particularly the "classical" music of the concert hall—coincided with, and was in many ways a response to, the heterogenization of American culture due to mass immigration. According to Levine, in "an industrializing, urbanizing nation absorbing millions of immigrants from alien cultures and experiencing an almost incomprehensible degree of structural change and spatial mobility . . . the arbiters of culture promised both relief from impending disorder and an avenue to cultural legitimacy."[42] Thus, the alliance between American high culture and European musical traditions on the one hand, and the American upper class and neurasthenia on the other, reveals a cultural crossroads that is uniquely and distinctly American.

At the center of that crossroads stood Ives. His personal and musical identity placed him at the highest level of society, and, by extension, associated him with "Anglo-American high culture"—not coincidentally, the art music traditions he had learned at Yale and to which he returned in full force in 1907: art songs, symphonies, and string quartets. Although he had written in these genres before, mostly under Parker's direction, Ives now fully embraced the musical language of "high culture" on his own terms—those of a self-consciously American composer. In his new musical voice, Ives reconciled the manner of European high culture—its forms and techniques—with the substance of American music through the use of hymns, fiddle tunes, band marches, and patriotic and popular songs. In conjoining the vernacular music that he learned as a child (and mostly associated with his father) with the Euro-American forms that he learned from Parker at Yale—a bastion of white male privilege—Ives's works act as a compositional analogue to his physiological reaction in the form of the "national" malady of neurasthenia.

Ives's "malady" provided a new musical, professional, and personal identity. Neurasthenia—as a set of symptoms and as a cultural construct—grew out of a fear of the modern world, the "overcivilization" of urban business centers and the frightening pace of progress. In such an environment, the impulse to idealize the past as a slower, more genteel time would seem a natural result. T. J. Jackson Lears, in his study *No Place of Grace*, ties neurasthenia to the paralyzing effect of "late Victorian sexual and social propriety" and the "impatient impulse to smash the veneer of Victorian convention." Indeed, Lears's description of early twentieth-century neurasthenics echoes both Ives's own life and later references in his writings through references to

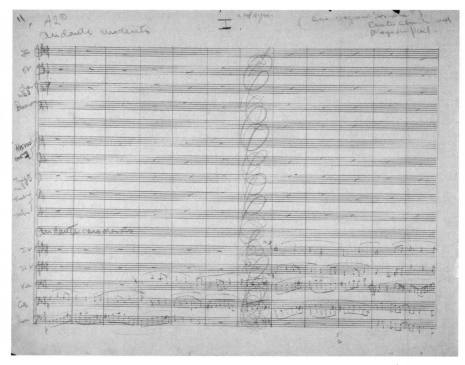

Page from full score of Symphony No. 2. Courtesy Yale University Irving S. Gilmore Music Library. Symphony No. 2 by Charles Ives © 1979 by Peer International Corporation. Copyright renewed. International copyright secured. Used by permission. All rights reserved.

rural life and Protestant camp meetings: "For the late-Victorian bourgeoisie, intense experience—whether physical or emotional—seemed a lost possibility. There was no longer the opportunity for bodily testing provided by rural life, no longer the swift alternation of despair and exhilaration which characterized the old-style Protestant conversion. There was only the diffuse fatigue produced by a day of office work or social calls."[43] Musically, Ives's impulse took root in new nostalgia for his own Danbury childhood. Socially, Ives's condition provided much-needed validation of his new standing as an independent, hardworking brain laborer, a man consumed by his business duties yet simultaneously sensitive and artistic. Personally, the illness provided one foundation in his courtship and marriage to a nurse aching to care for him.

But the recognition of Ives's illness clarified yet another central aspect of his identity—his social position. Ives the neurasthenic was, in fact, a member of the upper-class. His ownership of this identity reflects a reconciliation of the competing forces that had characterized his earlier musical career. As a member of the same upwardly situated class that supported Parker's works— the neurasthenic class, in effect—Ives was entitled to full participation in the European tradition, not to mention a well-placed marriage. At the same time, the disease's uniquely American profile and its nostalgic perspective validated the "nationalistic" borrowings from George's repertoire and style of music making.[44]

With this resolution came new compositional energy. First, he returned to where he had left off in 1902 and completed a second symphony, a more clearly "American" and highly romantic work than its predecessor. Ives's Second Symphony attained the clearest and most confident merger of Parker's language with George's materials. Ives extended the lessons learned in his First Symphony and packed quotations from patriotic and popular tunes, with a few hymn tunes scattered throughout, into a Euro-American form that Parker would have easily recognized, if not approved. Its lush orchestration and indulgent length reflects Ives's most significant flirtation with the expansive Romantic canvasses of Schubert and Bruckner.

At the same time, the self-conscious regionalism of the quotations and the work's unrestrained optimism convey a carefully constructed image of Americanism. Most prominent are themes based on minstrel tunes ("Massa's in de Cold Ground," "Turkey in the Straw," "Camptown Races") or gospel hymns ("Beulah Land," "Bringing in the Sheaves"), all prefiguring a rousing rendition of "Columbia the Gem of the Ocean" that explodes in the final movement.[45]

And yet, the Second Symphony is no mere appreciation of George's world, but a canny amalgam of musical forces from Ives's formative years. Consciously or not, Ives merges three contrasting, sometimes contentious American musical orbits. The source themes certainly invoke George, while the warm accessibility of the work betrays the lingering model of Dudley Buck, whose *"Star Spangled Banner" Overture* prefigured this nationalist blend decades earlier. Towering above both are Horatio Parker's "rules" and procedures, broken here and there but mostly intact, and wrapped in the same controlled Romanticism of Ives's most successful Yale works.[46] It is Parker's voice that frames Ives's earliest influences and reshapes them into a proper symphonic conception.

In fact, Ives's handling of the quotations and their role within this hierarchy is significant. The themes in the Second Symphony are transformations of

George's repertoire, not the real thing. Raw-material melodies are extracted from their everyday musical contexts, smoothed out and regularized to suit the demands of their new environment. In their transformation from amateur, participatory, often lower-class musicking into the upper, art-music echelons, these tunes shed their origins and much of their originality. Ives dresses them up in a new suit, combs their hair, and restricts their behavior to match the profile of a bona fide symphonic identity. Thus, the symphony's celebration of American identity masks the musical compromises necessary to achieve an acceptably coherent nationalist work in the late romantic orchestral tradition. In this European and American synthesis, George's music has been "cleaned up" almost beyond recognition to cohabit with that of Parker.

In what was yet another respectful offering to Parker and his world, Ives wrote a remarkably accessible and conventional piece whose refined sensuousness equals that of Parker's best works. Along with Harmony's songs, the newly married Ives seemed content to continue the genteel tradition, at least

Harmony Twichell and Charles Ives's wedding photo, June 9, 1908. Courtesy Yale University Irving S. Gilmore Music Library.

for the moment. The confluence of events reopened the cherished possibility that Ives could be a public composer after all, and he began searching for a venue in which to premiere his new sound. This time, he would be recognized as a composer of the future, able to write stirring and evocative American music that performers and audiences could appreciate—or so he hoped. For the first time since *The Celestial Country,* Ives had parts professionally copied as he prepared to reach out to his musical peers, this time in his new guise as a mature, responsible and economically successful composer whose work paid homage to the European, and specifically German, tradition.

On June 9, 1908, six years and eight days after he walked away from his musical career, Ives married Harmony Twichell. They would be devoted to each other for the next forty-six years with an intensity and exclusiveness that others found remarkable. With his marriage and all that it represented, Ives regained his equilibrium and plunged into his music with renewed energy and confidence. On the verge of their new life together, Harmony and Ives had no inkling of the obstacles they would face, or of the trials that would transform them both.

4

"A New Sweet World"

Saints smiled gravely, and they said: "He's come."
(Are you washed in the blood of the Lamb?)

That Saturday in March would prove challenging even for the perpetually busy players of the New York Symphony Society. It had been an unusually hectic week by the standards of the overscheduled orchestra and for Walter Damrosch, its inexhaustible leader. Damrosch was a second-generation conductor who with his father, Leopold, had enshrined German opera at the Metropolitan in the 1880s and 1890s: he had celebrated his twenty-fifth anniversary as a conductor with several public lectures, interviews, and concerts during the preceding week. The silver jubilee festivities culminated in a Carnegie Hall program on Tuesday, March 15, 1910, crowned with a congratulatory five-thousand-dollar check from Andrew Carnegie himself. This Saturday afternoon, March 19, 1910, the Society would complete its twelfth season with the last of a series of young people's concerts. The program would feature excerpts from Wagner's operas, in keeping with Damrosch's championing of the German tradition.[1]

In addition to its Wagner rehearsal, the ensemble would squeeze in a reading of a composition by a contemporary American that morning. Although Ives remained unknown as a composer, he had studied with one of Damrosch's closest friends, Horatio Parker. In fact, Damrosch had seen Parker just three days prior at a memorial service in New Haven honoring another Yale professor, Samuel Sanford, who had died two months previous.[2] Sanford was the treasurer and a significant patron of Damrosch's symphony in addition to his duties as head of applied music studies at Yale: no doubt, in the small Ivy League community, Ives had known Sanford during his New Haven days. In fact, Sanford's story offers a unique precedent for Ives's own, since

Conductor Walter Damrosch. Library of Congress Prints and Photographs Division, LC-DIG-ggbain-01153.

he was an independently wealthy musician and philanthropist who refused any remuneration for his services.[3] We do not know if Damrosch and Parker had a chance to discuss Parker's former student's progress at the memorial service of their colleague, but the network of contacts between Damrosch and two Yale music professors stands as a reminder of the many musical and personal connections between New Haven and New York.

At the rehearsal, Ives sat watching, perhaps nervous but surely eager to hear his own composition played by a professional orchestra for the first time. He had contacted Damrosch and persuaded him at least to read through the work en route to a public performance. As one of the leading conductors in the country, Damrosch wasted neither his valuable time nor that of his players on amateurs. But once Ives's credentials were established—almost certainly by Ives himself—the influential conductor agreed to give the work and its creator a chance. For Ives, getting the parts and full score prepared would have been a major undertaking, a commitment of time and money, but now came the payoff. Unlike his last big performance almost eight years earlier, at the premiere of *The Celestial Country*, this time Ives was not a participant: he had handed the work over to a full-time orchestra and conductor who were well versed in the European concert tradition. All Ives could do was listen. At least now, with his wife, Harmony, next to him, he wasn't enduring the experience alone.

He had had a choice of which work to present. The Second Symphony was already completed: in fact, contemporaneous fragments of professionally copied parts for the first and third movements of the work survive.[4] Yet Ives offered the First Symphony to Damrosch. It was a safer choice, one that Damrosch might approve, one more in tune with what his orchestra performed, and the one that stood the best chance of getting a public performance. And, it was the work most closely associated with Parker, and composed partially under the professor's influence. Curiously, as Ives remembered it, he offered the second, third, and fourth movements to Damrosch, but not the opening movement, which he wrote more than a decade earlier in Parker's class. Why Ives felt a need to decapitate his first symphony is unknown. Apparently he believed that, even lacking its opening and weightiest movement, the symphony might still be interesting to Damrosch. And, if this work was accepted and performed, there might be future opportunities for his other works and a new beginning for his public compositional career.

According to Ives, Damrosch made some positive comments on the work's instrumentation and "workmanship," and complimented the second movement as "charming." But the conductor "acted somewhat put out [and] got mad" when the second movement became more complicated. In the end, Damrosch declined to program the work because, in Ives's words, the more complicated passages would "take too much rehearsal time—for his pocketbook."[5] Ives's allusion to Damrosch's economic condition, in conjunction with the publicly announced check from Carnegie to Damrosch earlier in the same week, suggests that Damrosch could be the figure that Ives denounced in *Memos* two decades later. "Then another complaint from Prof. $5000 is the combination of notes in the chords. If he can't get his Jadassohn out and check it up, then it really isn't nice music etc. etc. 'He puts notes in a chord that don't belong in it—and he usually has too many notes . . . that is wrong!' (Grandma Prof. says). It is not, you g—d—sap!—takin' money for emasculating music and students."[6] A second candidate would be Damrosch's friend Parker, who split the ten-thousand-dollar prize for *Mona* with his libretticist Bryan Hooker. The identification of Damrosch and/or Parker as "Prof. $5000" clarifies Ives's long-standing resentment of two extremely important figures whom he knew personally, and who directly affected the composition and reception of his music. Ives's personal grudge against the financial aspects of classical music making by these two powerful leaders offers an ironic commentary as well, given Ives's own financial success. By the time Ives wrote this abrasive and abusive tirade, he was using his own ample pocketbook to fund performances of his own and others' works in the eastern United States and throughout Europe, regardless of the time needed to rehearse.

Interestingly, Ives's recollection of Damrosch's reading of the First Symphony in the manuscript of *Memos* begins mid-sentence (and mid-quote) after a missing page that seems to have referred to a no-longer-extant letter from Damrosch concerning the rehearsal, and that must have mentioned Ives's active role in contacting and persuading Damrosch to try out Ives's most conservative orchestral work.[7] But what we can conclude from the facts—that Damrosch, a good friend of Horatio Parker, rehearsed a work connected to Parker's class by an otherwise unknown composer whose most relevant credential for having an orchestral work performed by a major New York ensemble was his Yale pedigree—repeats Ives's earlier professional positioning for the premiere of *The Celestial Country*. Twelve years after his graduation, Ives continued to use his connection to Parker in his sporadic pursuit of professional recognition. Even more surprising, the validation he sought was based not on his contemporary, individual musical voice—the American-inspired, tuneful, confident Second Symphony—but the fragmented outgrowth of a student work later vehemently decried by its composer (in a more decisive condemnation than anything Damrosch gave it) as "if not the worst, one of the worst, poorest, weakest things I've ever written."[8]

"Just As I Am"

Ives's contact with Damrosch dates from two or three years after his renewed compositional activities and a year and a half after his marriage to Harmony. In the decade after their marriage in June 1908, the Iveses faced many challenges together. Harmony's mother died suddenly in 1910, collapsing during the funeral of family friend Mark Twain; her father suffered a nervous collapse early in 1913, after which Harmony accompanied him to a Vermont sanitarium.[9] While balancing the care of her neurasthenic father, Harmony structured her husband's time to provide rest cures. Ives worked steadily at building up the business with Mike Myrick, but Harmony used every opportunity to relocate her patient to wooded areas.

Their honeymoon in the Berkshires represents one such intervention; on later vacations Harmony guided her "nervous" husband to scenic locations in upstate New York to improve his "condition." One such vacation took place around six months after their wedding when the couple visited Saranac Lake. Comments from her mother indicate Harmony's direct role in structuring her new husband's treatment. "We have been thankful to learn of Charlie's betterment in condition, and have very highly approved the measure you adopted of taking him away from New York into the woods, though we knew it involved inconvenience, and probably loss, to him. It was wise to give the first interest the first place. We have considered, however, that, aside from your chief object in retreating to the Saranac Lake neighborhood, your sojourn there has doubtless, by way of compensation, been, on some accounts, a pleasure to you—you have so many friends thereabout."[10] There can be little doubt that the "chief object in retreating" to the woods was an ongoing rest cure, conscientiously administered by Harmony.

Within a few months, it would be Harmony, not Ives, who required extensive medical care. Husband and wife made minimal reference to the events, which remained shrouded in mystery until after Harmony's death in 1969. Ives's cryptic entry on the manuscript of "Like a Sick Eagle" reads, "H[armony] T[wichell] I[ves] in hospital—Sally singing 70 W. 11, April 29, '09." The entries in their shared diary, *Our Book*, mention that Harmony went into the hospital on April 20 and returned home May 15. Writing in 1974 (five years after Harmony's death), David Wooldridge intuited the nature of the condition, which John Kirkpatrick later confirmed through the confidence of a family member. Harmony had suffered a miscarriage, followed by a hysterectomy that ended the couple's hopes for a child of their own.[11] Although Kirkpatrick reports a "miscarriage," which rightly refers to the loss of pregnancy during the first trimester, the necessity of extensive surgical intervention strongly suggests that the pregnancy had progressed much further. Hospitalization was reserved only for the most serious complications, and obstetric surgery remained a desperate last resort.[12] That Harmony was hospitalized, and that she underwent such radical and dangerous surgery, suggests that her condition was life-threatening for her as well as their unborn

Sketch of the song "Like a Sick Eagle." Courtesy Yale University Irving S. Gilmore Music Library. Rights held by the Theodore Presser Company/Carl Fischer. Used by permission.

child. What Harmony and Ives may have experienced was a late-term loss or even a stillbirth, followed by potentially fatal complications.

Harmony and Ives faced the ordeal with tight-lipped stoicism. The brief entry in *Our Book* contrasts with earlier and later accounts of happier events—memories from their honeymoon, special dinners, and holidays.[13] For once, Harmony the professional caregiver was the patient. Her sister, Sally, who otherwise inhabited the role of family invalid, helped out at home while Harmony recuperated. In the aftermath, Harmony faced a crisis over her future direction. Over the next several years, she reverted to earlier patterns by becoming more active in their church. Although apparently skeptical about religion, Ives respected and supported his wife's faith, and attended church at least occasionally with her.[14]

Following this shattering event, Ives's compositions shifted to include more direct considerations of mortality, as well as works that are obviously and consciously based primarily on hymn tunes. One such response can be heard through the stark, deliberately listless song "Like a Sick Eagle," which uses a text by Keats, and on the manuscript for which Ives noted his somewhat coded remarks. The sinking vocal and piano parts operate outside of any traditional key, conveying a sense of disorientation, instability, transience, and surrender. In considering the fleeting nature of life, Ives solemnly addressed the loss of their child, the specter of his wife's death, and his own mortality.

The song "Mists" conveys a similar sense of loss. For it, Ives used a text that Harmony wrote after her mother's sudden death on April 24, 1910, almost exactly a year after Harmony's own crisis:

> Low lie the mists; they hide each hill and dell;
> The grey skies weep with us who bid farewell.
> But happier days through memory weave a spell,
> And bring new hope to hearts who bid farewell.

Harmony's invocation of weeping and farewells invoked her and Ives's earlier loss alongside this new heartbreak. Unlike earlier settings of Harmony's poetry—the conventional settings of "Spring Song" and "Autumn Leaves," for example—Ives's music for "Mists" is much more adventurous in its nearly complete avoidance of functional tonality, resorting to Debussy-like washes of parallel augmented chords.[15] While Harmony's text returns to a premarriage trope of parting, Ives's musical setting conveys something closer to lost—not new—hope. The phrase "happier days" is set to a loud, briefly functional major passage that surrenders to the same chromatic decline as "Like a Sick Eagle" in representing memory's spell, and perhaps again the inexorable ebbing of life. Both text and music invoke memories of the faded optimism and joy of a marriage barely begun, now engulfed in bereavement. Musically, his highly selective, nostalgically charged use of tonality suggests the latest phase in Ives's growing ambivalence toward the European tradition and his active questioning of this inherited system.

While commentators have noted links between these songs and the couple's immediate circumstances, we can now extend these links to another major composition from this period, one previously unconnected to the couple's struggles. Ives's most important work of mourning is the Third Symphony, which was begun probably around 1910–11. The work marks a sharp contrast with its ebullient predecessor, the boisterous, jovial, and optimistic Second Symphony: by comparison, the Third seems introspective, even occasionally somber, in character. Here, for the first time, Ives asserts a fully independent voice in the symphonic idiom. After the apprenticeship of the First, and the accommodation of the Second, the Third appears to have been written firstly for individual expression instead of a specific professional purpose.

Its deeply personal and spiritual meanings are clear in the work's subtitle ("The Camp Meeting") as well as each movement: "Old Folks Gatherin,'" "Children's Day," and "Communion." Building on the fragments of several earlier organ works, the Third Symphony's themes derive almost exclusively from hymn tunes: perhaps another reflection of the couple's renewed religious faith following their loss, while simultaneously commemorating Ives's memories of his own childhood and his father George. Several of the hymn tunes used in the work were the type performed at the camp meetings that George Ives led, particularly "Just As I Am." Yet, with this and other hymns, Ives had multiple connections to these works. The composer of "Just As I Am," William Batcheler Bradbury (1816–68), is buried in Bloomfield cemetery in Bloomfield, New Jersey, where Ives worked from 1898 to 1900. Several of the other hymn tunes were part of Ives's church repertoire after George's death, and would have been well known by his wife and her family too. As such, the symphony draws on a wide spectrum of hymn tunes in what appears to be an effort to knit together Ives's two families, those of birth and marriage, childhood and adulthood, father and father-in-law, mother and wife.

Both the first and last movements of the Third Symphony use an adaptation of sonata form in which the main theme appears in its entirety only at the end of the movement, referred to as either cumulative form (J. Peter Burkholder's term, which emphasizes the overall formal structure) or teleological genesis (James Hepokoski's term, which emphasizes the process by which the form is created).[16] The symphony's first movement uses as its main theme the hymn tune *Azmon,* for which the text "O For a Thousand Tongues to sing" is the most commonly used text; secondary themes are drawn from "What a Friend We Have in Jesus." The movement explores the connections between these musically similar hymns drawn from separate repertoires— one expounding on the triumph and glory of a bourgeois redeemer, the other voicing the grassroots, personalized, friendly religion of a small-town camp meeting—all within a framework derived from Ives's European models.

Beyond their musical relationships, the two hymn tunes suggest a more private subtext. Despite its optimistic tune and title, "What a Friend" deals with the bearing of "sins and griefs." The single complete statement of *Azmon* at the conclusion of the movement brings to mind its best-known text, ending on a phrase that, with its image of a triumphant birth, must have conjured mixed feelings for Ives:

> O for a thousand tongues to sing
> My great Redeemer's worth
> The glory of my God and King,
> The triumph of his birth.

While the hymn's text expresses victory, Ives's setting of the tune is larga-mente, with a solemnity that recalls "Like a Sick Eagle." Ives's employment of this hymn tune avoids the final cadence—on the word "birth"—throughout the movement. A further connection to his family's tragedies—and more specifically, the earthly care expressed in "What a Friend"—is suggested through an alternative text to the same tune that Ives probably encountered during his fifteen years as a seasoned organist:

> We bear the strains of earthly care,
> But bear it not alone;
> Beside us walks our Brother Christ,
> And makes our task His own.

When *Azmon* finally arrives in its full glory, Ives undercuts the concluding cadence. The tangible loss of the final cadence, in which the expected and deserved resolution is denied, became a feature of Ives's works in the early teens.

Ives's personal losses paralleled the larger sense of cultural upheaval in modern American society that resulted from the falling away of traditional systems of organization. In the later teens, both personal losses and the world-wide tragedy of the First World War would inform his best-known works. As in the Third Symphony, one measure of Ives's growing estrangement from the past would be his challenging, or even destruction, of European form and tonality, through the forces of his own identifiably American repertoire.

The hymn tunes in the Third Symphony provided the most extensive opportunity to reminisce about his own childhood, which Ives developed in the second movement, titled "Children's Day." By combining fragments of several different hymns from different traditions (the camp meetings as well as his own comparatively carefree days as an organist) Ives recalled his happier days. In fact, one of the main themes derives from the hymn "There is a Happy Land," whose "far, far away" land invokes the past:

> There is a happy land, far, far away,
> Where saints in glory stand, bright, bright as day.
> Oh, how they sweetly sing, worthy is our Savior King,
> Loud let His praises ring, praise, praise for aye.

"Just As I Am" appears briefly in both first and second movements, then serves as the main theme for the end-weighted third movement. Instead of the main tune's triumphant emergence at the end of the third movement, and the entire work, Ives provides an understated, prayerlike presentation of the hymn, finally whole and unencumbered by variations or embellishments.

By placing the most powerful and simultaneously simplest theme at the end of the work, the Third Symphony recedes formally, structurally, and ideologically. In this reading, the work progresses backwards, paring away unnecessary complexities to get to the core of personal meaning and expression. As such, Ives undermines the European tradition—which emphasized forward-propulsive compositions that culminate in large-scale orchestral climaxes, a la Beethoven's Ninth Symphony—with a modest hymn tune that he certainly knew before he left Danbury in 1893: thus, the work represents an attempted reconciliation between his pre- and post-Yale identities. In his central employment of this hymn tune, Ives conjures its personal meaning from his childhood with the text's explicit humility that acknowledges the honest simplicity and self-recognition of that now-lost world.

"Merely visitors"

Ives composed the Third Symphony in the midst of a growing musical debate in New York over American musical identity and foreign influence. In 1908–9, Gustav Mahler's conducting engagements at the Metropolitan Opera House and the New York Philharmonic triggered what had been a simmering argument about the role of Europeans—especially Germans and

Austrians—in the musical life of America, and particularly of Manhattan. On March 12, 1910, during one of his silver jubilee celebrations and exactly one week before his ensemble's read-through of Ives's First Symphony, Walter Damrosch had pointedly criticized "foreigners, who come here merely for the money" of conducting and performing. Delivered before an invited audience of two hundred, Damrosch's remarks, summarized by the *New York Times,* condemned the "present partiality for foreigners" as "a humiliating spectacle." Damrosch is quoted as saying, "I have dreams of opera in America at the Metropolitan Opera House, in which the director, conductors, artists, chorus, and orchestra shall all be Americans, either adopted or born, and not as now merely visitors who treat our country as but a temporary sojourn for which money, money, money is in many cases the principal motive."[17]

That Mahler was associated with both Damrosch's rival, the New York Philharmonic, and his former employer, the Metropolitan Opera,[18] which had rejected Damrosch's application as director seven years earlier, may have played a role in the German-American's gripes.[19] Moreover, during its founding season a year earlier, the press made much of the open animosity between Damrosch and the Philharmonic's primary patron, Mrs. George R. Sheldon. On hearing that Sheldon and her associates intended to establish "an opposition force to the New York Symphony Orchestra, of which Mrs. Sheldon was formerly a member of the board of directors," and that in Sheldon's opinion "there [was] at present no worthy orchestra in New York," Damrosch opined that "the agitation for the new orchestra seems to have been started by 'two or three restless women with no occupation, and more money than they seem to know what to do with.'"[20] Damrosch's patronizing and insulting comments would be greatly expanded in his autobiography's scathing account of Sheldon and her "pet artist."[21]

That the Philharmonic's choice of conductor was the Viennese Mahler over the German-born but Americanized Damrosch points up the lack of respect even powerful native musicians received in comparison with their European competitors. Damrosch's disapproval in his public speech of the "unrelieved and ugly decadence" of the operas *Salomé* and *Electra* targeted his Bohemian-Austrian rival again, as Mahler had championed these scandalous Strauss operas.[22]

Given the amount of sentiment voiced by Damrosch and reported in the media, Ives may have viewed the plain-talking conductor as a kindred spirit, one who was fighting for an American identity in the face of European imports. Damrosch's unembarrassed wrath, laced with gendered and nationalist overtones, recalls Ives's own much later railings against the "emasculation" of

American music and the detrimental effects of female sponsorship of the arts.[23] In this sense he and Damrosch appeared to be fighting the same battle.

If Damrosch wanted to support American artists, then why was he not more enthusiastic about Ives's symphonies—not only the first, but the second and the third, which Ives sent to Damrosch on later occasions?[24] Damrosch's criticisms were aimed squarely at Mahler as a conductor (and his New York supporters) along with contemporary works by Strauss, but not at the historical, dominant Austro-German repertoire as illustrated through his unrelieved championing of Wagner and Beethoven in his concerts.[25] Less than a decade later, Damrosch would prove indispensable in promoting American composers at home and abroad, but in this era he advanced the cause only of those composers most clearly allied with the "highbrow" tradition's homeland— namely the German-trained Parker, Chadwick, and their contemporaries.

The American identity of Ives's Third Symphony masks yet another dimension of this work as well as other quotation-based compositions from this period. Ives retained strong memories of the hymn tunes both from his childhood at the camp meetings and from his years as a professional organist. (That the majority of hymn tunes did not belong in both spheres due to class and denominational differences has already been discussed.) Other Americans of his generation, heritage, and religious background would have recognized segments of Ives's repertoire, at least in their fullest form, but not necessarily all of the camp-meeting hymn tunes as well as the middle- and upper-class hymns of his organist training. Another population of Americans—listeners schooled in European classical music—would recognize the symphony's late Romantic gestures and form. Yet one wonders how such a work could have been appreciated by the relatively small population, like Ives, who could understand all traditions on their own terms. If he ever looked at the score of Ives's Third Symphony, Damrosch may well have supposed the work was unintelligible to his concert audience because of its then unconventional combination of multiple classes of hymn tunes married to the symphonic tradition.

Ives's inclusive amalgam of hymn tunes with Romantic European traditions could be seen simultaneously as exclusive given what was happening in his own environment. Immigration to the United States from Eastern and Southern European countries peaked during the first fifteen years of the century. Millions of non-English-speaking, non-Protestant immigrants settled in Manhattan, particularly the Lower East Side, to the extent that an estimated 38 percent of New York's male population was foreign-born in 1909.[26] While Ives had encountered non-English-speaking immigrants before—after all, this was the demographic that his father taught long ago in Danbury—he did not directly address in his extensive writings the nation-changing waves of immigration that brought Italians, Greeks, Slavs, and Russian Jews within mere blocks of his residence and workplace. Instead, in his "American"-sounding, "classical" compositions from this era, we can hear Ives asserting a cultural authority that seemed to be under attack on dual grounds—that of the native-born Yankee whose family had arrived in the seventeenth century, as well as the Yale-educated, upper-class, neurasthenic businessman. It is this combination—signifying an idealized and homogenized Anglo-American history exalted through upper-class achievement—that would strike such a chord with a newly trained generation of post–World War II audiences when Ives's Third Symphony finally premiered in 1946.

Private and Public

With the Third Symphony, Ives attempted his most ambitious hymn-based composition to date. The work's unstable alchemy of European and American elements soon found its way into chamber works such as the Second String Quartet and the four completed violin sonatas. In each work, Ives wrestles with the balance of European form and American content while further exploring the rich history and personal significance of the hymn repertoire. Often, as in the case of the Third Symphony, Ives begins with his own church compositions dating from a decade or more earlier—fragments of organ preludes and religious songs—as the foundation for multimovement works that pledge allegiance to the European tradition in genre and title only. Many of the movements examine transatlantic relationships through cumulative form or teleological genesis, as in the Third Symphony: a simple hymn tune of American origin arrives at the end of a European-based process, only to remain unresolved at its cadence.

Harmony, her faith, and her religious family may have been responsible for rekindling Ives's interest in religious music of all types between 1908 and 1914. In addition to rethinking his organ works as a framework for the Third Symphony, Ives recopied and revised a number of earlier choral works during the early years of his marriage. Perhaps not coincidentally, Dudley Buck, Ives's pre-Yale role model for the successful church musician and composer, died in 1909. The obituaries that appeared in the New York papers provided an overview of Buck's position as teacher, organist, and composer, undoubtedly reminding Ives of his own earlier life and aspirations.[27] Sometime between 1908 and 1911, Ives appears to have recopied and recomposed several psalm settings, inserted new organ interludes into The Celestial Country, and composed new songs based on hymn texts such as "Serenity."

A related aspect of Ives's work involves the so-called "laboratory works."[28] These experimental compositions explore new compositional techniques in miniature forms. Often the intent is to portray a programmatic image, as in the baseball-themed *Scherzo: All the Way Around and Back* and *Take-Off No. 3: Rube Trying to Walk 2 to 3!!*, later incorporated into *Scherzo: Over the Pavements.* As Timothy Johnson has shown, both original works refer to specific players and teams active in New York between 1905 and 1908, and are roughly contemporary with a spate of popular baseball songs by commercial publishers, including the famous "Take Me Out to the Ball Game." In Ives's works, he represents specific plays—and players—through unconventional melodic, harmonic, and formal structures.[29] From the chromatic, polyrhythmic palindrome of *Scherzo: All the Way Around and Back* to the ragtime ostinati of *Take-Off No. 3: Rube Trying to Walk 2 to 3!!,* Ives uses the opportunities afforded by distinctly American programs to explore musical structures and procedures outside of the European mainstream.

Another approach was to explore working alternatives to the tonal system and/or received formal structures. For example, *Psalm 24* and *Central Park in the Dark* both employ an expanding and contracting pattern of intervals using a wedge shape for formal cohesion. Ives had already experimented with twelve-tone composition in a limited, tonal way, through the chromatic wedge of his "Credo" amen, one that duplicated a late-nineteenth-century barbershop technique called the "swipe."[30] Applying a twelve-tone approach without regard for traditional tonal relationships offered yet another way around, and out of, the European system. Experimental works such as *Over the Pavements, Psalm 24,* and the second *Harvest Home Chorale* organize pitch collections according to the revolving presentation of all twelve-tones, structured through expanding and contracting wedges.[31]

Ives was not the only composer to experiment in this way, but he was the only American. Arnold Schoenberg and Josef Mattias Hauer in Vienna and Nikolai Andreyevich Roslavets in Ukraine were all exploring the same concept within a few years of each other.[32] For each, twelve-pitch construction offered a cohesive alternative to tonality. In Ives's case—and possibly for Roslavets as well—dismantling tonality in these isolated works was a crucial part of questioning and circumventing the European tradition. Paradoxically, on the other side of the ocean Schoenberg viewed the eventual systemization of the same process (serialism), as one that would "ensure the supremacy of German music for the next hundred years."[33] Ives's challenges to the tonal system—in private on his own terms, and gradually more in his public works—represent a rejection of inherited European, and by implication dominant German, attitudes. Containing the process in his lab works nonetheless informed a rougher treatment of tonal organization in his large-scale compositions of the time, providing a kind of "Americanist" commentary when combined with hymn, patriotic, and popular quotations, the transformation of "ragging," or programmatic elements such as baseball.[34]

Ives may have had little hope of having his exclusively experimental works performed. Throughout his later career, Ives chose to promote works in recognizable European genres—symphonies, sonatas, art songs, and string quartets—even though their melodic and harmonic content veered from the norm. To this end, Ives used whatever contacts he could find to advance his cause even as he was nominally isolated from the larger musical community.

One such contact was Edgar Stowell, a violinist in the New York Symphony who had encouraged Ives to contact his conductor Damrosch. Ives met Stowell through Elizabeth Sprague Coolidge, a childhood friend of Harmony's who in later years would become a prominent patron of American music. According to Memos, the Iveses stopped to visit the Coolidges and met Stowell there—the connection is intriguing. Stowell taught music at New York's Settlement School under David Mannes, the founder of the Mannes Music School. In 1910 or 1911 Ives played an earlier version of part of "The 'St. Gaudens' in Boston Commons" movement for Stowell, who didn't like what he heard. So Ives pitched another work, attempting to interest Stowell in the first movement of the Second Symphony. Stowell liked the work enough to perform the movement publicly with his school orchestra, according to Ives. If his account is true, it would represent one more effort by Ives to have his music performed.[35]

Yet another attempt to interest a professional, well-connected musician in his work appears in Ives's contact with Max Smith. A classmate from Yale, Smith had put his own training with Parker to use as a music critic, first for the New York Press from 1903–16, and then for the New York American.[36] In 1912, Ives later recalled, he played for Smith two of the movements that would later become "Emerson" and "Hawthorne" in his Second Piano Sonata (Concord). Smith was not impressed. But despite his negative reaction on this and other occasions to his compositions, Ives continued to perform his works for Smith, no doubt hoping for encouragement and the advantages a professional musician and public critic could provide.

Added to these professional contacts were more informal readings, many organized through Ives's hired copyists at the Tams Theatre Agency on West 28th Street. Musicians corralled by the copyists (and paid by Ives) read through part of a movement of the Second String Quartet (in 1911 or later), and "Washington's Birthday" (1913 or 1914), which was read again in 1914 and 1915 in the Globe Theater, and yet again in 1918 or 1919 at the Ives home, lead by another violinist from Damrosch's orchestra.[37]

This sampling of contacts and informal performances, along with professional exposure of his music to Damrosch, offers a new view of Ives. After
returning to music around 1907–8, he revived his first career as a composer
(a career that he later claimed to have abandoned in 1902), and continuously presented his works to musicians that he hoped would be sympathetic.
Although he had less success during this second career than in his first, he
nonetheless received a large number of private and semipublic hearings of
his work by capable musicians of substance and reputation, no doubt due to
his own persuasive abilities.

Charles Ives in Battery
Park, ca. 1913. Courtesy
Yale University Irving S.
Gilmore Music Library.

That Ives was no wallflower when promoting his works should come as no surprise. After all, he wrote the advertisements and sales pitches for his insurance firm. He was the partner responsible for training sales agents, whom he equipped with an arsenal of original materials. These included Ives's own literature in the form of pamphlets, short stories, sample dialogues with prospective customers (called "prospects"), and illustrated advertisements that played on a wealth of insecurities—financial, personal, and emotional.[38] At the same time, Ives devised mathematical formulas designed to calculate a family's expenses and projected income over the course of a lifetime, estimating what would be needed to carry a family through should they lose their breadwinner. This should be the amount invested in life insurance, according to his 1912 pamphlet "The Amount to Carry" (later revised and expanded), and offered what a character in one of Ives's dialogues referred to as "authoritative data."[39] What Ives really imparted to agents was a multipronged strategy of persistence, professionalism, personal integrity, and a moralistic belief, according to one of his supervising agents, that "there was not a service . . . that was more important than the business of life insurance, because it instilled in the soul and mind of my fellow man the responsibility of meeting his obligations."[40]

Ives spent decades honing his skills as a trainer of salesmen, so all that was needed to energize musicians to support his work was the right sales pitch. Ives's efforts as a promoter of his own music would steadily increase through the second decade of the century as he attempted to interest ever greater numbers of musicians in his work, and as he expanded his contacts within the musical community. In these later attempts to promote his music (that is, after he had finished publishing accessible popular works in the early 1900s), Ives embarked on the same frustrating, fulfilling path as George Ives, Horatio Parker, and numerous other American composers and musicians. He offered a noncommercial product to a consumer society, but unlike his predecessors or peers, Ives had a uniquely useful background in the cutthroat world of business salesmanship. What made the difference finally, in the 1920s, was that Ives found the right product, the right sales pitch, and receptive customers in the form of a modernist community of composers and performers.

The Gospel of Transformation

As he reached out to members of the musical community, Ives was on the lookout for promising compositional material as well. On January 12, 1914,

The Independent published a review of Vachel Lindsay's poem, "General William Booth Enters into Heaven." Lindsay's stanzaic elegy memorializes the founder of the Salvation Army, a British organization that after its arrival in 1880 took on a uniquely American flavor. The colorful imagery portrays Booth entering into heaven accompanied by a cross-section of lower-class American society: convicts, drug and alcohol addicts, and assorted "unwashed legions" from "every slum"—the kind of people whom Harmony encountered in her career as a professional nurse. The verses included in the journal's review provided the basis for one of Ives's most convincing hymn-based works, in part because of Lindsay's incorporation of quotations from the camp meeting hymn "Are You Washed in the Blood of the Lamb?" as a recurring refrain in the text. Although later adapted for solo voice and piano, the work is far more effective in its original form, as a one-movement minicantata with full orchestra, chorus, and soloist.

Lindsay's text plays with the same metaphor of spiritual and physical transformation represented in the hymn tune, a theme that dominates late nineteenth-century gospel ideology. But Lindsay extends this dichotomy between the symbols of deep-rooted European religious and cultural privilege (grave "vermin-eaten saints with mouldy breath") and the unpredictable energy and drive of the Americans (a motley band of "bull-necked convicts" and "big-voiced lassies" banging on banjos). In a cameo appearance, Jesus blesses the unnoticing Booth and "his queer ones," all of whom are transformed in the creation of "a new, sweet world," a world defined by its historical, physical and musical boundaries as nineteenth-century America.

Lindsay's text could not have been better suited to Ives's compositional language, even if Lindsay himself had very particular ideas about how to set his own music—ideas which are not reflected in Ives's setting. Taking the metaphor of transformation as his musical impetus, Ives combines and contrasts two radically different hymn tunes (the obvious source, "Are You Washed in the Blood of the Lamb?" and a less obvious choice, "There Is a Fountain Filled With Blood") within a sonata structure. Thus, Ives recreates Lindsay's American/European opposition as the hymn-based thematic materials are subjected to the formal processes of the expanded, formally elastic sonata structure characteristic of the late Romantic tradition.

"Are You Washed" is a crowd-raising gospel hymn with call-and-response structures—a repeated refrain after each line of the verse, plus echoes in the tenor and bass voices throughout the chorus—that made it easy to sing for people who couldn't read either words or music, or both. Its melody continues this orality, so typical of camp-meeting hymns for obvious reasons of audience and context, through simple duplex rhythms, with three, four, or five repeated pitches at a time, and mostly pentatonic movement over a limited range. The text itself typifies the interactive, redemptive tone of the Second Great Awakening, in which direct communication—to "you" in the congregation—was of utmost importance.

By contrast, "There Is a Fountain" belongs to an earlier wave of revivalism that swept America in the late eighteenth century. Written by the English poet William Cowper in 1771, this folk hymn had been popular at revival meetings in the early nineteenth century before being arranged by the venerable Lowell Mason in 1832. In keeping with Mason's original compositions, his arrangement of this oral tradition work (the original form of which is unrecorded) joins a regular phrase structure with predictable and smoothly executed harmonies. By the late nineteenth century when Ives would have

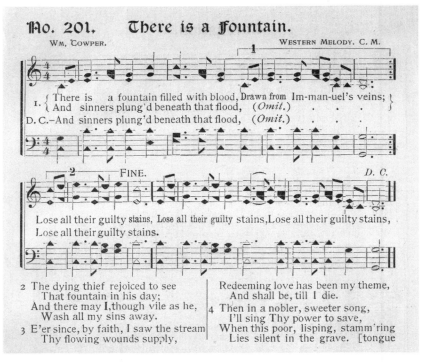

"There Is a Fountain Filled With Blood." Hymn source for Ives's setting of "General William Booth Enters into Heaven." Reprinted from *New Harvest Bells*, ed. W. E. Penn, W. H. Morris, and E. A. Hoffman. Eureka Springs, Ark.: W.E. Penn, ca. 1900.

"Are You Washed in the Blood of the Lamb?" Hymn source for Ives's setting of "General William Booth Enters into Heaven." Reprinted from *New Harvest Bells*, ed. W. E. Penn, W. H. Morris, and E. A. Hoffman. Eureka Springs, Ark.: W. E. Penn, ca. 1900.

General William Booth Enters Into Heaven

From a Poem by
VACHEL LINDSAY

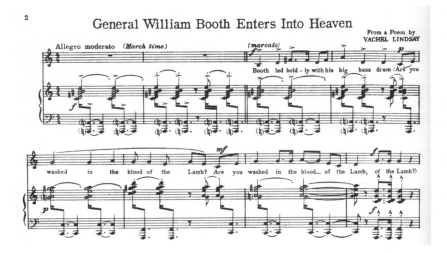

Three passages from Ives's setting of *General William Booth Enters into Heaven*: opening passage, beginning of the development section, and final verse. Rights held by the Theodore Presser Company/Carl Fischer. Used by permission.

Both small and large notes in voice part are sung, if there is a chorus.

[1916]

encountered the work, this hymn survived only in Mason's setting and was consistently attributed to him. Like his earlier setting of a different Mason hymn for string quartet (originally the first movement of the First String Quartet and later used as the third movement of the Fourth Symphony), Ives's musical selection would not have been a part of his father's camp-meeting repertoire. Mason's melody leaps ambitiously to a high E on no less than six occasions, a mercifully rare occurrence in congregational hymnody. Moreover, Mason's precise harmonic motion in block chords eliminates any possibility of call and response, while the precise part-writing and absence of a chorus precludes learning by rote within the oral tradition of the camp meetings. In its melody and ennobling text, "Fountain" (at least in its Masonesque incarnation, which would have been Ives's source) is a starchy, proper hymn tune dependent on notation and a literate congregation, and securely established in the upwardly mobile churches for which Ives worked after leaving Danbury, and which he and Harmony attended together.

Throughout his setting, Ives exploits the hymns' differences in origin, form, and context, most notably in collusion with the structural demands of sonata form. In the exposition, Ives sets the words "Are you washed in the blood of the lamb?" to the melody of "There Is a Fountain," thus exposing from the outset a conflict between the subjective gospel text and the firm, expansive melody advanced by Mason. As in earlier works, the cognitive dissonance between these two worlds represents yet another attempt to portray the duality of Ives's own America by combining lower- and middle-class musical traditions.

For the development ("Jesus came from the courthouse door"), Ives drops "Fountain," and focuses on the second phrase of "Are You Washed" ("Are you fully trusting in His [grace]"). By conjoining the hymn's own repetitive descending major third melodic structure with Lindsay's circular image ("round and round"), the uncannily apt setting encloses a static, calm oasis. Here is Ives's true vision of heaven, uncluttered by the march-based frenzy characterizing the surrounding sections and returning, without qualifications, apologies, or ennobling enlightenment, to the authentic music of his childhood.

In the recapitulation, each hymn tune and text reemerges transformed, irrevocably altered by their passage through the development section. The full melody of "There Is a Fountain" materializes from the fragments presented in the exposition, but with a compromised harmonization, and still joined with the text of "Are You Washed." The tonal bass line anchors the work in conventional hymnlike harmony (tonic, subdominant, and dominant), in an organ-pedal register. Undercutting the "pedals," the upper voices include a number of adjacent pitches along with the correct ones, as if the keyboard-ist were hitting "wrong notes," all in a snap rhythm that continues from the opening passage. At the conclusion of the hymn-tune statement, on the line "blind eyes opened on a new sweet world," Ives avoids a traditional cadence by substituting a deceptive landing on the subdominant.

The effect suggests that the "new, sweet world" of heaven—perhaps a reflection of Europe itself, or its colonial image in America—is an unsatisfactory, illusory, or unreachable destination for Booth and his misfits. Simultaneously, Ives has conjured the lost world of the old gospel hymns and their soothing message with unequaled clarity.

Immediately after, a ghostlike reappearance of the text, "Are you washed in the blood of the lamb?" finally reunites with its musical setting, albeit again in a compromised and only partially recognizable form. The final phrase begins with yet another statement of the "Fountain" theme, then veers unexpectedly into four repeated pitches—the final statement of the voice—which intone "blood of the lamb." In fact, the phrase alludes to the lower voices' call-and-response in the chorus that is so characteristic of "Are You Washed," and the part of the tune that the men at the camp meeting, including George Ives, would have sung. That this final phrase is surrounded by a conventional harmonization of "Fountain," offers a clue to its significance. In this final moment, Ives reconciles the two sources that have been in opposition since the opening of the piece—Mason's and Hoffmann's hymns, or more personally, the religious music of Ives's later life and George Ives's camp-meeting hymns—both of which are transformed through the mediation of European sonata form, a vestige of Ives's Yale education that is itself altered and transformed.

Ives's setting of *General William Booth* takes its cue from a central metaphor in the gospel tunes of his childhood: the transforming power of religion, community, and Christian love. Ives embeds this concept into the work by weaving together three interdependent sources—two hymn tunes and the formal process of sonata form—in such a way that none is complete without the others, and each is transformed by the contact. Beyond this layer of synthesis, the song emphasizes the vitality of oral tradition in contrast to the fixity of written tradition. This accounts for the ways in which the hymns intersect and mutate, since Ives was remembering performances of the tunes, and actively deconstructing and reconstructing them through remembrance, rather than quoting published sources verbatim. Thus, Ives's description of the variability of the hymn tunes sung at the camp meetings of his childhood offers an apt analogy for his capturing of the peculiar mutability of musical memory: "the music notes and words on paper were about as much like what they 'were' (at those moments) as the monogram on a man's necktie may be like his face."[41]

"A good plan"

The new incarnation of lower- and middle-class hymn tunes in *General William Booth* parallels Ives's own economic and social transformation. Their 1912 purchase of a country property in West Redding—not far from both hometowns of Danbury and Hartford—confirms that the Iveses had achieved a secure financial footing. The West Redding house allowed Harmony to enjoy extended and frequent visits from her family, including her father. Here again, formal religious practices took on a significant role. According to their nephew Bigelow, Reverend Twichell "used to visit often. He spent a summer down there. And while Reverend Twichell was living, they practiced the old-fashioned New England habit of family prayers. Before breakfast we all assembled in the living room, and old Joe Twichell would lead everyone in prayer."[42] For Ives, the West Redding retreat offered a perfect environment for pursuing his music undisturbed, away from the business of the city and the demands of his office. In the country, and with more real isolation from the distractions of work and the city, Ives found the energy and concentration necessary to fully flesh out major works, while beginning even more ambitious ones. Portions of the *Concord Sonata*, the Fourth Symphony, and the Holidays Symphony, to name only a few compositions, were begun or significantly worked out during the Iveses' early years at Redding.

During their second summer there, Ives used the Redding house for yet another invited reading of his music by a professional musician. Franz Milcke, a violinist, visited from nearby Hartford to play the violin sonatas. Ives's description is telling, as it echoes similar comments about Parker and Damrosch, but with a new, more pointed twist:

> Generally speaking, [the Third Violin Sonata] was a slump back, due, I am certain, to a visit in Redding in August 1914 from a typical hard-boiled, narrow-minded, conceited prima donna solo violinist with a reputation gained because he came to this country from Germany with Anton Seidl as [Seidl's] concertmaster. . . . Mrs. Ives knew him in Hartford, and as I'd had so much trouble with musicians playing my music, we thought it would be a good plan to get one of the supposedly great players. . . . The "Professor" came in and, after a lot of big talk, started to play the first movement of the First Sonata. He didn't even get through the first page. He was all bothered with the rhythms and the notes, and got mad. He said, "This cannot be played. It is awful. It is not music, it makes no sense." He couldn't get it even after I'd played it over for him several times. I remember he came out of the little back music room with his hands over his ears, and said, "When you get awfully indigestible

food in your stomach that distresses you, you can get rid of it, but I cannot get those horrible sounds out of my ears (by a dose of oil)."[43]

Milcke had been concertmaster of the Hartford Symphony for several years, and had conducted symphony concerts in New England. As a teenager, he had played in the Berlin Philharmonic Orchestra before emigrating to the United States in the late 1870s as part of a wave of German immigrant musicians who would change the performance, repertoire, and context of music in the northeast.[44] As in his encounter with Damrosch, Ives seems reluctant to admit his own considerable ambition in having a professional, well-placed musician recognize his work. Once again, Ives seems to have expected approval and private, possibly public, endorsement from this ill-fated encounter. In the absence of blanket approval, Milcke is dismissed as an angry, closed-minded, old-world philistine.

But here the trope of rejection takes on a more specific cast. Ives identifies Milcke specifically as *German,* by birth as well as by training. Unlike Ives's earlier German-American targets who endorsed the European tradition (such as Horatio Parker and Walter Damrosch), Milcke represents a more recent link to the Vaterland—a connection perhaps embedded in Ives's transcription of Milcke's awkward English. Thus, Milcke's rejection of Ives's music takes on a new significance. For his part, Ives clearly relishes the opportunity to express some reverse discrimination, in his glee that Seidl's concertmaster is unable to recreate sounds based on amateur performing traditions.[45] In this light, Milcke's incompetence allows Ives to turn the tables, implying that his music is simultaneously too earthy and too difficult for those like Milcke who lack a distinctly American musical education.

A musical manifestation of this attitude, to which Ives refers, appears in the Third Violin Sonata, another work in which American themes and European processes struggle for dominance. Although Ives later claimed the sonata was a "slump back" to a more conservative compositional style as a response to Milcke's criticism, he wrote the piece as a direct challenge to Milcke's European training and aesthetic sense. The work's three movements use themes derived from gospel hymns that, unlike Ives's other extended works at this time, all share the same social, contextual, and musical identities. The first and last movements use Lowry's "I Need Thee Every Hour" from 1872 for their main themes, while the middle movement combines the immediately recognizable "Beautiful River" of 1865, again by Lowry, and Sankey's "There'll Be No Dark Valley" from 1892. It is worth noting that all four tunes were written, and experienced their greatest popularity, during George Ives's lifetime. And, all of them were written by Americans as well.

Unlike the Third Symphony and *General William Booth,* the Third Violin Sonata does not reconcile upper- and lower-class hymns, nor does it "elevate" gospel tunes associated with the camp meetings by combining them with elite musical sources. As if to reinforce the distinction in musical class, performers, and context, Ives "rags" the gospel hymns in the second movement, referencing his own contact with what was viewed as lower-class identity. Furthermore, by utilizing variants of the same melodic and rhythmic patterns that he learned at Yale, Ives infuses the work with technical and interpretative dimensions that a musician like Milcke (or any similarly trained musician in the European tradition) could not grasp.

The victorious, even angry final statement of "I Need Thee Every Hour" in the Third Violin Sonata's last movement appears as a deliberate contrast to the peaceful emergence of "Just As I Am" at the end of the Third Symphony. In fact, all three movements present the full theme at the end, again illustrating the virtue and undiminished power of the American hymn—and perhaps its growing independence—as an expressive source over more standardized European themes.[46] But here, the reconciliation between theme and process, content and form, present and past, seems less secure. Certainly the Third Sonata contains some of Ives's most consonant writing in years—no doubt, what he later tried to dismiss as an embarrassing "slump back." But despite extended tonal and quasi-impressionistic segments, the dissonance level slowly climbs, the violin and piano occasionally slip out of sync with each other, and the sonata as a whole, especially in the conventionally written sections, is permeated with a sense of loss and nostalgia. In sonic terms, Ives seems to be taking one last look before moving inexorably forward into a hostile and fearsome future.

Milcke's visit to Redding took place in August 1914, just as the First World War began. What is commemorated in Ives's iconic retelling of the Milcke encounter—the battle between German traditionalism and American innovation, between vested European authority and the struggle for validity by a cultural colonialist—would be played out over the next four years on a tragic scale. For his part, Ives vacillated between bullish patriotism and heart-heavy pacifism, and struggled with the dual legacy of the American and European traditions, the inheritances of Danbury and Yale, George and Horatio. By the end of the war, in the wake of worldwide and personal destruction, Ives would disavow nationalism in total, even as he completed and published some of his most "American," and most popular, compositions.

5

A Tragic Day

There's a land that is fairer than day,
And by faith we can see it afar;
For the Father waits over the way
To prepare us a dwelling place there.

—from "In the Sweet By and By"

Ives later claimed that, in spite of the grind of working two careers, the relationship between music and business was mutually beneficial. "My work in music helped my business and work in business helped my music."[1] His efforts at work paid off: by 1915, Ives & Myrick was one of the biggest companies of its kind in the United States.

Even as his company flourished, however, a slow panic was building over the possibility of the continuing war in Europe. Initially, the threat of war proved only a mild inconvenience, even an exciting novelty, for Americans. According to the *New York Times* of August 1, 1914, the prospect of war affected the vacation plans "of many a 'cure' guest and Continental automobilist who had hitherto felt no misgivings about returning to America at his leisure." For those vacationing in Germany, the "unprecedented spectacle of seeing the world's greatest military nation girding itself for war provided the greatest conceivable excitement for American tourists in Berlin this week."[2]

The next day's front page announcement of the official declaration of war between the "Triple Alliance" of Germany, Austria-Hungary, and Italy, and the "Entente" of France, Russia, and Great Britain made no mention of American interests—or reactions—at all.[3] Although papers stateside reported developments in the European war regularly, the main focus on America's role concerned its economic interests and the continuance of trade. As six European countries braced for what would become the bloodiest war yet, the *New York Times* reported that the "greatest concern that is felt at this time is for some adjustment of affairs so that some part of the European commerce of the United States may be taken care of and some means be provided for keeping up money exchanges."[4]

Soon, editorials expressed a new anti-German sentiment. Germany was denounced for challenging "practically the whole of Europe to submit to her dictation." Germany and by extension the Austro-Hungarian empire were consistently painted as the aggressor, while "the two great representative democracies of England and France have borne themselves with the greatest calm and dignity."[5]

The United States continued to identify itself as "neutral" despite its alliance with Great Britain, while American German-language newspapers were dismissed as "German propaganda."[6] Even during its neutral period American papers loudly condemned "the Kaiser's enterprises of blood and slaughter," maintaining that "all the American people stand like a rock against Germany in the war she has permitted, encouraged, and provoked. If the pro-Germans among us insist on butting their heads against that rock, it will be bad for the heads."[7]

"That beautiful shore"

The nation's worst fears were realized on May 7, 1915, when German forces sank a merchant ship that may have been carrying ammunition to the British. The *Lusitania* had already skirted danger on its April crossing from Liverpool to New York when it had sailed under the American flag (despite its British registration) to avoid engaging German submarines. In fact, the sinking of the *Lusitania* and the loss of over a thousand passengers and crew marked the culmination of several months of escalating rhetoric among Germany, Britain, and the United States.

American citizens reacted swiftly to the tragedy. Politicians and the media unleashed a torrent of anti-German sentiment that had been brewing for years: "[I]f the dispatch without warning of torpedoes against the great *Lusitania* with 2,000 human beings on board is to be accepted as a true manifestation of the German spirit, if Germany proclaims it, if she has deliberately determined that all the world shall know that this is the way in which she proposes to make war, that this is her attitude toward law, this is the measure of her humanity, then all neutral nations are on notice that the complete defeat of Germany and eradication of the military spirit of Germany are essential to their peace and safety."[8] As Ives recounts, the news stunned everyone. The people in the office, on the street, and on the elevated train he took between home and work "had something in their faces that was not the usual something. . . . That it meant war is what the faces said, if the tongues didn't." Coming home that night, as Ives waited for his train at Hanover Square station, a memorable event occurred:

> As I came on the platform . . . a hand-organ or hurdy-gurdy was playing in the street below. Some workmen sitting on the side of the tracks began to whistle the tune, and others began to sing or hum the refrain. A workman with a shovel over his shoulder came on the platform and joined in the chorus, and the next man, a Wall Street banker with white spats and a cane, joined in it, and finally it seemed to me that everybody was singing this tune, and they didn't seem to be singing in fun, but as a natural outlet for what their feelings had been going through all day long. There was a feeling of dignity all through this. The hand-organ man seemed to sense this and wheeled the organ nearer the platform and kept it up fortissimo (and the chorus sounded out as though every man in New York must be joining in it). . . .
>
> Now what was the tune? It wasn't a Broadway hit, it wasn't a musical comedy air, it wasn't a waltz tune or a dance tune or an opera tune or a classical tune, or a tune that all of them probably knew. It was (only) the refrain of an old Gospel Hymn that had stirred many people of past generations. It was nothing but—"In the Sweet Bye and Bye" [sic]. It wasn't a tune written to be sold, or written by a professor of music—but by a man who was but giving out an experience. . . . [T]his remnant of American folk art . . . has been so long belittled and despised by too many nice, respectable, well-intentioned but unimaginative Americans with arrested muscles above the neck, especially those who have too much to say in musical and other circles today,—and who say, think, deride, or approve only what some business-man-musician-European (with a bigger reputation than anything else) has carefully told them to say, think, deride, or approve.[9]

For Ives, the strangers' singing of the hymn vindicated the work against long-remembered criticisms uttered by Parker at Yale against this very work and the "Moody and Sankey" gospel hymn in general. But Ives's condemnation extends beyond Parker to "some business-man-musician-European." Although Parker championed the European tradition that he had learned firsthand in Germany, and he had married a German citizen, he was not himself a European. Perhaps Ives was collapsing several German-centric critics in this portrait: Professor Parker of nearly two decades earlier; Dr. Damrosch, to whom Ives had recently sent his latest completed symphony, the Third; and "Professor" Milcke, whose bruising comments had occurred only months earlier at Redding.

The choice of the hymn tune by the singers is significant as well. The hymn tune's central metaphor—in heaven, "we will meet on that beautiful shore"—stood out as a particularly moving response to the shipwreck.[10] But beyond that imagery, the distant shore represented the future destination of American soldiers, thousands of whom would die fighting Germany. For Ives, the "beautiful shore" of high European culture—discovered in his youth at the Columbian Exposition, acquired at Yale, and musically debated ever since—had proven disillusioning. Instead, it was the "folk art" of his father that created a coherent community moment, one that cut across lines of class and religious belief in a moment of tragedy. The protestant hymn tune of his rural childhood—a piece of music that represented a preimmigration past, one that was now associated with white Protestant homogeneity—held the power to reshape the Hanover Square train platform and its diverse population into a town square of the most democratic dimensions.

Ives and his fellow New Yorkers were now involved in the "European" war, a conflict that was decried as having been started by the "barbaric" and "uncivilized" behavior of the Germans. In the wake of the *Lusitania* incident, openly anti-German sentiment flowered in the United States. As Ives's prewar compositions testify to an increasingly uneasy balance between the forms and genres most closely associated with Austro-German composers, and thematic content drawn from the increasingly distant American past, his major works of the late teens actively questioned the validity and power of both lineages.

"Country Air"

The day after the Hanover Square impromptu gospel-sing memorialized in Ives's second orchestral set, the Iveses left for an extended summer in Redding, where their country property provided an escape from the mounting stress of the outside world. Charles had peace to work, and Harmony welcomed the relaxing country environment necessary to treat her husband. The annual relocation, and possibly their growing prosperity, seems to have revitalized Harmony's social conscience. During their third summer in Redding, with America's entry into the war looming, the Iveses hosted a large, poor, urban family named Osborne through New York's Fresh Air program. The Fresh Air impulse was a continuation of Lillian Wald's Riverhold initiative providing impoverished children with their own rest cure in the country.

The Osbornes stayed on the Ives property in summer 1915. In the most conspicuous return to her premarriage activities, Harmony began caring for

Harmony with Edith, ca. 1916. Courtesy Yale University Irving S. Gilmore Music Library.

the youngest of the Osborne children. According the Iveses' nephew Brewster, fifteen-month-old Edith "was with a family of six or seven children and was the youngest. . . . Edith's mother was having a difficult time with her as she was a sickly child, and Aunt Harmony took her into the house and cared for her. Aunt Harmony had been a nurse and loved the idea of having a child to care for. They both became fascinated with Edith and arranged with Edith's family for an eventual adoption. Edith became the center of their lives for many years after that. She seldom left home as she was not physically well and, in fact, was handicapped with illness all of her life."[11] There is no evidence that Edith ever saw her birth family again.[12]

Later reports of Edith's ill health require the same close examination as reports of Ives's own health issues. While members of the extended family maintained that Edith was "sickly," indeed "handicapped" throughout her life, John Kirkpatrick says only that Edith remained with the Iveses because she was "still in need of country air," an explanation that echoes the neurasthenic rest cure.[13] The earliest extant photograph of Edith reveals an alert, even luminous toddler (under Harmony's tender yet possessive gaze) who does not appear to have any debilitating illness. Edith's childhood friend Monique Schmitz Leduc makes no mention of any ongoing illnesses, only that she was "gentle and in some ways poetic, a little bit mysterious, and in a way not terribly full of childishness."[14] As a young lady, Edith was described as pretty and charming, somewhat rebellious against her parents, and anxious to experience life during the family's travel in Europe—hardly a physically challenged shut-in. Before her 1939 marriage to George Grayson Tyler, the son of a judge and himself an up-and-coming New York lawyer whom Edith met at church, Leduc was surprised to find her "a young woman who was shopping for a trousseau, who had her two feet on the ground."[15] Edith was healthy enough to live what seems to have been a normal life with her husband, and she gave birth to her own child—something her adoptive mother was unable to do—at the age of thirty-two.

While Edith's own circle may not have mentioned her illness out of modesty, another possibility must be raised. The Iveses' adoption of Edith rested on her needing the medical care offered by Harmony, a trained nurse. If Edith was not medically ill, if she was suffering from what her adoptive mother perceived as neurasthenia, or if she was actually ill but recovered from her illness quickly, her good health would remove a legitimate reason for the Iveses to keep her.

It is possible, of course, that Edith was suffering from an illness, and that the Iveses believed they could best help her through adoption. Yet they might have taken other, less intrusive or drastic steps to aid both Edith and her family. They might have paid for a visiting nurse or live-in help to care for Edith and assist her remaining siblings as well as her biological mother, who was certainly overworked. Charles could have arranged employment directly through Ives & Myrick, or otherwise intervened to find Edith's father a better paying position. Their choice to remove Edith from her family may have pivoted on a specific emotional motivation masked by exaggerated fears of Edith's "illness": that Harmony and Charles wanted to raise a child together. Edith's rescue from illness and poverty hid the Iveses' very personal motivations. The Osbornes acquiesced, but for a price. According to Ives's secretary and personal bookkeeper Kathryn Verplanck, the Osbornes "bothered him to death for more money," which Charles paid out of fear of losing Edith.[16]

The Ives family soon settled into a regular routine. Extended summers, some lasting over six months, were spent at Redding. Ives took the train into New York, writing during the commute, while Harmony and Edith enjoyed the country air. During the school year, the family relocated to their comfortable townhouse in midtown Manhattan. Charles took the elevated train to work each day, and returned in the evening eager to work on his compositions. According to Christine Loring, who worked for a time as personal secretary to the Ives family, "Mr. Ives would come home from a strenuous day in the insurance business, have his meal, and then go the piano and forget all about time until the wee small hours. He would be completely absorbed in his music. . . . [T]heir little girl [Edith] had learned to adjust. He couldn't take any interruptions because he was listening to what was inside him. He'd play, and the little girl was allowed to sit there underneath the piano and play with her dolls, but she must not make a sound."[17] Edith would learn to play the piano, and grow to be "very fond of her father's music," according to her husband.[18] While the schedule was grueling for Ives, and one marvels at Edith's childhood patience with (and interest in) her father's music, this charming domestic scene underscores the family's devotion to each other.

As Edith became a part of the family, her new parents celebrated her arrival through several songs. Harmony wrote texts grounded in nineteenth-century Romantic imagery, just as she had in the days of their courtship and early marriage, which Ives set to elegantly crafted music. "To Edith" and "Two Little Flowers" both use flower imagery familiar from the Lieder texts that Ives reset in Parker's classes, now converted to domestic settings about childhood innocence. Both songs maintain a gently blurred tonality and rolling piano arpeggios—complete with left-hand crossovers—that would be at home in a collection of Debussy preludes. In the case of "Two Little Flowers," which depicts Edith and her friend Susanna playing together, the effect of simplicity is achieved despite the subtle rhythmic tension between the piano accompaniment and voice, which resolves only at the description of the two as "fairest, rarest of them all."[19]

In what may be his most successful song to Edith, Ives adapted portions of Longfellow's poem to his own children, "The Children's Hour," to reach a textual and musical climax on the line "Edith with golden hair." Here again, Ives writes an impressionistic but basically tonal work that belies the more explosive modernist works underway at the same time. In its dreamy textures and appropriately naive word-painting ("the patter of little feet" is set to dainty triplets, while the accompaniment descends chromatically to represent the children coming downstairs; "laugh" is set to an endearing little chromatic flourish), "The Children's Hour" reveals Ives as a consummate craftsman of miniatures, who could compose in a restrained formal and harmonic language with utter conviction, without the dense network of allusive quotations that characterize such large-scale works as "General William Booth."[20]

The Iveses recorded the official adoption of Edith, now two-and-a-half years old, on October 18, 1916, just days before Ives's forty-second birthday. Despite having reached what appeared to have been both a financial and a legal settlement, Edith's family—and their ongoing potential to cause "trouble" for the Iveses—would prove an ongoing source of anxiety through the 1920s.[21] But as Americans braced for a bloody and uncertain war, at least this one aspect of the Iveses' lives seemed secure.

"The Foe"

International tensions proved a progressively volatile issue leading up to the 1916 election. Incumbent Democrat Woodrow Wilson ran on the motto "He kept us out of the war," against the Republican nominee Charles Evans Hughes, whose campaign was overshadowed by the omnipresent Teddy Roosevelt, who argued strongly for American entry into the conflict. Wilson was declared the winner by just a few thousand votes after several days of speculation and uncertainty. Yet, despite Wilson's stance, it was generally assumed that entry into the war was unavoidable and a nationwide draft inevitable.

A second election issue involved "hyphenation," which turned on the continuation of old world identities in the new—an idea that had been debated for some time, but that had become more sensitive for millions of German-Americans beginning with the outbreak of war in 1914. Put simply, in 1916 Hughes and the Republicans needed the votes of large German-American populations in the Midwest to swing the election, and thus courted "the hyphen vote" in states such as Wisconsin. For his part, Wilson used Hughes's association with "the German-American alliance" to advance both a progressivist endorsement of national unity while simultaneously undermining the Republicans as pro-German.[22] Entering into the hyphen debate was a new study on immigration and its impact on "the future welfare of the nation."[23] Frank Julian Warne's *The Tide of Immigration* recommended that the interruption of immigration by the war offered an opportunity for severely limiting future immigration, which "should be restricted by legislation within the narrow channel of the legitimate demand of our industries for skilled labor."[24] A review of Warne's book that appeared in the *New York Times* just a few days before the election equated the issue of immigration regulation with hyphenation and, by inference, the war, stating that limitations will "solve the group of problems arising out of the fact that we have among us the hyphenated American, the man who holds a double allegiance and is a new menace to our democratic institutions."[25] Debate over America's role in the war against Germany, immigration, and ethnicity thus introduced critical questions of American identity that continued to inform political rhetoric well after the election of 1916.

Coeval with the outbreak of the war and the referendum on Americanism in the 1916 election, Ives was fleshing out several major compositions that expressed his own, unhyphenated identity in conjunction with a new emphasis on musical militarism.[26] During these years Ives composed or significantly expanded from earlier sources the first two movements of *Three Places in New England,* and three of the four movements of the *A Symphony: New England Holidays,* more commonly known as the *Holidays Symphony.* Ives's focus on these programmatic, full orchestral movements in the early years of the war is intriguing, since each movement integrates specific, multilayered militaristic imagery in musical quotations and explicit programs. The hymn tunes that figured so prominently in earlier, prewar works are now largely eclipsed.

Perhaps the best known example from this early war era is Ives's *Three Places in New England,* whose three movements—"The 'St. Gaudens' in Boston Common (Colonel Robert Gould Shaw and His Colored Regiment)," "Putnam's Camp, Redding, Connecticut" and "The Housatonic at Stockbridge"—celebrate regional locales, often imbued with military significance and blended with moments from Ives's own family life.[27] The final movement is probably the earliest, in its subtle invocation of hymn tunes as well as its textual connections to Ives's 1908 honeymoon with Harmony: Ives himself explained the work as a commemoration of "a Sunday walk that Mrs. Ives and I took near Stockbridge, the summer after we were married."[28] By contrast, the second movement, "Putnam's Camp, Redding Connecticut" (which was substantially realized only in 1914 or later) celebrates the site of a Revolutionary War battle practically visible from the backyard of Ives's country house. "Putnam's Camp" realizes its military identity by embedding marching and patriotic tunes played by a series of marching bands in what Ives refers to as both a historical recreation of the Revolutionary War battle, and a child's dream of the event on a late-nineteenth-century July Fourth celebration—thus invoking the memory of George Ives while paralleling a larger act of simultaneous meaning and memory in different eras of American warfare—a multilayered experience that Ives understandably represents through multiple, independent, yet interconnected musical strata.

By reaching back to earlier wars for inspiration, Ives remained in step with larger societal currents. In her research on "The 'St. Gaudens'" movements, Denise Von Glahn details the growing significance of the Civil War in print media beginning in 1909 and continuing the six-year period leading into the First World War.[29] Ives's "The 'St. Gaudens'" memorializes the fallen Union Army officer and his all-black regiment that inspired almost a half-century of literary tributes by Ralph Waldo Emerson and Robert Underwood Johnson among others, as well as the 1897 sculpture mentioned in Ives's title. While other commentators have connected the Civil War–era topic with Ives's father George, Ives's poem that accompanies the work suggests a more contemporary interpretation:[30] The poem begins "Moving,—Marching—Faces of Souls!" and later includes an image of a "man on horseback, carved from / A native quarry of the world Liberty." The Civil War past connects with the present conflict particularly through the use of the key word, Liberty—a word used in both the poem for the first movement, and Ives's program for "Putnam's Camp" in which an apparition of "the Goddess of Liberty" encourages Putnam's soldiers to fight on. In fact, the word Liberty emerged during the First World War as a metaphorical rallying cry, and came to be used in every possible nationalist context (as we will see below): thus its prominent appearance in Ives's writings concerning the first two movements of *Three Places in New England* stands as a wartime signifier.

Yet another example of Ives's use of military imagery both contemporarily and historically involves the remaining three movements of the *Holidays Symphony*. Together with the earlier hymn-based "Thanksgiving" movement, Ives portrays a year in late nineteenth-century New England using movements named after exclusively American holidays including "Washington's Birthday," "Decoration Day," and "The Fourth of July." While parts of these works may have existed in earlier forms, substantial sources for "Decoration Day" and "The Fourth of July" indicate that Ives fully conceptualized the movements during the First World War.[31] Locating the works regionally and historically in his childhood masks the militaristic history and subtext of each movement. In fact, each holiday memorializes the military victories of the Revolutionary War and the Civil War. Beyond this, "Decoration Day" and "The Fourth of July" are soaked in quotations from a specifically military repertory (most easily recognizable) that synthesizes Ives's recollections of these holidays in his childhood (and his father's central role in both as a bandleader) from the past with the emerging rejuvenation of American military identity in the face of the European war.[32]

The war infiltrated Ives's consciousness to the extent that in 1917 he wrote what could be considered the core of a war-based song cycle. As in other war-era works, the songs "Tom Sails Away," "The Things Our Fathers Loved," and "In Flanders Fields" voice patriotism and protest simultaneously. Here, however, the songs portray the effect of the war on everyday Americans, even an idealized family whose son goes off to fight in the war.

Ives's insurance pamphlets had long addressed the concerns of the so-called common man and woman. Now he expanded this model to include a traditional family of four that duplicated his own birth family. Although the family is identified only in "Tom Sails Away," the placement and context of the group of songs suggests a continuous connection. The first song, "Tom Sails Away," is narrated by the older son (Charles himself in his birth family), who recalls his childhood on the day his younger brother Tom (Moss Ives, or perhaps one of Moss's older sons) sails off to the war. "The Things Our Fathers Loved" is another memorial work, with an unidentified narrator that could be Tom himself musing on the country he has left behind and the reasons for his journey to the front. "In Flanders Fields," a setting of the by now famous poem by a Canadian lieutenant colonel and doctor, John McCrae, delivers the denouement: "Tom" has been killed in action, and due to his sacrifice we must complete his work and find meaning in his death. To this trilogy could be added the raucous "He Is There," a rousing march applauding the bravery of the soldiers and the rightness of their mission, and the postwar composition "An Election," in which a father muses that the sacrifice of his son (Tom again, in this interpretation) was for nothing.

Throughout the war songs, Ives violently juxtaposes distinctly American quotations first with each other, and then with select formal, timbral, and registral references to European models. In "The Things Our Fathers Loved," for example, the first half of the song combines quotations with specific regional implications, many of them popular during the Civil War, from "Dixie" and "My Old Kentucky Home" to "On the Banks of the Wabash" and "The Battle Cry of Freedom."[33] The opening section could portray the recent military history of the Union and Confederate armies, while conjuring the geographical roots of a motley group of troops from all over the country, brought together by a shared goal. On the word "Now!" the work addresses the present threat directly. The hymn tune "In the Sweet By and By" emerges in the vocal line, marchlike, against a dense, chromatic arpeggiated late-Romantic pianistic texture. Ives's employment of this specific hymn is significant given its fairly recent association with the sinking of the *Lusitania* and the entry of the United States into the war. His placement of a unified, complete American melody in opposition to a European-styled accompaniment that threatens to overwhelm it embodies the contemporary reality of national unity in the face of a foreign war.

Moreover, Ives's own text for the song captures the contemporary flavor of

Ives's song, "The Things Our Fathers Loved," mm. 12–17. From *Charles Ives: 129 Songs*, edited by H. Wiley Hitchcock. Music of the United States of America, vol. 12. Middleton, Wisconsin: A-R Editions, Inc. 2004. Used with permission. "The Things Our Fathers Loved" by Charles Ives © 1955 by Peer International Corporation. Copyright renewed. International copyright secured. Used by permission. All rights reserved.

a country gearing up for battle. The song's superscription, "and the greatest of these was liberty," places the most significant word at the very end of the superscription, thereby amplifying its meaning.[34] "Liberty" occupied a central position within American rhetoric within and beyond the political arena. The war was financed by a series of Liberty Loans, the first beginning in April 1917. For average citizens, the word "liberty" offered an opportunity to express distinctively anti-German sentiment, sometimes in unexpected (and what would prove prescient) ways. Throughout the country, anything associated with Germany was renamed. Sauerkraut and hamburgers became "liberty cabbage" and "liberty sandwiches." Even German measles were transformed into "liberty measles" by what one scholar described as "an unimaginative physician in Attleboro, Massachusetts."[35] Ives's use of the word "liberty" as the song's subtext thus reflects current civil and political sensibilities.

In addition to confronting the enemy, the war songs offered Ives an opportunity to consider the historical and current complexities of his nation. "Tom Sails Away" combines similar metaphors of opposition, here between the American past and present. Ives's text begins (and ends) with a reference to "scenes of my childhood," which is built on a multidimensional quotation from "The Old Oaken Bucket," an 1819 poem set to music in 1870. Ives anchors his composition in the earlier work by quoting both its music (first the opening passage in the accompaniment, then in voice and piano together) and its text, since the original poem begins, "How dear to my heart are the scenes of my childhood." This musical and textual concept permeates the song as scenes from the small town are replayed to variations on the tune.

Although the text might seem to be a representation of Danbury in the 1870s and '80s, there are many other possible connections to Ives's present circumstances. Indeed, the song takes on richer meanings when heard as a fusion of old memories and more recent reality. The narrator recalls a spring day on the hill, "mother with Tom in her arms is coming towards the garden; the lettuce rows are showing green," and the children running down the lane to meet "Daddy . . . coming up the hill from the mill." (The mill and father are central to the original song's text as well.) Ives may be reaching back to his earliest years, seeing his mother Molly carrying his younger brother Moss. At the same time, he could have been placing Moss's five sons, his own nephews, at the center of the songs. Of the five boys, Richard (born 1902) and Brewster (born 1903) would face the draft if the war lasted more than a year or two. That the family was involved in the war effort is obvious in their group photograph in military uniform, complete with baby sister Sarane in the gear of a Red Cross nurse. Yet another version of this scenario had oc-

Moss Ives's children in uniform, ca. 1917–18. The boys (left to right) are Bigelow, Moss, Richard, Brewster, and Chester; daughter Sarane is in front. Courtesy Yale University Irving S. Gilmore Music Library.

curred within the past two years: Harmony carrying Edith in her arms at Redding, where the family tended their spring garden with great enthusiasm and to which Ives returned nightly, driving up the lane from the train station after spending his day at the insurance office.

The complex opposition between past and present builds tension through the song, as the impact of the looming war tears at the idyllic family, past and present. In fact, the "scenes of childhood" are more active and vivid in Ives's setting than the clear, cold, frightening present. Old military tunes ("Columbia the Gem" and "Taps") as well as new ones (George M. Cohan's wartime hit "Over There") replace the "Old Oaken Bucket" quotations in a somber, almost funereal tribute to Tom, who has sailed away "over there." Thus the song text collapses moments as well as music from Ives's past and present in uniquely personal terms, yet in such a way that would have resonance for many families nationwide who were watching their loved ones leave for the front.

Two of the three songs ("Tom Sails Away" and "The Things Our Fathers Loved") were professionally lithographed, indicating that Ives's interest in having his music performed and distributed escalated in 1917. Apparently Ives's business partner Mike Myrick arranged to have baritone McCall Lanham and pianist William Lewis perform "In Flanders Fields" in April 1917 at a meeting of insurance executives.[36] Lanham was a longtime church musician who taught singing at the American Institute for Applied Music: one of his colleagues was the organist Harry Rowe Shelley, whom Ives had known since their Danbury days over a quarter century earlier.

In fact, the meeting was one of many that occurred that month surrounding the official declaration of war on April 7. The New York–based national insurance industry faced a daunting challenge as American troops shipped off to war. Many soldiers had existing policies at regular, low-risk rates, and many more were purchasing policies before leaving for the war. Without additional funding, the insurance industry faced millions of dollars in unexpected claims due to deaths in training, transit, and battle. Mutual, Ives's parent company, had already attempted to offset future losses with the introduction of a new disability clause aimed at injured soldiers that Ives and Myrick's own advertisements publicized. But now insurance executives debated the financial risks of adding surcharges to existing and new policies based on comparisons with British and Canadian models. According to an article in the *New York Times* from April 28, 1917, "[r]epresentatives of most of the insurance companies in the United States met yesterday afternoon and last night at the Hotel Astor with a committee from the National Association of Insurance Commissioners to consider the question of insuring soldiers and to devise a uniform type of war-risk insurance to be adopted throughout the United States. About 100 were present." Within this debate, patriotism vied with budgetary caution. The discourse clearly centered on profit margins for shareholders, on protecting the industry's own interests. Yet one executive at the meeting of April 27, 1917, argued that the business should be less concerned with profits and more active in its patriotic duty. This was probably the meeting at which Ives's "In Flanders Fields" was performed, and it is tempting to see his choice of text and use of patriotic quotations as an admonition to his fiscally focused colleagues.[37]

"The relentlessness of fate"

That the war figured large in Ives's musical output and thinking is apparent even in works without a specific war-related program or text such as the Fourth Symphony and the *Holidays Symphony*. Beyond this, the Piano Sonata No. 2, possibly the best known and most studied Ives composition, had the war as its backdrop as well. No single piece has dominated Ives scholarship as much as this extended solo composition, subtitled "Concord, Mass., 1840–1860" and commonly known as the *Concord Sonata*. Apart from its musical importance, the *Concord*'s significance was established through its publication history, performances, and the unique accompaniment of a written book, the *Essays before a Sonata,* prepared by Ives in 1919 in part to "explain" the work, and his musical credo, to a larger audience.

As is true for so many of Ives's major works, the chronology of the *Concord* defies easy summation.[38] Ives dates sources for the work as early as 1902,[39] but most of the sonata was completed only during the First World War, with other sources filling in the intervening years. The four movements of the *Concord*—"Emerson," "Hawthorne," "The Alcotts," and "Thoreau"—began life as a series of orchestral overtures dedicated to each of the New England Transcendentalists. ("The Alcotts" movement celebrates the family that included father Bronson Alcott as well as his more famous daughter and *Little Women* author, Louisa May Alcott.) Ives's dates for these abandoned overtures range from 1904 to 1911, while the extant sources suggest that the completed sonata grew out of sketches and drafts for the earlier compositions that date from 1907 to 1911—overlapping with Ives's courting of and early marriage to Harmony. For Ives, the subject matter of the *Concord* represented a continuation of his Yale studies under William Lyon Phelps, in what was a rare · validation of New England regionalism—history, religion, philosophy, and beliefs—within the classroom context, and in comparison with more venerated and authoritative European models.[40]

Ives began to adapt portions of the orchestral works into a broad-ranging and technically demanding piano sonata early in the second decade of the century. The majority of extant sketches for the sonata itself, however, appear to have been created between 1915 at the earliest, and fall 1919, when Ives finished copying the entire work into a complete autograph manuscript.[41] Thus, the most significant progress on the composition occurred during and immediately after the First World War. As we shall see, Ives's reactions to the war permeate the program and musical materials of the sonata in unexpected and previously unrecognized ways.

On the surface, Ives places his program for the sonata before the American Civil War, which is supported by most of his musical borrowings ("Columbia the Gem" from 1843, and the venerable hymn tunes *Martyn* from 1834 and *Missionary Chant* of 1832). In reaching back into the past, Ives conjures his own idealized America, a pre–Civil War history based on the world view of the rural or small-town, protestant Transcendentalists, their region and nation, as yet unaffected by immigration or even the abolition of slavery. Yet, a crucial engagement with the present informs Ives's invocation of the past, creating a sense of contradiction, paradox, and simultaneity.

The first contradiction involves the meaning of Concord, Massachusetts, itself.[42] Historically the location represented two opposing yet interrelated ideals of the American experience. First, Concord symbolized the country's proud military history, emergent nationalism, and openly Revolutionary spirit; a place where armed confrontation of British troops on April 19, 1775, began with the "shot heard 'round the world," a phrase reused to describe the assassination of Archduke Ferdinand and the beginning of the First World War. Some sixty years after the Minutemen, the town began to acquire further symbolic resonance. Ralph Waldo Emerson established Concord as his home base; over the next quarter century, he would be joined by Henry David Thoreau, Nathaniel Hawthorne, and Amos Bronson Alcott.

The "second revolution" of American Transcendentalism advanced by these writers and philosophers reflected a unique amalgam of seemingly incompatible elements. Adaptations of German Romanticism merged with highly selective interpretations of Asian belief systems and American Christianity. Emerson, a graduate of Harvard's already elite divinity school, expressed an interest in the common person and voiced a desire for a classless society. The transcendentalist belief that divinity resides within every person coexisted with an emphasis on intuition over scientific knowledge and self-reliance over institutional authority.

Yet, despite the universalist overtones, Ives adapts the tone, structure, and content of transcendentalist writings to forge a uniquely American voice in the *Essays,* as Thomas Owens convincingly demonstrates.[43] Anchoring the work in a place known simultaneously for brass-knuckles warfare against a foreign entity, and the advocacy of nonviolent resistance (voiced in Thoreau's *Civil Disobedience* of 1849), Ives may have been offering a complicated reflection of his own time. The pacifist militarism—or militaristic pacifism—of *Concord* is particularly evident in the substance of its quotations and the manner of their employment. As in other war-era works, Ives uses quotations representing America's recent intramilitary past by drawing on music popular during the Civil War, and more personally associated with his father George. For example, "Columbia the Gem of the Ocean," written at the time the Concord group was active, originally referred to the nation's naval power and was later associated with the Union Army. Ives extends his musical references to the war by incorporating several measures from his own pro-military song "He Is There" into the "Hawthorne" movement. Thus, the quotations reflect a unique blend of historicism and currency, regionalism and nationalism.

Further echoes of the work's wartime genesis involve the related rhetoric of slavery, democracy, equality, and war. The Transcendentalists were active abolitionists, and slavery was a part of the world that Ives portrays in the sonata: yet, he avoids drawing on this identity explicitly in his celebration of antebellum America. Perhaps the most significant reference, paradoxically, occurs in one of the work's central themes, a song that originated within the climate of minstrelsy. Foster's "Massa's in the Cold Ground" was born of the racially defined oppositions of white minstrel troupes imitating and parodying the slaves that the abolitionists were attempting to free. By using parts of Foster's song within the "Emerson" movement, the meaning of the deceptively straightforward minstrel tune is called into question and is transformed for an America at war over half a century later. Foster's text is a representation of slaves celebrating the death of their master: Ives's employment of the tune could be interpreted as celebrating the death of European dominance, and the liberation of American music.

Concord extends its wartime commentary in its treatment of sources from the European, and specifically German, tradition within a specifically American context. In describing the subject of the final movement, Ives states that Thoreau was "a great musician, not because he played the flute but because he did not have to go to Boston to hear 'the Symphony.'"[44] Here, in an essay written while America was at war with Germany, Ives collapses Thoreau's flute-playing on Walden Pond with a symbolic critique of late-nineteenth-century cultural colonialism that emphasized the supremacy of German composers and musicians above all others.

In fact, the backdrop of the Great War provided Ives with an unprecedented context for considering issues of European and American autonomy, interaction, and power. These tensions are summed up in Ives's multifaceted uses of the opening of Beethoven's Fifth Symphony. The famous quotation stands at the musical, intellectual, and programmatic core of the *Concord*. As one of only two quotations to appear in every movement, and one of only two quotations identified by Ives (the other being Foster's "Massa's in De Cold Ground"), Beethoven's motif—which was added to what Ives called the "human faith melody" only in or after 1915, and thus only after the start of the war—offers a musical remnant of continuous significance stretching from Ives's earliest years to the present.[45] Throughout the sonata, Ives enshrines the work in a pianistic reduction similar to the arrangements of Beethoven's symphonies that he played as a teen. In so doing, Ives reclaims the nineteenth-century American amateur performance context of this work from the forces of the early twentieth-century concert establishment that insisted on "authentic" readings of the work by trained, professional symphony orchestras.

Another aspect of Beethoven's famous motif is clearly referenced by Ives in his prose, in the *Essays,* and in a less-familiar musical quotation. Ives connected the Fifth Symphony opening with Emerson's beliefs, saying that "in those four notes lies one of Beethoven's greatest messages. We would place its translation above the relentlessness of fate knocking at the door, above the greater human message of destiny, and strive to bring it towards the spiritual message of Emerson's revelations, even to the 'common heart' of Concord—the soul of humanity knocking at the door of the divine mysteries, radiant in the faith that it *will* be opened—and the human become the divine!"[46] Alongside the spiritual significance of Beethoven's motif, Ives embeds a pun on the "fate knocking" theme. In "The Alcotts," Ives employs the melody of another minstrel tune, "Stop That Knocking," in a lyric, perhaps nostalgic, version that leads into the movement's central statement of the Beethoven theme.[47]

Ives's choice could be coincidental, but there are no overriding musical reasons to use "Stop That Knocking," while the programmatic possibilities—of an American popular song asking "the greater human message of destiny" to stop its knocking—are intriguing. In its broader terms, the gesture may replicate Ives's approach in *The Celestial Railroad* and the second movement of the Fourth Symphony: that one way to deal with divine mysteries is to escape into worldly pleasures.[48] Perhaps Ives is suggesting that a minstrel tune can participate just as equally in the transformation of humanity into "the divine" as a great composition by Beethoven, suggesting again that "the fabric of existence weaves itself whole." At the same time, this musical pun juxtaposes a humorous, popular American source with reverential European art, setting up an unlikely homespun challenger to the latter's sanctity.

A similar juxtaposition characterizes the main theme of the work, referred to by Ives as the "human faith melody." This label eerily echoes the "human life values" expounded in Ives's insurance writings, and combines American and German quotations in such a way as to emphasize their similarities. The theme is presented in full in "The Alcotts" movement after fragmented introductions in the two earlier movements, and repeated almost complete in the flute melody that closes "Thoreau" and the entire work.[49] In its structure, the "human faith melody" joins Beethoven's Fifth Symphony, *Martyn,* and

Missionary Chant, three culturally distinct but melodically similar quotations that all begin with a repeated pitch followed by a leap of a descending major third. Ives describes the melody using a combination of local, regional, and universal terms, avoiding explicitly *nationalist* terms while nonetheless exalting American over European identity, with Beethoven as the lynchpin:

> There is a commonplace beauty about "Orchard House"—a kind of spiritual sturdiness underlying its quaint picturesqueness—a kind of common triad of the New England homestead, whose overtones tell us that there must have been something aesthetic fibered in the Puritan severity—the self-sacrificing part of the ideal—a value that seems to stir a deeper feeling, a stronger sense of being nearer some perfect truth than a Gothic cathedral or an Etruscan villa. All around you, under the Concord sky, there still floats the influence of that human faith melody—transcendent and sentimental enough for the enthusiast or the cynic respectively—reflecting an innate hope—a common interest in common things and common men—a tune the Concord bards are ever playing, while they pound away at the immensities with a Beethoven-like sublimity, and with, may we say, a vehemence and perseverance, for that part of greatness is not so difficult to emulate.[50]

In the face of the overwhelming crisis of the day—rooted as it was in nationalism, militarism, and isolationism—Ives struggled to express universalist views despite the pervasiveness of a wartime context. The "vehemence and perseverance" of the previous years combines with "the self-sacrificing part of the ideal" in a reference to the recent war; the "stronger" sense of American over European values underscores the still-recent victory; and the "innate hope" longs for transformation into the divine. All pro- and anti-war elements coexist, just as Beethoven's motif joins with the "common" hymn tunes in an effort to transcend the limits of nationality, class, and memory.

Simultaneously, in another attempt at transcendental universality within a specifically American context, Ives's use of the Beethoven motif—along with several other acquisitions from the American-European public repertoire of the late nineteenth century—reclaims the authoritative German repertoire. The convergence of local and global elements extends to the personal as well. Ives's program for "The Alcotts" describes the movement as portraying "the memory of that home," suffused with Beth Alcott "playing at [Beethoven's] Fifth Symphony" on the spinet, as her father, "Concord's greatest talker" indulged in "a kind of transcendental business, the profits of which supported his inner man rather than his family."[51] This scenario contains a multitude of related images over several decades. George Ives was the father who "supported his inner man rather than his family," while Charles himself "played at" Beethoven symphonies, learning them from organ scores but probably practicing them on the piano in the family's parlor as well.[52]

At the same time, Ives's portrait of "The Alcotts" reconstitutes the harmonious domestic image of his own adult family alluded to earlier, by conjoining the small-town past of Concord and Danbury with the Manhattan present. Ives is now the father, a successful insurance man whose wealth not only provided for his family but created it through ongoing payments to the Osborne family. Having assimilated the Fifth Symphony, he plays his own Beethovenian creation while his own daughter Edith listens silently beneath the piano in their Manhattan townhouse, reducing the regional, national, and universal dimensions of the work to a deeply rooted, uniquely personal moment.

In this sense, Ives's *Concord Sonata* is literally conservative as it seeks to conjoin crucial moments throughout Ives's life, from the potpourri concerts popular during the Concord group's heyday and during Ives's childhood to his own musings in wartime New York. The juxtaposition and free mixture of hymns, minstrel songs, and marching tunes with Europe's best known works—symphonies and operas, in keyboard arrangements—recreates the sonic and tactile backdrop of Ives's earliest memories, now passed on in a new form to his own child. By stitching together such disparate elements, and defending the combination through his interpretation of transcendentalist ideals, Ives celebrated and enshrined a lifetime of otherwise unknowable memories.

"At business steadily"

Throughout 1917 and 1918, Ives was hard at work in both the musical and business spheres of his life. Within the tense environment of the First World War, Ives's music crystallized a previously conflicted American identity in the wartime songs, *Concord Sonata,* "From Hanover Street North," the Fourth Symphony, the *Holidays Symphony,* and in other period works.

At the same time, the war seems to have hastened Ives's already numerous activities as a promoter and disseminator of his own music. The premiere of "In Flanders Fields" for an audience of hundreds of insurance executives, and by professional musicians, is merely one example of his intentions. Two war songs were professionally lithographed, obviously with the view of circulating the works and having more performances. On April 22, 1917, only days before the premiere of "In Flanders Fields," Ives's Third Violin Sonata—written as a reaction to Milcke's criticisms a few years earlier—was performed at "a small invited concert" in the chamber recital room at Carnegie Hall.[53] While the song premiere a few days later could be considered a patriotic effort, no similar claim can be made for the reading of the Third Violin Sonata, which could just as easily have taken place at the Ives home. One wonders at exactly who else was invited to this concert—whether the guest list included music critics or other professional musicians. But again, Ives had to be the instigator in arranging the event, from contacting and providing music for the performers (David Talmadge, the violin teacher for Ives's nephew Moss, and Stuart Ross, an active professional accompanist) to renting the hall. Talmadge had read over the first three violin sonatas on various occasions, and Ives claimed that he was the only person in the "twenty-five years after Father's death [that is, from 1894 to 1919], who showed any willingness to try to get my music, or took any interest in it at all."[54] Later, Ives would be remembered by commentators such as the composer Lehman Engel as someone who "had literally lived with no performances of any sort for almost all his life, in utter loneliness."[55]

While Ives's statement may be technically truthful, it belies his almost continuous effort to interest others in his music, and to hear performances of new or developing compositions throughout his entire life, except for the period 1902–8. In addition to the song and violin sonata performances in April 1917, the Iveses arranged for "rehearsals" of Ives's chamber works at their house. According to Mrs. Artur Nikoloric, an American pianist and teacher, "Mrs. Ives asked if I would like to come sometime to a rehearsal of Mr. Ives's works. He had written quartets and various other kinds of chamber music and had rehearsals at their house. It happened that he was going to have a rehearsal the following week. . . . I went and was very much impressed. It was a rehearsal of either quartet or quintet."[56] Nikoloric specifies that she attended this rehearsal "during the war" (i.e., before 1918), and her language suggests that it was not a unique event, nor was it tied to the public performance of the violin sonata. What is apparent is that Ives was actively recruiting—and presumably paying—musicians to perform his works, both in public and private.

As Ives was pressing for more exposure and performances of his music, he made the astounding and seemingly contradictory decision to enlist. A surviving carbon of a letter from September 4, 1918 to a Mr. C.C. Whittelsey, the "Assistant Personal Secretary" of the YMCA, indicates that Ives had applied to that organization to serve six months in France, but that "Doctor Bradshaw," a staff physician at Mutual, would not pass Ives on a required physical exam.[57] Ives's actions could be interpreted as philanthropic and patriotic, since the reason cited later for his attempted enlistment was to drive an ambulance.[58]

Yet other evidence mitigates this view. Feder suggests that Ives's overwhelming urge to see battle may have stemmed from a desire to replicate his father's own service during the Civil War.[59] Moreover, Ives, on the cusp of his forty-fourth birthday, intended to leave behind his wife and child, as well as his business as it faced a time of tremendous uncertainty and economic threat. What Harmony and Mike Myrick thought of this decision is unknown, but it is tempting to read Dr. Bradshaw's refusal to approve Ives as a much-needed but apparently ignored reality check. Accounts of the American ambulance corps indicate that the vast majority of volunteers were in their twenties, and a significant number were Harvard and Yale graduates. Thus, Ives's presumed interest in volunteering could have stemmed from a desire to recapture his youth and to rekindle the competitive Yale spirit.[60] Although seemingly self-sacrificing and patriotic on the surface, Ives's actions might have been seen as equally selfish and irresponsible as his enlistment would provide an escape from his everyday life as a middle-aged insurance executive, husband, and father.

Perhaps most intriguing is the timing of Ives's decision to apply during the summer of 1918, and his possible intentions. Nowhere is it mentioned in the extant draft of the September 4 letter that the purpose of his attempted enlistment was to drive an ambulance; this is a later interpretation.[61] In fact, Ives's nephew Bigelow specified that Ives was a poor driver whose abilities were limited to traveling only from the Redding house to the train station. He said, "I recall with particular amusement the times when Uncle Charlie would attempt, and I use that word advisedly, to drive the old Model T car. He was really one of the world's wildest drivers, and he had this Model T Ford which he kept there in Redding just to drive between the house and the West Redding Station. On one occasion he tried to go up to Bethel with it. That was quite an extensive drive of six miles or more, and farther than he usually went."[62] Bigelow's recollection raises the question of Ives's capacity to serve as an ambulance driver anywhere near the chaos of a war zone.

There may be other reasons why Ives was so eager to get to the French front. Through the summer of 1918 the press predicted that President Wilson would announce a nationwide draft. On September 1, he did so, calling on all American men between the ages of 18 and 45 to register.[63] At the furthest edge of the age range, Ives would have been legally required to register on September 12 along with a million other New York men. Although the chances of his being drafted immediately were slim, there was no guarantee that he could avoid being sent to the front as a soldier, especially if the war continued for another year or more. By comparison, volunteering to serve must have seemed preferable to the specter of enforced service. The draft drawing, which would determine who was sent to the war, was set for October 2, 1918. However, President Wilson began it earlier, and the first report of the event appeared in the *New York Times* on October 1, 1918.[64]

Yet another explanation for Ives's action may be connected to the role of American musicians in the Great War. In August 1918, when Ives originally applied to serve in France, Walter Damrosch was setting up a training school for American musicians in France, where he had traveled through the auspices and with the support of the YMCA. Ives's decision to apply coincided precisely with reports of Damrosch's efforts to train bandleaders and bandsmen through a school at Chaumont with the support of the French and American military; this wartime institution was a precursor to the school at Fontainebleau that would train generations of American composers beginning with Aaron Copland.[65] News of Damrosch's plan to open a "big training school for Americans," one that would train "10,000 musicians [who] will go home to the United States after hostilities with more knowledge of and enthusiasm for music than they ever had before," appeared in the *New York Times* on August 24, 1918, six days before Whittelsey wrote to Ives asking for his medical certificate.[66] The appeal of men, military, and music may have contributed to Ives's urgency in getting to France in late August 1918.[67]

Conditions at work contributed to his intense desire to enlist—or escape—as well. The summer of 1918 saw the insurance industry's high anxiety over war claims exacerbated by the growing impact of the influenza outbreak in what would become the largest pandemic to that date.[68] "The Spanish Lady" killed an estimated twenty-one million people worldwide, with over half a million casualties in the United States alone. American troops were infected at the rate of one in four both in military camps at home and abroad. One unusual feature of the disease was that it proved especially lethal to young adults and those "in the prime years of life"—not just the very young or old. For the insurance industry, the influenza pandemic posed an unprecedented threat in that millions of dollars would be paid out for life insurance claims to beneficiaries of the plague's otherwise low-risk victims. Combined with insecurity over war claims, the influenza pandemic threatened even corporate high rollers such as Mutual.

The influenza scare reached New York in early fall 1918. On September 28, the *New York Times* reported that new cases of influenza had doubled in the previous twenty-four hours. On October 1, influenza cases reached their peak in Boston, and nine days later, New Yorkers were advised to avoid public places at all times and to wear gauze masks to avoid infection.

In the midst of the influenza panic, growing reports of war casualties, industry uncertainty and fear—and on the very day that Walter Damrosch's school for American bandleaders and musicians opened in France, and the draft drawing concluded—Ives suffered a debilitating breakdown. While later commentators described his October 1 health crisis as a heart attack, it was more likely a much more serious recurrence of what would then have been called cardio neurasthenia, which was first diagnosed and treated in 1906. Ives himself believed that he had had influenza, a belief that in itself would have been consistent with the documented reactions of neurasthenics to an influenza epidemic.[69] Given the sheer number of stress factors in Ives's life on that date, such an attack seems understandable, even unavoidable in retrospect.

Soon after this breakdown, the Iveses relocated to Asheville, North Carolina, for an eight-week rest cure from January until March 1919. The isolation provided Ives with the uninterrupted opportunity to complete the *Concord Sonata,* one of his largest and most significant works, along with the accompanying *Essays.* On returning, he remained out of the insurance office for another six months—long enough to finalize the autograph of the whole sonata, to arrange for a private printing by the music engravers at the Schirmer company, and even to begin planning a second publication, which became the *114 Songs* collection.

Ironically, Ives's concentrated efforts to publish these two works—publications that would have a huge impact on later evaluations of his music—coincide with yet another transformation in his compositional style after his 1918 breakdown. Most of his new compositions would be written in an aggressively modernist style with minimal connections to either European concert music genres or borrowings from American sources. Ives's break with his own past after World War I parallels a larger worldwide shift. In his new compositions, Ives would all but abandon the recognizably American musical style of works such as the *Concord Sonata* in the wake of worldwide political reorganization and the emergence of the United States as an imperial power in its own right. Thus, the music expresses pervasive nationalism through the opposition of specifically German and American thematic sources, even as the *Essays* address postwar concerns such as the creation of democracy abroad.[70]

Although unplanned, Ives's yearlong health sabbatical yielded impressive results. The publication of the *Concord Sonata* and the *Essays,* and probably his initial plan for publishing the song collection, would prove crucial for realizing the goal that he had pursued for nearly a decade, through the wartime performances and rehearsals and even earlier in his pursuit of performances with Damrosch, Smith, and Milcke. That goal was to reintroduce his music to a broader musical community, to achieve recognition and legitimacy in the opinion of his peers, and thus to resume a professional composition career which he had never completely abandoned.

6

Revising a Life

Nature is man's enemy;
Nature is man's friend.
Nature shows us part of life;
Nature shows us all the grave.

—Ives's text of the song "On the Antipodes"

On November 28, 1922, an audience heard two of Ives's recently published songs in a recital at New York's Town Hall. George S. Madden, a baritone, chose "Du alte Mutter," which was sung in an English translation, and "A Night Thought." Both works were drawn from the volume *114 Songs,* which Ives had had printed and distributed the previous summer. Fifteen months later, Madden returned to the volume for two more Ives songs. He sang "The Greatest Man" and "The White Gulls" in another Town Hall recital on February 28, 1924.

Considering later accounts of the rejection of Ives's music, what is remarkable about Madden's concerts is they were rather unremarkable. Madden seems to have been a serviceable baritone who performed as a soloist in recitals and in choral works (such as a New York production of *Elijah* "in costume at Mecca Temple"). A review of one of his concerts states that Madden had "a natural voice of ample power and range, which however is often somewhat unmanageable and lacking flexibility." In his first solo recital, Madden grouped Ives's songs with other works by earlier and nearly contemporary Americans, most notably Stephen Foster and Edward MacDowell, along with "European classics and popular ballads of other days." A later concert combined "modern songs by American composers and classic and modern selections of the German, French and Russian schools."[1] In the absence of any riotous response (a la Stravinsky's *Sacre du Printemps*) combining critical furor and outright audience rejection, Madden's concerts—historically significant as two of the earliest, independent, documented public performances of complete Ives works—have remained in the background of later, more adventurous, and critically debated premieres.

In their first New York appearances,[2] Ives's songs were paired with traditional and contemporary offerings, both European and American, and apparently emerged as uncontroversial. This was, in part, due to Madden's propitious choice of repertoire. The first concert presented two of Ives's most predictable, tonal, conservative Euro-American Lieder written in the shadow of Parker.[3] The songs chosen for the second recital, however, may be even more intriguing. "The Greatest Man" is one of Ives's novelty songs. Written from a child's perspective, the naively charming, rural American dialect characterizes Anne Timoney Collins's poem first published in the *New York Evening Sun* on June 7, 1921.[4] Ives sets Collins's text in a deliberately simple style, imitating the singing style of a child while having the accompaniment play the singer's melody as if to keep him or her on pitch. Its lilting "half-boasting and half-wistful" melody uses a Victorian-sounding chromatic rocking gesture throughout, underscored by obvious image painting in the piano, such as the classic hunting horns on the line "Dad's some hunter, too." The song is notated without a key signature but remains anchored throughout to a G major tonal center.

"The White Gulls" originated in a relatively recent *New York Evening Sun* issue as well, where it was printed in August 1920. "The White Gulls" employs striking atonal constructions that nonetheless recall the quiet blurring of Debussy, from the (mostly) whole-tone scales that descend through the piano introduction (mm. 1–3) to the symmetrical, chromatic parallel wedge that opens and closes on the phrase "As they spread their wings and fly" (mm. 7–8). However, the conclusion of "The White Gulls" recontextualizes the central sonority (m. 8) from a beautifully colored but harmonically ambiguous rolled chord to a luxurious dominant-function chord (which can be read as a dominant eleventh in first inversion) that resolves unambiguously—and unironically—to a simple, grounded B-flat major chord. Like "The Greatest Man" then, "The White Gulls" ends with a harmonically extended but ultimately reassuring tonal cadence.

The reasoning behind Madden's choices and, indeed, even the path by which he discovered *114 Songs,* are unknown. What is clear is that he chose two unproblematic works that originate in Ives's earliest, pre-1902 career, followed by two works that postdate Ives's 1918 breakdown. Absent from the collection is anything that suggests Ives's most experimental approach, or the modernist-nationalism style that dominated his output for roughly the decade between 1908 and 1918. In drawing from the two opposite ends of

124. THE WHITE GULLS

Unknown
(trans. Maurice Morris)

Ives's song, "The White Gulls," mm. 1–8. From *Charles Ives: 129 Songs*, edited by H. Wiley Hitchcock. Music of the United States of America, vol. 12. Middleton, Wisconsin: A-R Editions, Inc. 2004. Used with permission. Rights held by the Theodore Presser Company/Carl Fischer. Used by permission.

Ives's compositional career to that point, Madden seems to have intuitively avoided the repertoire that must have seemed most problematic in the post–World War I world: songs that often recreated the violence of the immediate past, in a conflict now understood to have grown out of the nationalist spirit that is so prevalent in many of Ives's most popular works.

Early Publications

After more than a decade of trying to interest musicians in his work, Ives decided to take another approach. He paid the engravers at Schirmer's music to print a large composition, then paid to distribute the work to anyone and everyone connected with music that he could find. In a sense, the publication of the *Concord Sonata* and an accompanying volume of *Essays Before a Sonata* represent a nearly thirty-year effort to publish and publicize his keyboard works: an effort that began in 1892 with the *Variations on "America,"* and came to fruition only with the 1920 publication of *Concord.*

Once again, Ives had a myriad of choices as to which piece to publish. Certainly the piano sonata was a large-scale work, but there were other pieces that fit that description as well—not least of which were the Second or Third Symphonies, the Third Violin Sonata, and a collection of the songs. His decision to introduce the *Concord* to a national audience may have been based, in part, on his own performing skills as a pianist. *Concord* was the largest piece that he could hear played all the way through, over and over as he worked on it, which couldn't be said of the songs or ensemble works. The work then offered Ives the unique opportunity to hone and revise the composition based on hearing it performed. In fact the sonata represents the most completed work in Ives's output during this period.

At the same time, the published form of the *Concord* represents a compromise in its 1920 edition, particularly in comparison with a second edition published in the early 1940s. According to Block's comparison of the first and second editions of the work, Ives removed prominent statements of motifs derived from Beethoven's Fifth Symphony; these were restored in the second edition.[5] Ives's decision to downplay Beethoven's motif in the 1919 autograph score used for the 1920 printing is intriguing given the recent end of the First World War and the nationwide discomfort with Germanic culture. Ives reveals the same anxiety within the *Essays,* which act as a combination of musical apologia, literary validation, and sales pitch. Having written a clearly nationalist, even militaristic piece that must be introduced to a war-weary, antinationalist society, Ives struggled to validate the work by emphasizing the universalist and modernist aspects of transcendentalism within a clearly conservative Americanist rhetoric.[6]

Ives's first fully funded publication failed to find an audience.[7] Part of the reason may be purely practical: the work lacked Ives's own efforts as a performer of his own music. Composers such as Henry Cowell and Leo Ornstein—both of whom were introducing unconventional, modernist works from the midteens through the early twenties—toured as pianists and introduced audiences to their new compositions in person. While the reception of Cowell and Ornstein's music was not always positive, at least their public performances allowed their works to be heard.[8] Ives had no such advantage.

The choice of work may have had something to do with the lackluster responses from both the conventional and the new music communities as well. Reviewers for mainstream periodicals including *Musical America* and *Musical Courier* (to be quoted below) rejected the work on sight, complaining (among other things) that the work lacked time signatures and bar lines. At the same time, the sonata retained too many obvious connections to the Romantic, Euro-American tradition to be seen, or heard, as completely modernist. It had a long and detailed program at a time when Schoenberg was advocating a return to absolute music and Stravinsky was on the verge of writing musical "objects" such as the Octet; it used a traditional genre and was identified with the pianistic catalogue dating back to one of its clearly identified inspirations, Beethoven; and its American-sounding quotations connected with a nationalist ethos, at that time still represented by Euro-American composers such as George Chadwick, Amy Beach, and Arthur Foote. With very few exceptions, most commentators in the 1920s and '30s chose to focus on works like the Fourth Symphony movements and individual songs that avoided the pseudo-Romantic nationalism of the sonata in words and music, and that supported the new vision of Ives as the father of modernism. *Concord* would languish for nearly two decades before a pivotal performance gained it the current status in the composer's canon.

By contrast, *114 Songs* fared much better. Its wide variety of styles, narrative topics, and texts met the needs of a large and musically diverse audience. Regardless of their style, the songs were compartmentalized miniatures that could be attempted, if not expertly realized, by a population ignored by modernist composers: the amateur singer and accompanist. Moreover, with a text, Ives's experimental approaches made much more sense. The rippling water and flying wedge of "White Gulls," for example, could be easily understood as effective word painting rather than modernist anarchy, especially given a safe tonal resolution at the end.

Like its predecessor, the published edition of *114 Songs* reveals Ives to be a composer seeking acknowledgment by his peers and audience. By including many of the chanson and Lieder resettings written at Yale under Parker's tutelage, Ives implicitly recognized the value of these works and his education. Indeed, while publicizing the *Concord Sonata*, Ives had clearly identified himself as a student of Parker, just as he had done almost two decades earlier at the premiere of *The Celestial Country*. Even into the 1930s, Ives continued to use his connection to Parker (who had died in 1919) as a kind of pedigree: Henry Bellamann's 1933 profile of Ives describes his "hearty respect" for Parker.[9] Ives could have easily packaged only his most radical works and published a smaller, more manageable collection. Instead, he included all works dating back some three decades, even as he avoided saying anything negative about his Yale instructor. On the whole, the two publications reflect an aspect of caution evidenced in Ives's earlier attempts at making his work known by professional musicians: to offer the widest possible stylistic and chronological spectrum in the hope that anything will prove acceptable.

The first copies of *Concord* were distributed early in 1921, and *114 Songs* followed about a year and a half later. By fall 1923, at least eight reviews of the publications had appeared, and Ives had made direct contact with many interested musicians. At least three of the reviews were caustically dismissive; that these appeared in the largest publications (*Musical America, New York Sun,* and *Musical Courier*) must have been a bitter pill for Ives. The *Musical America* review, for example, stated that the *Concord* was "without doubt the most startling conglomeration of meaningless notes that we have ever seen engraved on white paper."[10]

Of the remainder, several reviews were cleverly written in a partially humorous style, yet they refrained from dismissing the music or the composer altogether. While a reviewer for the *Rocky Mountain News* confessed that the *Concord Sonata* and *Essays* left him "at sea," he nonetheless admitted that "the composer's statements are witty, informative and make unusually fascinating reading. They give personal observations of the characters mentioned that should find a place among the biographical literature. They are well worth reading."[11] While a 1922 *Musical Courier* review of *114 Songs* remained highly critical, at least it showed a more careful reading of the volume and offered the comparison that "Ives is the American Satie, joker par excellence."[12] The *Music & Letters* review of *Concord* in 1921 similarly balanced sarcasm—"Mr. Ives' style is sadly familiar here . . . at any rate in households where the baby or the cat has access to the piano"—with gestures of encouragement—"the few pages that are in any way concerned with music have good sense under their verbiage. . . . [The sonata] is well worth trying."[13]

Moreover, a particularly perceptive review of the *Concord* appeared in the Cleveland newspaper *The Plain Dealer* written by the musician and author Henry Bellamann. Bellamann seized on the *Concord* almost immediately, and featured portions of the work in two lectures in late 1921 or 1922 in Columbia, South Carolina, and Atlanta, Georgia.[14] Other letters of congratulation and encouragement, if not always unambiguous praise, were sent to Ives from scattered musicians who received one or both publications.[15]

For a composer with no name recognition, no reputation, no personal appearances promoting his own music, and working without the support of a sponsoring institution, well-connected peripheral patron, or peer group— essentially, working without any public identity or network to assist him— Ives managed to promote his music rather well. His financial investment in printing and distributing the two publications—in effect, acting as his own patron—paid off with some performances, several reviews of his work in varied publications over a large distance (and aimed at different audiences), as well as requests for more copies of his music.[16] Ives was able to make other contacts as well, as with the violinist Jerome Goldstein. Ives's 1922 letter to Goldstein eventually resulted in a 1924 performance of the Second Violin Sonata as part of a three-concert series featuring the "Modernists." Paired with sonatas by Milhaud and Pizzetti, Ives's work appears to have been introduced by Goldstein as "embodying the transcendental idea of the Concord group" at its Aeolian Hall debut, in an early instance of wholesale application of transcendentalism to all of Ives's works.[17]

The number and variety of contacts that Ives made independently are impressive for someone reentering the professional music scene just shy of his fiftieth birthday. But he needed to connect with someone who had greater influence in the music scene, and such a person showed up, rather miraculously, in the form of E. Robert Schmitz. Schmitz was a French pianist and conductor who immigrated to New York after the end of the First World War. In 1920 Schmitz founded the Franco-American Society, later renamed as the Pro Musica Society, to promote modernist works primarily by French and American composers. The society grew to include a few dozen regional chapters throughout the United States, and in doing so supported the introduction of modern music to such far-flung destinations as Poughkeepsie, Detroit, and Los Angeles.[18] Working in the central hub of New York City, Schmitz was well connected through his activities as a performer and organizer to the burgeoning new music scene. By 1923 he was established as a champion of modern music, a frequent recitalist, conductor, lecturer, and promoter. Although most of his efforts to that time focused on French composers such as Honegger, Milhaud, and Ravel, Schmitz was also working on behalf of John Alden Carpenter, and participated in concerts promoting Charles Tomlinson Griffes's compositions.[19]

Given Schmitz's connections, his chance arrival in Ives's office appears suspiciously fortuitous.[20] According to Kirkpatrick, Schmitz "met Ives while in search of insurance." Perlis's oral history collection expands on the random nature of the encounter: "Schmitz first visited Ives at his office in 1923 in search of an insurance policy, and to Schmitz's great surprise, he found a composer behind the desk. Ives was invited to become a member of Pro Musica."[21] Since Ives never personally sold insurance policies, one wonders how he and Schmitz ended up on either side of Ives's desk in the first place. An agent in the Ives & Myrick office, in the course of selling a policy to Schmitz, could have found out about his musical background and took him in to meet Ives. This explanation, however, again depends on an element of chance since Ives's own secretary claimed that not everyone in the office was aware of his musical life.[22] As Ives's works had been reviewed in New York papers and music journals during the previous two years, it seems likely that Schmitz had a motive other than purchasing life insurance in his visit to the Ives & Myrick offices that day.[23]

Whether or not the encounter between Schmitz and Ives was accidental or planned, it proved mutually beneficial. For Ives, Schmitz proved a source of new ideas gleaned from his experience with modern musical developments in France. He brought not only organizational expertise but an exceptional pianistic technique to his study of Ives's music. Schmitz's daughter Monique (who became close friends with Edith Ives) remembers that

> when we got together at the house on 74th Street, Father and Mr. Ives did a great deal of work together—always playing and talking around the piano. They alternated at the piano. One would push the other one off—not literally, of course, but I remember they would change places at the piano or else bring another chair to the piano, and the two of them would go at it with four hands. I presume that they were working on orchestral scores. They were sight-reading from large formats that were not published. Father was a very good sight reader. This came from the Paris Conservatory, where he studied as a boy. . . . By that time, Father had tackled some music which had prepared him for Ives, and I think this was why he was so valuable to Ives. When Father had occasional objections, he made them straight to Ives. There were some parts that he felt could be done another way at the piano—the same exact notes but distributed in the hand differently so that it might be a little easier to play. . . . Ives would answer with "Never mind."[24]

Schmitz's friendship and professional encouragement may have provided the inspiration for a new composition by Ives, the *Three Quarter-Tone Pieces,* which premiered in February 1925 at an Aeolian Hall concert sponsored by Schmitz and the Franco-American Music Society. Written for two pianos tuned a quarter-tone apart, these three movements represent the first work in two decades that Ives began, completed, and had premiered within a short span, about two years. In terms of his entire output, the *Three Quarter-Tone Pieces* represents the only large work for piano written after the *Concord Sonata,* and the only complete multiple-keyboard work—perhaps an expansion of Ives's experiences playing four-hand piano with Schmitz.[25] The final movement, "Chorale," quotes prominently from "America," in effect creating a late career counterpart to Ives's first significant keyboard work of thirty years earlier, the *Variations on "America"* for organ. Despite their obvious differences in musical language, both works were written for public performance and with the intent of establishing Ives's compositional career: by the mid-1920s, now as a "modernist."

In fact, Ives wrote many new works in a consciously modernist style during the early 1920s. Some were conceived in collaboration with his new circle, as in the *Three Quarter-Tone Pieces* for Schmitz or his settings of Bellamann's texts in "Yellow Leaves" and "Peaks." Other new songs such as "On the Antipodes" demonstrate Ives's full command of a nontonal compositional language filled with crashing dissonances and violent cluster chords, while bluntly attacking the "nice and sweet" music of the past: unknown to his audience, and probably to the composer's own amusement, he borrowed some of this "nice and sweet" music from his own early conservative music, namely the cantata *The Celestial Country* for this phrase.[26] Similarly, the song "The One Way" caustically mocks conservative music and its supporters: its subtitle reads, "The True Philosophy of all NICE Conservatories of Music and NICE Mus. Doc's 'IM.B.CDGODAMLILY.'"[27] In his latest incarnation, Ives intended to prove himself to a new audience not only through his musical style, but also in his willingness to vividly destroy any relic of the past, even or especially his own.

For Schmitz, Ives's contribution was clear. Monique states bluntly that "Ives came to the financial rescue of Pro Musica any number of times."[28] Ives refused to be acknowledged publicly for his crucial role as patron, a pattern that would be repeated throughout the remainder of his life. Although this could in part be attributed to his shyness, or his desire to remain outside of public view, another reason could be Ives's discomfort serving as both composer and patron. Of course, Ives paid for concerts that included his own music as well as works by others. But while he was willing to help the entire new music scene in general, Ives the composer benefited most from the efforts of Ives the patron. Within three years, Schmitz and Pro Musica premiered three large works by Ives. In addition to the newly composed *Three Quarter-Tone Pieces* for two pianos, the first and second movements of the Fourth Symphony appeared in a 1927 concert and *The Celestial Railroad,* a recomposed solo version of an earlier piano concerto, was introduced in 1928. Ives was the only composer to appear on all three programs—a significant distinction given that the concerts included works by Stravinsky and Debussy.[29]

Another reason for Ives's discomfort over his role as patron may stem from his choice in 1902 to "give up music" and pursue a full-time business career. Schmitz, Lou Harrison, Henry Cowell, John Becker, Arnold Schoenberg—all supported modern music without compromising, either as full-time enablers or front-line composers. All would receive Ives's monetary gifts. In fact, Ives's generosity had an enormous impact on the midcentury contemporary scene since it provided direct economic support for numerous composers who subsisted primarily without institutional underwriting.[30] In trading the difficult life of an American composer for the financial success of a business-man, Ives accrued the kind of financial security that someone like Schmitz could never attain.

In the decades that followed, Ives replicated his relationship with Schmitz on an ever expanding basis, as he used his new contacts to complete, revise, promote, perform, publish, and record his music. In Ives, many modernist American composers would find a mentor, a patron, and a symbol of an in-digenous, exaggerated experimental past. Still other composers, musicians, and entrepreneurs would find opportunities in Ives's open wallet. And in a young Californian, the eccentric and unconventional Henry Cowell, Ives found a kindred spirit in whom he placed absolute trust, and a fellow com-poser whose personal vision of Ives shaped the composer's legacy more than any other single factor.

"Indubitably American"

The Pro Musica premieres had an immediate and tangible impact. New York critics began to take notice of Ives's music. Although initially skeptical of Ives, later reviews by Olin Downes (for the *New York Times*) and Lawrence Gilman (for the *New York Herald Tribune*) were remarkably sympathetic toward the music. While Downes's 1925 review of the *Pieces* remarks that the work "had little interest," his 1927 column on the Fourth Symphony movements describes the work as having "something more genuine behind it" than Milhaud's *Les Malheurs d'Orphée,* an orchestral arrangement of music from the chamber opera that was performed at the same concert. Downes concluded that "there is something in this music: real vitality, real naiveté and a superb self respect. . : . It is genuine, if it is not a masterpiece, and that is the important thing."[31] Gilman remarked that the symphony "is as indubitably American in impulse and spiritual texture as the prose of Jonathan Edwards; and, like the writing of that true artist and true mystic, it has at times an irresistible veracity and strength, an uncorrupted sincerity."[32] The reviews reflect the maturing of attitudes toward the New York modernists in the short space of a few years, while Gilman's emphasis on American aspects of the piece works in tandem with the gendered praise of the music's "strength."[33]

Another aspect of Downes's and Gilman's endorsements of Ives's music may be the tentative authority implied through Ives's sponsorship by a prominent music society. Since Ives's publications early in the decade, several New York societies had sprung up around the cause of new music. Initially these organizations took turns endorsing Ives and his music. His migration between shifting and opposing groups reveals yet another aspect of his works' reception at this time. Ives proved a mainstay of Schmitz's Pro Musica concerts in part due to his patronage role; his works were featured on the programs of the Pan American Association and the International Composers Guild (ICG) as well. However, his works were all but excluded in concerts offered by the League of Composers, and in the Copland-Sessions concerts.[34]

In one sense, Ives and his music were critical in the debate between the ICG, Pro Musica, and the Pan-Americans on the one hand, and the League and Copland-Sessions concerts on the other. Members of the first group saw themselves as American modernists fighting the European influence of neoclassicism, which emerged as the dominant style of the League and the composers Aaron Copland and Roger Sessions. Two significant figures in the debate included Dane Rudhyar, whose "utopian vision of an ethnically diverse society" was modeled on American identity, and Carl Ruggles, with whom Ives enjoyed a supportive friendship. As Carol J. Oja notes, both Rudhyar and Ruggles "allied themselves against specific opponents in the avant-garde—most notably Varèse and Schoenberg."[35] In 1930 and 1931, Ives's *Three Places in New England* and "Americanist" songs "The New River," "Indians," and "Ann Street" were paired with those of Rudhyar and Ruggles in programs presented by the Pan American Association, but did not appear in the League's programs through the early 1930s.[36]

The chasm between these modernist groups can be seen in broader terms

as well, as not only potentially anti-European but also anti-immigration.[37]
A review of the works featured in the Pan-American and Pro Musica concerts is notable for its emphasis on several composers whose American roots
stretched back generations, including Cowell and Ruggles. Thus, both Ives's
genealogy and his quotation-based music such as *Three Places* fit with this
group despite generic and formal connections to European Romanticism.

At heart, the Pan American Association was organized to counter the
continuing prominence of European composers even in American societies
such as the ICG and League. Neither had been particularly active in promoting the Austro-German school in the early 1920s, immediately following
the war.[38] Yet by the mid-1920s the ICG featured a mix of modernists that
favored French and German composers over Americans. The formation of
the Pan American Association in 1928 marked a tidal change in modernist societies, as the group existed to promote the works of "citizens of the

Henry Cowell (left) with Ives. Courtesy Yale University Irving S. Gilmore Music Library.

countries of North, Central and South America."[39] Steering the group was a young American composer who had already decided to declare war on European domination. For the next decade, Henry Cowell devoted himself to elevating American modernists to an equal or even superior position over their European contemporaries. Cowell's animosity toward Europe had been brewing since the teens, when he and his teacher, Charles Seeger, had "spent no small amount of time in planning assaults, in the form of concerts, upon New York, Paris, and Berlin" in an attempt to establish a foothold for the American school.[40]

It would be Cowell more than anyone else who enabled Ives's arrival as modernist composer. Until 1936, Cowell continually recruited musicians to perform Ives's works. He single-handedly ran the journal *New Music Quarterly*, begun in 1925 in what Cowell's biographer described as "a calculated assertion of America's cultural equality."[41] Ives would become the journal's single most important patron, as well as bankroll a series of related concerts and recordings. In return, *New Music* published the second movement of Ives's Fourth Symphony in 1929, with Cowell acting as "editor," despite the fact that the work was virtually reproduced without alteration from a copyist score. Thanks to Cowell's contacts, the score represents Ives's first orchestral work to be published in any form and circulated to the broadening community of contemporary composers, and commentators regularly discussed the work following its appearance in print and performance.

For his part, Cowell delivered to modernist circles a much-needed hero. In Cowell's articles about Ives, we see Ives through the eyes of someone other than himself. In Cowell's writings, Ives underwent a startling transformation from a nervous, hermetically creative New York businessman into a deep-rooted Connecticut Yankee who preserved long-lost regional music in his compositions. George Ives became all important, and Horatio Parker all but disappeared. Historical and contemporary Europe receded in favor of an indigenous experimental tradition. In Cowell's war against Europe, Ives was the most effective weapon.

Central to Cowell's approach is a remarkable reconfiguration of Ives as quintessentially American through his genealogy, upbringing, and quotations, and the use of experimental techniques independent of influence from contemporary Europeans—emphases that are either absent or only partial in earlier assessments, such as the 1927 reviews by Downes and Gilman (quoted above). In several publications from the early 1930s, Cowell described Ives's use of "folk-themes" and "typical American usages" as quotations, coupled with the precedence over Schoenberg and Stravinsky in his use of polytonality,

atonality, and complex rhythmic structures.[42] This two-pronged approach—
in which Ives emerges, paradoxically, as *both* an American nationalist and as
an experimental iconoclast—as well as Cowell's proclamation that Ives was
"the most potent and original figure" in American music, created a feedback
loop as other reviews and profiles during the 1930s echoed the same pro-
American, anti-immigration, and anti-European tropes about Ives.

No doubt Cowell expanded on biographical material and descriptions of
specific works that Ives provided for him. But the Cowell-Ives collaboration
was even more symbiotic than might be obvious. For all that Cowell did,
Ives provided steady financial support. Beyond the practical results, Cowell
stoked Ives's need to be part of a younger, daring group, instead of feeling
like a retired insurance manager already past the half-century mark, yet em-
barking on a new public career. In many ways, it would be Ives who followed
Cowell's leadership, not the other way around, despite their difference in age,
experience, and economic condition. And Ives would once again revise his
life and output to satisfy Cowell's great expectations.

"Adding and changing"

By the late 1920s, Ives had what he had always wanted: access to performers
and venues through an increasingly dedicated and well-connected assistant;
an expanding circle of peers, critics, and admirers who responded intelli-
gently and with growing respect to his works; and enough income that he
did not have to worry about making a living from his music. The tables had
turned from his life during the teens. Now, he was a full-time composer and
part-time insurance executive, not the other way around. In this new and
provocative environment, Ives enjoyed a surprising level of productivity
despite what was described as ill health.

During the mid- and later 1920s, Ives finished, and in the process often
revised, earlier works which he then paid to have performed and published.
One of the most extensive examples involves portions of the Fourth Symphony.
Through the mid-1920s Ives continued to work on three of the four movements
of the Fourth Symphony, the third movement being the string quartet fugue
written for Parker at Yale and incorporated into the symphony with minimal
revision.[43] The finale was copied around 1923, while the first two movements
of the Fourth Symphony premiered in 1927, and Ives seems to have continued
incorporating new ideas as he prepared these movements for performance.
While the finely honed Third Symphony retained accessible harmonies and
clear formal articulations, its colossal successor launches an unprecedented
acoustic assault, one with clear ties to Ives's post-1918 modernist outlook.

In support of its program—what Ives described as the questioning of existence—the Fourth attains a previously unknown density of musical material,
unparalleled even by the thickets of the *Concord*. The first movement ("Prelude") poses the question of existence, and each of the following movements
offers one possible response. The second movement, the "Comedy," offers a
vision of the secular world based on Hawthorne's "The Celestial Railroad."[44]
Musically, the second movement builds on the "Hawthorne" movement of
the *Concord Sonata*, now exaggerated and expanded to the breaking point
in a swirling collage of marches and hymns, ragged beyond recognition.
As Swafford notes, the "Comedy" movement contains "the most elaborate
extension of polyrhythm in Ives's career, or in the career of Western music
for years to come," while the texture represents "the closest Ives ever came
to . . . sheer sonic turmoil."[45] Since this movement expresses a stronger and
more explicit modernist aesthetic than Ives had attempted before 1918, it is
tempting to see it as being aimed squarely at the New York circle that supported and attended the movement's 1927 premiere.

The third movement fugue offers another solution to existence, that of
religion and "formalism and ritualism," with Ives's old classroom fugue embodying the virtues of discipline. Ives's finale offers an "apotheosis of the
preceding content, in terms that have something to do with the reality of
existence and its religious experience."[46] Undergirding the final movement is
a percussion battery that plays throughout in independent strata, supporting
an extended collage of hymn tunes that recontextualizes material from the
previous movements.[47] The Fourth Symphony thus concludes with a summation, while the work as a whole presents an overview of Ives's musical
history that integrates decades of materials and processes.

Concurrent with substantial work on the Fourth, Ives continued to extend
his experimental language, now buoyed by the new ideas of the New York
modernist scene. Most of the surviving sources for the *Universe Symphony*
date from 1923 or later, and contain some of the most far-reaching language in
Ives's output. Less a practical composition than an abstract conception—one
that Ives seems to have left intentionally incomplete and unrealizable—the
Universe was intended to depict, in Ives's words, "the creation the mysterious
beginnings of all things, known through God to man [/] to trace with tonal
imprints the vastness, the evolution of all life, in nature of humanity from
the great roots of life to the spiritual eternities [/] from the great inknown
to the great unknown[.]"[48] Ives's concept has similarities to Scriabin's *Mys-
terium* in scope and intent. Since Scriabin was becoming better known in
American circles, Ives owned at least a few Scriabin scores, and he read an
article in the mid-1920s on Scriabin's significance as a composer, it is pos-

sible that Ives knew more than a little of his deceased Russian counterpart despite protests to the contrary. At the same time, Ives's *Universe* presents an extension of the cornucopia of experimental techniques that he had been testing for over a decade already, most notably symmetrical and nontraditional chordal structures, twelve-pitch organization, rhythmic cycles, and multiple independent strata.[49] Thus, the Fourth and *Universe* represent two streams of Ives's work—the public and the private, the performable and the esoteric. Each work offers a type of musical compendium of Ives's orchestral writing: the fullest realization of the post-Romantic ideal on the one hand, and the most ambitious synthesis of coherent rhythmic, harmonic, melodic, and formal alternatives to the inherited system.

In 1920s New York, Ives was a creative and active composer making connections within the modernist community, so it is understandable that he was influenced by the ideas of those around him. Indeed, it would have been remarkable, or even disappointing, if Ives had chosen to retain without modification a compositional style already over a decade old—that is, the language and approach evident in the first edition of *Concord*—despite exposure to new ideas. Here, as in so many other aspects of his life, career, and musical style, Ives enjoyed the best of both worlds. The substance of his earlier compositions (including unconventional notation, form, melodic structure, and harmonic language) dated from the midteens, thus justifying earlier dates that Ives provided. Yet, some of the superficial dissonances may have been added on very late in the process during the mid-1920s, thus ensuring that Ives's new colleagues would recognize and applaud its modernity.

At the same time, Ives's actions could be interpreted as revisionist in that he incorporated later ideas into an earlier work but retained the earlier date. Here, Ives's actions may have a strange parallel in the later activities of his new associate. As Michael Hicks has shown, in the 1950s and '60s Cowell engaged in a campaign to redate some of his earliest cluster chord pieces from the later teens and early 1920s back to the early and midteens, apparently to prove precedence.[50] The similarity between Cowell's redatings and those of Ives is striking, and one can only speculate as to how the activities of both composers might have been related. Whether Cowell encouraged Ives to stress the earliest possible date for a radical idea and then used the same technique himself, or if Ives followed Cowell's example will never be known.

What is certain is that Ives could justify earlier dates for later works by emphasizing earlier dates of no longer extant sources, or for sources that had been substantially surpassed. Perhaps more importantly, Cowell publicized these early dates through his activities as the primary chronicler of Ives and his music, despite having first-hand knowledge of Ives's ongoing compositional activities by the late 1920s. As one of the central beneficiaries of this aspect of the Ives myth, Cowell had a deeply personal agenda in emphasizing the earliest dates as well, regardless of how much was added or changed later.

The same can be said for most of the works that Ives revisited during the 1920s and even later, of which his orchestral set *Three Places in New England* may be the best known and most performed. Elliott Carter, Ives's younger protégé—essentially, his only student—remembers seeing Ives alter a score of the work as follows:

> A matter which puzzles me still is the question of Ives's revision of his own scores. I can remember vividly a visit on a late afternoon to his house on East 74th Street . . . this must have been around 1929. [Ives] was working on, I think, *Three Places in New England,* getting the score ready for performance. A new score was being derived from the older one to which he was adding and changing, turning octaves into sevenths and ninths, and adding dissonant notes. Since then, I have often wondered at exactly what date a lot of the music written early in his life receives its last jolt of dissonance and polyrhythm. In this case he showed me quite simply how he was improving the score. I got the impression that he might have frequently jacked up the level of dissonance of many works as his tastes changed.[51]

Carter's recollections have been questioned in light of his later relationship to Ives, one in which he struggled to deny the influence of the older composer.

Yet, apart from the suggestion that Carter is lying about this incident, the manuscript itself supports his memory of Ives altering the score. In fact, Ives did revise the score in 1929 in order to rescore the work for a chamber orchestra from its full score version, which involved (among other things) adding a piano part. In the process, Ives's alterations primarily serve to concentrate some of the most dissonant passages—previously spread out over an entire orchestra—into one condensed piano part, thereby emphasizing unconventional intervallic structures that were previously present, but not as noticeable in the original instrumentation. (This is not always the case; for example, there are perfectly consonant octave passages in the piano that defy Carter's description.) What Ives appears to have done is to cobble the piano part together by taking a pitch from a string part, and uniting it with a pitch from the winds or brass, often creating an interval of a ninth or seventh in the process. Thus, Carter's description is probably accurate, yet the difference is in emphasis rather than content.

On the whole, the more stringent piano part can be distracting at times, like a superficial modernist patina that interferes with the rest of the chamber orchestra. Works like this, that are based on previous works from the 1900s or even earlier, that were reworked and recycled through the 1910s, and finally finished in the 1920s, occupy what can be thought of as a three-dimensional chronological space analogous to the spatial and collage effects in some of these compositions. The resulting heteroglossia, or creation of multiple, simultaneous voices, explains much about the coexistence—peaceful or otherwise—of early, middle, and late period styles. A particularly good example of this phenomenon is the circa 1924 source for *Psalm 90,* which presents a singular summation of Ives's compositional language. Ives chose the seventeen verses of the biblical source that contrast the immortality of the divine with human mortality. Ives's choice of text may be related to his own declining health. Through the 1920s, Ives would battle diabetes, cataracts, and recurring heart palpitations. By the 1930s, his combined health problems would limit his ability to effectively read and clearly write his own music and correspondence; the former activities would be assigned to copyists and supporters, while the latter duty of copying out Ives's correspondence would fall chiefly to Harmony and, to some extent, Edith.[52]

At the same time, Ives's preoccupation with mortality in *Psalm 90* could be connected to the suicide of David Twichell, Harmony's brother and Ives's old friend and roommate, in August 1924. According to Harmony Ives, *Psalm 90* is the only work with which her husband was completely satisfied: an understandable sentiment given the masterly treatment of the text and integration of thirty years of compositional approaches.[53] The work synthesizes the most experimental concepts, also visible in the *Universe* sources, with surprisingly effective tonal sections that reach back to Ives's first career as a composer and organist. Passages of unmeasured chant coexist with dissonant wedge shapes, rhythmic cycles, and nontonal chords. The closing passage's hymnic simplicity arguably presents Ives's most peaceful compositional expression, a benediction that prefigured his withdrawal from musically progressive New York circles, even as he redirected his creative energies into the marketing of his own myth.

"In the Mornin'"

Elliott Carter's recollections date from the end of Ives's active composing career. By 1929, Ives's world was in flux yet again. With the crash of the stock market, the American economy and the insurance industry in particular faced yet another crisis after the fast-growing, profitable bull market of the mid-1920s. Ives was only in his mid-fifties but his recent public success as a full-time musician must have made it impossible to return to the office full time. He arranged with Myrick to retire from their firm in 1930 at the age of fifty-six: undoubtedly, this was merely a formalization of what had been a gradual withdrawal from the business.

After a few overtly experimental new compositions—the *Three Quarter-Tone Pieces* and "On the Antipodes" among them—Ives gave up writing new compositions in a predominantly modern voice, preferring instead to promote his older works with an adjusted dimension of modernism. This reaching back to the past parallels similar works written during an equally uncertain time: his compositions during the war more than a decade earlier had confronted current realities by revisiting—or escaping to—mid-nineteenth-century Transcendentalists as well as his own early life in Danbury. Simultaneously, it is intriguing to see Ives withdrawing from original compositional activity just as his works began to be accepted. Perhaps, sensing that the tides were turning in favor of the modernists, Ives lost creative interest in a winning cause, and turned his energy to the new underdog—the conservative, tonal idiom.

That impulse appears in two of Ives's final compositions, both of which are arrangements. In 1925, Ives arranged an accompaniment for daughter Edith's melody and original text, entitled "Christmas Carol" (not to be confused with Ives's earlier setting of "A Christmas Carol" from *114 Songs*). Edith's middle-school classmates premiered the work, undoubtedly before an audience not of cutting-edge modernists but of doting parents. Accordingly, Ives provided a "nice" accompaniment, apparently without cringing. An arranged transcription of the spiritual "In the Mornin'," dating from 1929, again rejected the modernist aesthetic in favor of old-fashioned nineteenth-century pragmatism. The circumstances of how Ives came to know this work, which he labeled a "Negroe [sic] Spiritual," are unclear, but apparently he wrote down the words and text based on a performance of the work by Mary Evelyn Stiles, and specified that she knew the work "from her father, Major Robert Stiles, of Richmond, Va., who heard it when a boy. It is quite probably considerably over 80 years old."[54] Unknown to Ives, the spiritual had been published several times in the nineteenth century.

More interesting is Ives's ethnographic attempt to record an oral tradition outside of his own white New England repertoire that originated in a parallel past, that of African Americans in Virginia. In its clear tonality and predetermined form, Ives's fragmentary arrangement of "In the Mornin'" avoids all pretense, any clear invocation of European art forms or styles, and at the same time any manipulations of preexisting material—nationalist or otherwise— that shaped many of his largest works. Using truly borrowed material, Ives in his last works finally regained his undiluted, uncompromised, uncontentious, and unironic compositional voice, the voice of innocence he had left behind so long ago and had struggled to regain for decades. It was time to quit.

Beyond Advocacy

"Is she a good singer? These owners might like to, you know, talk with a good singer like that."

"She's a good singer, but she sings songs that don't have any real melodies. You know, Charles Ives. Anton Webern. Alban Berg. Sometimes she sings some Schubert."

"I've heard of him," said Luciano.

—excerpt from Jane Smiley, *Horse Heaven*[1]

Through the 1920s and early 1930s, reviewers offered good, bad, and indifferent evaluations of Ives's output. Some of the challenge of establishing a reputation lay in his unique status as one of the oldest but least known (and least accessible) composers within the New York scene. Another disadvantage involved the continuing unavailability of scores and the lack of polished performances. But this would change as more works were performed and published, and as the details of his life became better known, primarily through the direct efforts of Ives himself with substantial help from Cowell. By 1939, critics had revised their appraisals and begun to advocate for Ives's "cause," a turnabout steered through Ives's own promotional work on every front.

Ives's earliest efforts to shape and reshape the narrative of his life and work through prose were intertwined with his activities as a patron. In the earliest examples, the *Essays Before a Sonata* and the "Postface" to *114 Songs*, Ives the publisher appealed to the widest possible audience for his compositions using two approaches. In the *Essays* he conjoined his newly problematic nationalism with the universalist and pacifist philosophical foundation of Transcendentalism, while the "Postface" pays homage to all manner of traditional inspiration, both European and American—and along the way, offers the public his pedigree, by way of his education with Parker.

By the mid-1920s, Ives must have known that a more aggressive experimentalist tone would prove successful, at least in capturing the interest of the growing modernist crowd: hence, the article "Some Quarter-Tone Impressions," written to pave the way for the *Three Quarter-Tone Pieces*. Instead of appealing to the average, or conservative, musician, Ives's article intentionally reached out to his new peer group by emphasizing the futuristic aspects of musical composition, and by conspicuously placing himself and his works within that context.

Later writings appear to have been undertaken as a direct or indirect response to Cowell. In 1931, Ives redirected his composing energy into the creation of the highly influential collection of autobiographical writings that would become the *Memos*. Here, Ives rewrites his story to fit the prototype of the original American composer—a model provided and disseminated by Cowell above all others. In many ways, *Memos* functions as a personal letter to Cowell. Ives emphasizes his outright contempt for European and Euro-trained composers, especially Horatio Parker, while reconstituting George Ives as an amazingly progressive thinker, a late-nineteenth-century modernist in his own right whose stunning record of accomplishments—in using quarter-tones, polytonality, polyrhythm, and so on—attacked the European establishment at its Romantic roots.

Like *Essays* and "Postface," *Memos* offered another extended sales pitch directed at a specific audience for a specific purpose. But unlike the earlier writings, *Memos* reveals a disturbing pattern of revisions, omissions, and shifting emphases. Many of the alterations form a type of de facto collaboration with Cowell, as the change in focus and content reflects Cowell's values at the time. In addition to the pronounced pro-American, pro-innovation, anti-European partiality, Ives's emphasis on George dovetails with Cowell's lifelong obsession with creating and idolizing father-figures, in the wake of a difficult relationship with his own father, Harry Cowell.[2]

Moreover, in *Memos* Ives emphasized his connections to amateur musicians and music making, denying or deemphasizing both his Yale pedigree (by claiming that he learned nothing there) and his affluence. Both would have served as a badge of elitism. By omitting, revising, and understating the facts, Ives echoed Cowell's own political views as well as a dominant 1930s aesthetic that sought to reconnect art with the working and lower classes.[3]

And, both Ives and Cowell discuss the noncompositional aspects of music in amazingly misogynistic terms. Cowell, in a 1934 publication, dismisses the "society women" who, through their power, money, and influence decree that new music "must be slightly exotic, must be emotional and waft delicate through the sex-centers, arousing sex emotions pleasurably, but not in an unseemly way. It must create a slightly drugged mood—cast a spell. It must not be intellectual, nor induce thought. It must incite no radical feelings. It must be just modern enough so that it can be called frightfully original, but it must have no experimental modern qualities."[4] Ives freely mixes misogyny with fears of emasculation and homophobia throughout *Memos*, from the very first page, which contains his rant about the critic Philip Hale as "a nice and dear old lady."[5] A more extensive passage echoes Cowell's own complaints, that even great composers "had to live at least part of the time by the ladies' smiles—they had to please the ladies or die. And that is the reason—through their influence—that no one can prove (not even the ladies) that there has been great music ever composed. . . . Music is a nice little art just born, and they ask 'Is it a boy or a girl?'—and one voice in the back row says 'It's going to be a boy—some time!'"[6] As Walter Damrosch's earlier diatribes indicate, misogyny toward female patrons was not new in the American music world. But Cowell, Ives, and even Varèse (whose primary support came from female patrons) extended their antiwoman rhetoric as part of a modernist world view.[7]

Added to this are two new themes in Ives's writings, ones that echo Cowell's own views at the time. Ives refers to the rejection of his works over the years by musicians trained in the European tradition, from Parker, Damrosch, Milcke, and Max Smith up to Hale's dismissal of the 1931 concert performances of *Three Places in New England,* conducted by Slonimsky in a tour financed by Ives. While these incidents certainly happened, all are presented in an uncompromisingly one-dimensional way. More importantly, all prefigure the much more recent rejection of the American modernists, including various incidents in which Cowell's music was rejected or mocked. And, in an extension of the trope of precedence over European experimenters, Ives emphasizes his isolation from other music and musicians through the teens. As has been shown by Michael Hicks, Cowell's biographer, this is a revision of fact, one that anticipates Cowell's own claim of isolation from such influences as Leo Ornstein during the teens.[8]

After three years of intensive work on the project, Ives appears to have abandoned *Memos* sometime after 1934, possibly after Cowell's conviction and subsequent prison term in San Quentin (from 1936 to 1940) after pleading guilty to charges of child molestation.[9] Almost two decades later, Cowell and his wife, ethnomusicologist Sidney Robertson Cowell, published a life-and-works book on Ives, which appeared in 1955. For the book, Ives handed over the incomplete manuscript of *Memos* to use as a source. In fact, Ives's act of generosity is hardly surprising since in *Memos* he shaped his own narrative, and by providing the collection to Cowell, he guaranteed a level of control over even his posthumous reputation.

But with Cowell's imprisonment in 1936, Ives lost a close friend, his most faithful supporter, his publisher and editor, and his most significant connection to the American musical world. Cowell had proven Ives's main conduit to the performers, critics, and scholars who were only beginning to understand his music. By this time, Ives had become isolated from all but a small circle of friends and family. Harmony and Edith now interceded in almost all of his contact with the outside world. Both dutifully recopied his letter drafts in what Owens called "mediated correspondence," while screening incoming information. Indeed, Harmony went so far as to withhold the knowledge of Cowell's arrest from her husband, confiding to her confidante Charlotte Ruggles (and wife of composer Carl Ruggles) that "it is the only secret I've ever had from him." When Ives did learn of the arrest and conviction, he was devastated: according to Harmony, he said, "I thought [Cowell] was a man [but] he's nothing but a g—d—sap!"[10]

Cowell's abrupt, if temporary, departure shook the family to its core and left a critical vacuum in terms of circulating and promoting Ives's works. This vacuum would prove short-lived, as another champion stepped into the role only a few months later, and in so doing changed the course of Ives's reception for the next several decades.

"Quietly and obscurely"

The figure who would become most closely identified with Ives had been studying the *Concord Sonata* for several years before meeting Ives in person. John Kirkpatrick had discovered the work in Paris a decade earlier through Katherine Heyman, who had brought the score with her from New York. Heyman—yet another central female in the modernist scene—was a pianist and teacher who sponsored readings of modernist composers (including Schoenberg and Scriabin) at her Manhattan home in the mid-1920s; her performances of part of the work had introduced Ives's music to a young Elliott Carter.[11] In 1935 and '36, Kirkpatrick played parts of the sonata in public, and in 1937 he finally met Ives. The two would enjoy a warm if somewhat formal friendship until Ives's death in 1954; perhaps after the Cowell affair, Ives was reluctant to get too close to another well-meaning supporter.[12]

Two years later in January and February 1939, Kirkpatrick performed the complete sonata in two well-publicized concerts, each time to a stunned audience that included critics Olin Downes and Lawrence Gilman. Gilman's review in the *New York Herald Tribune* proclaimed the *Concord Sonata* "a masterpiece of American music" and Ives "probably the most original and

JOHN
KIRKPATRICK

Piano Recital

TOWN HALL
113 West 43rd Street

FRIDAY EVENING AT 8:30
JANUARY 20th

Sonata in C major, Op. 53   BEETHOVEN

I. allegro con brio
II. Introduzione, adagio molto
    Rondo, allegretto moderato—prestissimo

Concord, Mass., 1840-60   CHARLES E. IVES

SECOND PIANOFORTE SONATA (1911-15)
("an attempt to present one person's impression of the spirit of transcendentalism that
is associated in the minds of many with Concord, Mass., of over a half century ago")

I. **Emerson** ("a composite picture or impression")

II. **Hawthorne** (an "extended fragment" reflecting "some of his wilder, fantastical
   adventures into the half-childlike, half-fairylike phantasmal realms")

III. **The Alcotts** ("a sketch")

IV. **Thoreau** ("an autumn day of Indian summer at Walden")

FIRST PERFORMANCE

STEINWAY PIANO

Tickets: Box seats $2.75, Orchestra $2.20, $1.65, $1.10, Balcony $.83
Tax included   At Box Office

Management RICHARD COPLEY, Steinway Bldg., 113 West 57th St., New York, N. Y.

Detail from the program of John Kirkpatrick's Town Hall performance of the *Concord Sonata*, January 20, 1939. Courtesy Yale University Irving S. Gilmore Music Library.

extraordinary of American composers."[13] In fact, Gilman's portrait of Ives reveals the fruits of more than a decade of promotion by Ives and his circle in its emphasis on innovation, Americanism, isolation, and neglect, now capped with the image of an aging revolutionary vindicated by the revelation of past creative efforts.

> Charles Ives is sixty-four years old, and for nearly half a century he has been experimenting with musical sounds, and writing them down on paper, working quietly and obscurely (as revolutionary spirits in the regions of the mind so often work), known only to a few inquisitive students and observers who at first suspected, and were afterward sure, that this astonishing artist is one of the pioneers of modern music. . . . Charles Ives is as unchallengeably American as the Yale fence. . . . This sonata is exceptionally great music—it is, indeed, the greatest music composed by an American, and the most deeply and essentially American in impulse and implication.[14]

In addition to paying homage to George Ives, Gilman quotes extensively from *Essays* while discussing the transcendentalist program of the work.

The new image—a conflation of Ives as a transcendentalist, isolated, innovative Americanist—dominates every review of Kirkpatrick's concerts, including those by Downes, Irving Kolodin, and Francis Perkins. A nationally circulated notice in *Time* magazine of January 30, 1939, describes the "practical Yankee" as "grizzled" and "bristle-bearded," attributes his "long obscurity" to "his horror of publicity," and laments that the sonata has been "almost entirely neglected since he completed it in 1915." No reviews remark on Ives's self-publication and circulation of the work in the early 1920s— surely evidence to contradict, or at least question, "his horror of publicity." And most reports neglect to mention the gradual acceptance of his work by composers, musicians, and critics over nearly two decades that counters the tropes of isolation, neglect, and obscurity.

Kirkpatrick's landmark performances of *Concord* established the tone for evaluations of Ives's music for several decades. Although the score and *Essays* had been available for nearly two decades already, the sonata had generally been ignored by prominent writers (especially Cowell) and performers who chose to focus instead on orchestral works and songs. On the eve of the Second World War, perhaps commentators found the heritage of transcendentalism comforting. Certainly the Romantic genre and overt musical and programmatic nationalism of the work found a more receptive audience than in the early 1920s. Even the work's unconventional aspects could have seemed less objectionable to critics and audiences jaded, and perhaps softened, by contact with all means of ultramodernism during the intervening years.

Kirkpatrick's performances and later recordings of the *Concord Sonata* ensured the canonization of Ives (despite Carter's statement to the contrary), and established Kirkpatrick as the clear successor to Cowell, who was still in jail. Over the next few decades, the sonata became the most studied work in Ives's output, and the composer and his entire output were recast endlessly in transcendentalist terms. After Ives's death, Kirkpatrick spent years organizing Ives's manuscripts, painstakingly piecing together every extant source; tracking down and obtaining wayward correspondence or other documents; transcribing manuscript memos and letters; editing numerous musical publications; reconstructing a detailed if problematic chronology of Ives's life and works; and, of course, performing, recording, publicizing, and writing about Ives and his works. Among his efforts, the 1960 *Temporary Mimeographed Catalogue* of the archives served as the central volume for researchers for over forty years, until James Sinclair's catalogue appeared in 1999.

Obviously, Kirkpatrick's activities extended far beyond those of a curator. He edited, annotated, and supplemented *Memos* to such an extent that the added material dwarfs Ives's original manuscript.[15] He edited or coedited a large number of Ives's compositions as well—in some cases, modifying sources significantly, or suggesting entirely new musical passages.[16] Above all, Kirkpatrick functioned as the closest link to Ives, the person most clearly associated with him, and his most active and powerful champion—all of which stemmed from the victorious performances of *Concord* in 1939.

Redemption

The high-profile reception of Kirkpatrick's concerts represents the beginning of the first peak period for Ives's music nationally. Through the 1940s and early '50s, American concert audiences raised to appreciate the European symphonic repertoire recognized familiar elements in Ives's music. Works such as the Second and Third Symphony, as well as the First Orchestral Set, worked as both modernist and "middlebrow."[17] Their clear connections to Romanticism balanced less traditional harmonies, rhythms, and forms— innovations that were already being surpassed by the next generation of American modernists such as John Cage and Lou Harrison—while patriotic and hymn-tune quotations resonated with the unprecedented nationalist spirit of the Second World War.

Most of Ives's works that were performed and recorded in the 1940s and '50s were written in a clearly identifiable Romantic genre—symphonies, sonatas, string quartets, and art songs. A new generation of concert audiences had become comfortable with classical music (via the pervasiveness of network radio and its powerful personalities, especially Toscanini) as one part of a repertoire that coexisted with popular song, church hymns, ragtime, and jazz.[18] Given the truly unique social and cultural conditions of the time, Ives's nationalist style was remarkably well-suited to the audiences of the Second World War era.

The Third Symphony, for example, didn't succeed in spite of its style, but because of it. When the work premiered in 1946, its symphonic celebration of Protestant hymns, using a strikingly traditional harmonic vocabulary, represented an idealized small-town past characterized by national pride and the fiction of religious and racial homogeneity. The awarding of the Pulitzer Prize in 1947 coincided with the rise of America as an economic, political, and cultural empire in its own right, along with a new surge in nationalism (an outgrowth of the Second World War) and the creation of "white" identity.[19] The Second Symphony enjoyed similar success when it premiered in 1951 in a celebrated New York Philharmonic concert conducted by Leonard Bernstein, an event that will be considered in more detail momentarily.

Ives's fortunes parallel the "rise and fall" of classical music in America, in terms of widespread interest in and performances of his music. Indeed, Joseph Horowitz linked "the absence of a native canon" to the decline of interest in American classical music after 1950.[20] With the April 1954 premiere of the *Holidays Symphony,* most of Ives's completed, performable orchestral music had been premiered by the time of his death, after which there was a relative lull in high-profile premieres for over a decade.[21] The premiere of the Fourth Symphony in 1965 fared better, helped by the mainstream press who dutifully trotted out the old bromides: a half century of neglect, technical experimentation decades ahead of its time, the vindication of the "craggy" American Yankee. Interestingly, soon after the premiere a new generation of scholars, performers, and composers began championing Ives's most experimental works in Vietnam-era America, replacing the nationalistic, patriotic repertoire with the studies and chamber works most befitting an iconoclast.

As a result of these continuous efforts, Ives's music reached another peak with public audiences in the mid-1970s, thanks in large part to the intersection of Ives's own centennial year (1974) with preparations for the American Bicentennial of 1976. The most critical publication of this period is Kirkpatrick's edition of the complete *Memos,* which collected essentially an extended letter to Cowell and a few other supporters, giving public voice to ideas and sentiments Ives may never have intended to circulate. Regardless, the volume, collated and vastly expanded by his most constant champion, revitalized interest in the person as well as his music.

After nearly a decade out of the public eye, Ives's music regained center stage between 1974 and 1976 in many highly publicized concerts, series, conferences, and even a documentary for PBS that drew almost entirely on *Memos* from the 1930s. In these efforts, Ives's nationalism took precedence— not surprisingly, given the intense focus on all things American during the years surrounding the Bicentennial. Again, not surprisingly, much of the promotion of Ives and his music was significantly underwritten by the U.S. government in the mid-1970s, both directly and indirectly. In fact, Ives's music may have received more government sponsorship between the 1930s and the 1970s than the music of any other American composer. Ives's choral music regularly appeared in Federal Music Project concerts of the 1930s as part of Franklin Delano Roosevelt's Works Progress Administration initiative, a broad-ranging program that sought to create a de facto history of American music through performances, recordings, and publications. In the late 1950s and early '60s—that is, during the Cold War—the State Department, along with the Rockefeller Foundation, funded Henry Cowell's tours abroad as a "cultural ambassador" in which he publicized Ives's compositions (along with many others) to international audiences. In the mid-1970s, the U.S. government contributed substantially to a wide array of Ives-related events and publications, among them an Ives concert series at the Library of Congress and funds from the National Endowment for the Humanities that supported the Ives oral history project.[22] Partially as a result of this funding, Ives's music and his Americanist, experimentalist image became entrenched in both the academy and the public imagination.

"Some Questions"

By the late 1980s, when Maynard Solomon's article questioning of the truth of Ives's dates appeared, Ives was already safely established as an American pioneer and revolutionary in the concert hall and through a vast array of recordings and publications. Ives's music even migrated into more mainstream vehicles, more like his successors Aaron Copland and Samuel Barber. Two major 1999 films—the German *Lola rennt* (released in the United States as *Run Lola Run*) and the big-budget Hollywood feature *The Thin Red Line*—incorporated the perennial favorite *The Unanswered Question* into their soundtracks.[23] The same work was used as a visual punch line in an episode of the television series *Frasier* in 1997. (As Frasier roams the streets of Seattle agonizing over his own unanswered question, he encounters an advertisement for a concert of the Ives work, which serves to further aggravate his dilemma.)[24] The casual mention of Ives's name and music alongside equally renowned twentieth-century composers in the Jane Smiley novel *Horse Heaven* (cited at the beginning of this chapter) of 2000 confirms his status, even though the passage must be read with irony. The character who is speaking, an American horse trainer, is familiar with the unjustly neglected composer (even as he describes Ives's music, inaccurately, as unmelodic) while the horse's Italian masseur, Luciano, has obviously never heard of Ives at all. Ives has even made it into the *USA Today* Crossword puzzle, as the four-letter answer to the clue "American composer."[25]

Despite the questions of the chronology of his works, Ives continues to function as both a figurehead and a maverick—paradoxically, an established rebel—within the constellation of American music. Among the many symbols of the continuing authority of his works is the endorsement of his music by two prominent, public American musicians. John Adams has identified his own work as a composer with that of Ives, and championed the elder composer through conducting appearances and recordings. Michael Tilson Thomas, in many ways Bernstein's successor, recorded Ives's symphonies for Sony and emphasized Ives's experimental bent in concert series such as the "American Mavericks" in 2000.[26] The two collaborated on Adams's *My Father Knew Charles Ives,* a commission from Thomas's San Francisco Symphony that premiered in 2003, and that Adams described thus: "*My Father Knew Charles Ives* is about my musical childhood, growing up in a small New England town, playing in marching bands with my father and being exposed to the work of Thoreau, Emerson and Ives at an early age. . . . There are three movements, each with an Ivesian title: 'Concord,' 'The Lake' and 'The Mountain.' . . . The work is written for Michael Tilson Thomas, a friend and, like me, an admirer of Charles Ives." [27] Such well-situated admirers who place Ives in the same category as Thoreau and Emerson underscore his current status as a father-figure to contemporary American musicians.

In 1920, Ives embarked on the next stage of his public career after having secured a solid financial footing in insurance; in 1998, Ives's posthumous legacy made a similar transition. In that year, the National Academy of Arts and Letters bestowed the first Charles Ives Living award, a three-year stipend of over two hundred thousand dollars presented to a composer of merit to "concentrate fully on composition." Perhaps ironically, the first award was made to Martin Bresnick, a composer on the Yale faculty who represented Horatio Parker's legacy as much as, or more than, that of Ives. In fact, the award is funded by Ives's donated royalties, earned over six decades of commercial recordings, printed music sales, and public concerts (often subscriber series), all against the backdrop of establishing Ives and vindicating his struggle for recognition.

The amassing of this considerable wealth during the second half of the twentieth century underlines the central role that Ives's music has come to play within the United States and around the world. As such, the establishment of a generous, ongoing composition award in his name using the funds raised through the appreciation of his music seems both fitting and ironic. In sum, the Charles Ives Living award stands as a paradoxical monument to the self-patronized composer, while confirming that his comparatively widespread fame—through film soundtracks, a mainstream novel, and television series, and in the efforts of performers, scholars, and listeners around the world—would seem to render any further efforts at special advocacy unnecessary. Indeed, Charles Ives has been woven into the fabric of contemporary American culture.

Ives Today, Ives Tomorrow

Ives's music has been impossible to categorize effectively because of the contradictions and apparent lack of any dominant aesthetic at any particular period in his career. However, the revised chronology allows a new, somewhat clearer understanding of how he approached composition at various times in his life, and thus substantially redraws the outline of his career, particularly in contrast to the earlier defined tropes of the Ives Legend that emphasized his isolation, American identity, the neglect of his music, and the precedence and centrality of his experimental works.

Ives's first period stretched from approximately 1886 to 1902 and encompasses three overlapping subperiods. His Danbury training (1886–94) includes study with his father (resulting in first works such as *Holiday Quickstep* and a few tentative forays into alternative musical structures, such as the Communion Service's "Credo") and keyboard teachers, his earliest employment as an organist, and his first compositions as an organist-composer ("Rock of Ages," "As Pants the Hart," *Variations on "America"*). Ives's Yale period (1894–98) encompasses his study with Parker and many compositions for publication and performance ("For You and Me," "Crossing the Bar") in addition to works originating in his classes (the fugue for string quartet later used in the First

String Quartet and as the third movement of the Fourth Symphony, reset-tings of Lieder and chansons). After graduating, during his early New York years (1898–1902) Ives struggled to reconcile what he had learned in college with his earlier influences (First Symphony, *The Celestial Country*). From approximately 1902 until 1907, Ives appears to have written almost no new works, thus supporting his contention that he "gave up music" in 1902.

His second period lasted from approximately 1907 to 1918, and can be subdivided into two overlapping periods. First, beginning with the works written during his courtship and early marriage (1907–14), Ives developed a distinctive nationalist voice in works that became increasingly unconven-tional (in harmonic and formal terms) and nostalgic (Second Symphony, Third Symphony, the Third Violin Sonata, "Thanksgiving"); the primary source materials for these works were drawn from hymn and gospel tunes. During the First World War (1914–18), this modernist-nostalgic nationalism took a decidedly militaristic turn in works that invoke America's previous and current wars through texts, programs, and patriotic quotations ("The Fourth of July," "Decoration Day," *Concord Sonata,* the war song trilogy). Throughout, Americanism vies—often violently—with the tonal and formal dictates of the German and larger European tradition.

Ives's final main compositional period spans the years from approximately 1919 to 1929. During this decade, Ives rejected the national tradition in most of his new works. Instead, he embraced both ends of the musical spectrum, by attempting to recapture an earlier innocence ("The Greatest Man," "In the Mornin'") while writing completely new, self-consciously modernist works (*Three Quarter-Tone Pieces,* "On the Antipodes") and substantially revising earlier ideas in a modernist vein (*Universe Symphony*). As he sought and received the kudos of the New York experimental musical community, Ives revised some of his own earlier works according to his continuously evolving aesthetic values, as well as those of his new supporters and audiences (parts of the Fourth Symphony and *Three Places in New England*). After 1929, Ives's musical activities were limited to occasional revisions rather than wholesale re-writing, even while his distortions in *Memos* revised his life and influences.

Why and how much Ives actively continued to reshape his own narrative late in life, in response to and in collaboration with his younger colleagues, still remains to be fully understood. But what emerges from the larger tra-jectory of Ives's life and career is the difficulty—perhaps even, at times, the futility—of distinguishing between "revision," "correction," and "completion" when discussing the compositions such as the Fourth Symphony on which Ives worked during the 1920s. Despite later claims to the contrary, Ives was in all respects a practicing composer during the decade after his breakdown in 1918; and despite later descriptions, Ives appears to have been healthy enough during this period to produce a significant amount of music, both in completions of earlier works and entirely new ones. If he returned to a work that he had written ten years earlier and changed it, it was the work of an active composer engaging in the creative process, not a charlatan seeking to deceive the listeners and scholars of the future.

The ramifications of Ives's later activity—whatever the label and intent—are evident in one of his most famous works, the Second Symphony, which contains no fewer than three compositional stages stretching over more than four decades. In its original source from around 1908 to 1910, the Second Symphony ended with a completely conventional tonal cadence. Ives added a quotation from "Columbia the Gem" to the last measures of the work in an undated later source; at some later date again, he affirmed the quotation when he copied this idea into a photostat of the score sent to Bernard Herrmann in 1938. Both sources, however, maintain a perfectly tonal final cadence. The last incarnation is found in the published score from 1951, where a quotation from "Reveille" joins with a very dissonant final cadence, a surprise tutti "splat." This latest version consisting of two quotations and the cluster chord appears to have been added in 1950 when Lou Harrison and Henry Cowell were preparing the final score for Bernstein's premiere. Ives turned seventy-six that year, and he seems to have indulged in a little fun, probably with the encouragement of one or both younger composers. At the very least, the revisions to the work's ending are collaborative in nature. After all, the brass chord is none other than Cowell's own signature construction, a cluster chord—a construction that Ives had known and used before meeting Cowell, but that is nonetheless absolutely incongruous with the remainder of the Second Symphony and that does not appear in the original sources.

The later revisions to this otherwise conventional work could be dismissed as superficial alterations. However, this work must be considered along-side the many other changes to Ives's compositions in the decades following publication of the *Concord Sonata* and *114 Songs*. More importantly, these changes convey an image of Ives that was very important to him and to his supporters—indeed, to the whole field of American experimental music. Rather than allow his conventional ending to stand honestly on its own terms, Ives and/or Cowell obliterated the pat tonal cadence that had existed for at least three decades, adding one final dose of dissonance. Indeed, this musical moment expresses an "in-your-face" attitude guaranteed to shake up the audience of the New York Philharmonic while simultaneously reiterating

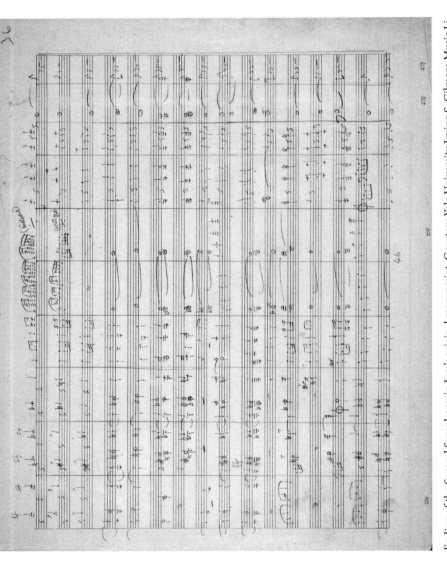

Ending of the Second Symphony in Ives's original manuscript. Courtesy Yale University Irving S. Gilmore Music Library. Symphony No. 2 by Charles Ives © 1979 by Peer International Corporation. Copyright renewed. International copyright secured. Used by permission. All rights reserved.

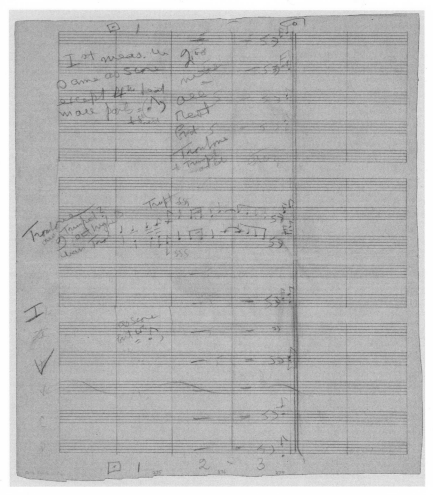

Undated revision to the ending for the Second Symphony with "Columbia the Gem."
Symphony No. 2 by Charles Ives © 1979 by Peer International Corporation. Copyright
renewed. International copyright secured. Used by permission. All rights reserved.

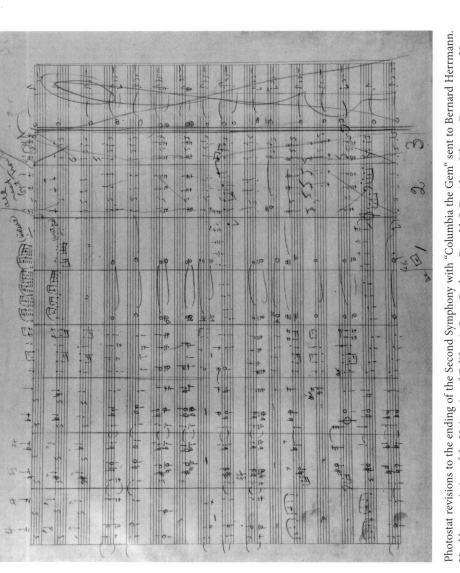

Photostat revisions to the ending of the Second Symphony with "Columbia the Gem" sent to Bernard Herrmann. Used by permission of the University of California Santa Barbara, Donald C. Davidson Library, Department of Special Collections. Symphony No. 2 by Charles Ives © 1979 by Peer International Corporation. Copyright renewed. International copyright secured. Used by permission. All rights reserved.

Ending for the Second Symphony published by Southern Music Publishing Co. Inc. in 1951 and premiered by Leonard Bernstein in the same year, with "Columbia the Gem," "Reveille," and the final cluster chord (clarinets and trumpets are in B-flat: horns are in F.) Symphony No. 2 by Charles Ives © 1979 by Peer International Corporation. Copyright renewed. International copyright secured. Used by permission. All rights reserved.

Ives's legendary status. When the work premiered under the baton of Leonard Bernstein, then a young and popular conductor who negotiated the slippery turf between the authority of the German-dominated canon and the new opportunities of American composition, the final chord was greeted with surprised laughter.

That many of Ives's earlier works were slightly or substantially altered during his post-1918 career has been known for some time. But fully appreciating this fact, in conjunction with later portraits constructed by Ives and others, ultimately changes our view of Ives and his historical position. A portion of Ives's output fits neatly into the early or late periods, but many of his works—especially those like the Second Symphony and *Three Places in New England* that receive significant attention from performers and audiences and that represent the public Ives—do not fit entirely, or cleanly, into one stylistic period. This represents one of the central challenges of rethinking Ives's music: accepting that many of his most important works cut across the arc of his compositional life in complex and probably unknowable ways. Many large compositions that were revised in the 1920s and later contain disparate stylistic layers that coexist and interact outside of any linear evolutionary narrative, much like a pin piercing several folds of fabric simultaneously.

Another challenge is abandoning our impulse toward advocacy when it comes to realistically reevaluating Ives's music in light of the revised dates of his works. In this new model, Ives is neither a cold-hearted cheater nor the irreproachable father of American experimentalism whose own motivations and agenda lie beyond critical evaluation, a figure of power and pity whom well-meaning scholars and musicians have vigorously defended in recent years. Instead, Ives emerges as an extremely complex individual—a flawed, brilliant, naive, shrewd, insecure, compassionate, ambitious, deceitful, trusting, earnest human being—who wove his life and his times into some truly remarkable compositions. Understanding Ives and his music from this unvarnished perspective may yet prove the greatest challenge of all.

Notes

Abbreviations

CEI   Charles E. Ives
HTI   Harmony Twichell Ives

Introduction

1. All of these ideas can be found in the Ives biography written by Jan Swafford and available on the composer's Web site: http:///www.charlesives.org (accessed December 8, 2005). Rossiter refers to this group of beliefs as the Ives Legend in his landmark study, *Charles Ives and His America* (New York: Liveright, 1975), 241, 248–50. I have expanded and revised Rossiter's core ideas here.

2. Rossiter, *Charles Ives and His America*, 248–50.

3. Robert P. Morgan, "Ives and Mahler: Mutual Responses at the End of an Era," *19th Century Music* 2 (1978): 72–81; Morgan, "Rewriting Music History: Second Thoughts on Ives and Varèse," *Musical Newsletter* 3, no. 1 (January 1973): 3–12 and no. 2 (April 1973): 15–23; J. Peter Burkholder, "The Evolution of Charles Ives's Music: Aesthetics, Quotation, Technique," Ph.D. dissertation, University of Chicago, 1983; Burkholder, *All Made of Tunes* (New Haven: Yale University Press, 1995); Geoffrey Block and J. Peter Burkholder, eds., *Charles Ives and the Classical Tradition* (New Haven: Yale University Press, 1996).

4. J. Peter Burkholder, "Ives and Yale: The Enduring Influence of a College Experience," *College Music Symposium* 39 (1999): 27–42; Gayle Sherwood, "The Choral Works of Charles Ives: Chronology, Style, Reception," Ph.D. dissertation, Yale University, 1995; Larry Starr, *A Union of Diversities: Style in the Music of Charles Ives* (New York: Schirmer Books, 1992).

5. In addition to Rossiter's book, which focuses on specifically American aspects

of Ives's life and music, see Michael Broyles, "Charles Ives and the American Democratic Tradition," in *Charles Ives and His World,* ed. Geoffrey Block and J. Peter Burkholder (Princeton: Princeton University Press, 1996), 118–60; Thomas Clarke Owens, "Charles Ives and His American Context: Images of 'Americanness' in the Arts," Ph.D. dissertation, Yale University, 1999; Sherwood, "'Buds the Infant Mind': Charles Ives's *The Celestial Country* and American Protestant Choral Traditions." *19th Century Music* 23, no. 2 (Fall 1999): 163–89; and Denise Von Glahn Cooney, "A Sense of Place: Charles Ives and 'Putnam's Camp, Redding, Connecticut,'" *American Music* 14, no. 3 (Fall 1996): 276–312; Cooney, "Reconciliations: Time, Space and American Place in the Music of Charles Ives," Ph.D. dissertation, University of Washington, 1995; Cooney, "New Sources for The 'St. Gaudens' in Boston Common (Colonel Robert Gould Shaw and His Colored Regiment)," *Musical Quarterly* 81, no. 1 (Spring 1997): 13–50.

6. Stuart Feder, *Charles Ives: My Father's Song* (New Haven: Yale University Press, 1992), 285–91; Gayle Sherwood, "Charles Ives and 'Our National Malady,'" *Journal of the American Musicological Society* 54, no. 3 (Fall 2001): 555–84.

7. For example, in his 2004 profile of Ives in the *New Yorker,* Alex Ross once again emphasized Ives's innovations and his radical American identity ("Pandemonium," *New Yorker,* June 7, 2004).

8. Maynard Solomon, "Charles Ives: Some Questions of Veracity," *Journal of the American Musicological Society* 40, no. 3 (Fall 1987): 463.

9. For immediate responses within the scholarly community, see J. Peter Burkholder, "Charles Ives and His Fathers: A Response to Maynard Solomon," *Institute for Studies in American Music [ISAM] Newsletter* 18, no. 1 (Fall 1988): 8–11; J. Philip Lambert, "Communications," *Journal of the American Musicological Society* 42, no. 1 (Spring 1989): 204–9; and Carol K. Baron, "Dating Charles Ives's Music: Facts and Fictions," *Perspectives of New Music* 28, no. 1 (Winter 1990): 20–56. For mainstream articles, see Donal Henahan, "The Polysided Views of Ives's Polytonality," *New York Times,* June 10, 1990; Alex Ross, "Vindicating Ives on Dates and Music," *New York Times,* August 20, 1996; David Schiff, "The Many Faces of Ives," *Atlantic Monthly* 279, no. 1 (January 1997): 84–87.

10. See Gayle Sherwood, "Questions and Veracities: Reassessing the Chronology of Ives's Choral Works," *Musical Quarterly* 42, no. 1 (1989): 209–18.

11. In some ways, Solomon's article continues earlier criticisms of the quality and nature of Ives's work—as in, for example, Virgil Thomson's 1970 article "The Ives Case," in which Thomson cites the "fatal scars" evident in Ives's works from his "divided allegiance" between music and business. Thomson, "The Ives Case," *New York Review of Books* 14, no. 10 (May 21, 1970): 9–11; reprinted in *American Music Since 1910* (New York: Rinehart and Winston, 1971), 22–30; and in *A Virgil Thomson Reader* (Boston: Houghton Mifflin, 1981), 460–67. I am grateful to Jonathan Elkus for suggesting this connection.

12. J. Peter Burkholder, James B. Sinclair, and Gayle Sherwood, "Charles Ives:

Works," in Grove Music Online, ed. L. Macy (available at http://www.grovemusic .com; accessed November 24, 2007).

13. Rossiter, *Charles Ives and His America*, 248–50.

14. "converse": Memo on the first page of the score of the Second String Quartet; quoted in James B. Sinclair, *A Descriptive Catalogue of the Music of Charles Ives* (New Haven: Yale University Press, 1999), 143.

Chapter 1: The Discovery

1. Norman Bolotin and Christine Laing, *The World's Columbian Exposition: The Chicago World's Fair of 1893* (Urbana: University of Illinois Press, 2002), 8: source unknown.

2. William E. Cameron, *The World's Fair* (Philadelphia: National Publishing Co., 1893), 392; and Reid Badger, *The Great American Fair: The World's Columbian Exposition and American Culture* (Chicago: Nelson Hall, 1979), 93, quoting Columbian Art Company, *Artistic Guide to Chicago and the World's Columbian Exposition* (Chicago: R.S. Peale, 1891), 300.

3. Danbury Museum and Historical Society, "Danbury Fair" (available at http:// www.danburyhistorical.org/DanburyFair.html; accessed September 26, 2004).

4. As Laurence Levine notes, "The clear distinction we tend to make today between bands and orchestras did not obtain for most of the nineteenth century." The division of these two by instrumentation and repertoire was a feature of the chasm between "high" and "low" music late in the century. Levine, *Highbrow/Lowbrow: The Emergence of Cultural Hierarchy in America* (Cambridge, Mass.: Harvard University Press, 1988), 104–14.

5. "Dime museums," Armond Fields and L. Marc Fields, *From the Bowery to Broadway* (New York: Oxford University Press, 1993), 7, "a joke," Frances Hall Johnson, *Musical Memories of Hartford* (Hartford: n.p., [1931] 1970), 14, 16. The musician is Dudley Buck (discussed below).

6. Vivian Perlis, *Charles Ives Remembered: An Oral History* (New Haven: Yale University Press, 1974; reprinted with a foreword by J. Peter Burkholder, Urbana: University of Illinois Press, 2002), 3, quotes Ives's cousin Amelia Van Wyck on the family history; Feder, *My Father's Song*, 9–30, provides the most detailed history of the family and its individual members, including George Ives's siblings. See also Rossiter, *Charles Ives and His America*, 3–23.

7. This paragraph summarized from Levine, *Highbrow/Lowbrow*, 113–15.

8. See Feder, *My Father's Song*, 31–43, for a vivid account of George's Civil War service, including his court-marshal for destroying his cornet.

9. See ibid., 83, which mentions George directing the Saint Peter's Band that consisted of first- and second-generation Irish and Italian immigrants.

10. Many "Old School" Baptist sects disapproved of camp meetings, revivals, and the preacher-musician team of Dwight Moody and Ira David Sankey specifically. A

leading writer of the time proclaimed the revivals swept "like a raging pestilence over the length and breadth of our land." Gilbert Beebe, quoted in R. Paul Drummond, *A Portion for the Singers* (Atwood, Tenn.: Christian Baptist Library & Publishing Co., 1989), 112–13. These churches, which had disapproved of using any music in worship services until the late nineteenth century, included only a few gospel songs in their repertoire because of doctrinal conflicts as well. These "primitive" Baptist sects were found throughout New England, the Midwest, and the upper Southern states.

11. Levine, *Highbrow/Lowbrow*, 40.

12. Ibid., 89–90.

13. See Carol Baron, "George Ives's Essay in Music Theory: An Introduction and Annotated Edition," *American Music* 10, no. 3 (Fall 1992), 246–47, for George's questionings of European theorists. Baron stresses George's views, as set forth in this pedagogical essay, as "independent and even radical" (244), rather than as commonsense applications and modifications of received theoretical practice.

14. The following paragraphs are summarized from Betty Chmaj, "Fry versus Dwight: American Music's Debate over Nationality," *American Music* 3 (1983): 63–84. For an additional consideration of Fry's nationalist agenda, see Denise Von Glahn, *The Sounds of Place: Music and the American Cultural Landscape* (Boston: Northeastern University Press, 2003), 36–50.

15. Quoted in Chmaj, "Fry versus Dwight," 66.

16. Ibid., 73.

17. John Kirkpatrick, *A Temporary Mimeographed Catalogue of the Music Manuscripts and Related Materials of Charles Edward Ives, 1874–1954*, (New Haven: Yale University Music Library, 1960), 214–15.

18. Ives's later claims, that "Father kept me on Bach and taught me harmony and counterpoint," and that "[George] started all the children of the family—and most of the children of the town for that matter—on Bach and Stephen Foster" are probably true only in the most literal sense (Ives, *Memos*, 49, 237). The copybook contains a few Bach chorales used for harmony exercises, but Ives's most extensive study of Bach came through his organ lessons with other teachers (see below). George's essay on music theory contains little that is groundbreaking, experimental, or even original. The essay—dated 1894 by Baron—paraphrases an 1863 publication, indicating that George did not keep abreast of new studies during a period that saw a sea change in music practice, education, and thought in the United States. Baron, "George Ives's Essay in Musical Theory," 240–42.

19. Perlis, *Charles Ives Remembered*, 16.

20. Feder, *My Father's Song*, 95, claims that Moss (Charles's younger brother) and George participated in performances of the work.

21. Ives, *Memos*, 49.

22. Feder, *My Father's Song*, 107.

23. This paragraph summarized from Barbara Owen, *The Organ in New England*

(Raleigh, N.C.: The Sunbury Press, 1979), 255–58. For a different perspective on Ives's role as organist, and the importance of his organ music in later compositions, see J. Peter Burkholder, "The Organist in Ives," *Journal of the American Musicological Society* 55, no. 2 (Spring 2002): 255–310.

24. Owen, *The Organ in New England*, 255, 269.

25. In "The Organist in Ives," Burkholder suggests that Ives modeled some passages of his *Variations on "America"* on Lemmens's *The Storm*. If this is true, then Ives was seeking less to emulate a European master directly, as Burkholder suggests, but rather once again following in the footsteps of his American contemporaries. Ochse recounts that "the notorious 'storm' scenes continued to receive enthusiastic responses" through the 1890s in American organ recitals. Orpha Ochse, *The History of the Organ in the United States* (Bloomington: Indiana University Press, 1975), 197; citing Henry Lahee, *The Organ and Its Masters* (Boston: L.C. Page & Co., 1902), 279.

26. Owen, *The Organ in New England*, 271.

27. *The Musical Independent*, October 1869; quoted in ibid., 256.

28. Theodore Thomas quoted in Levine, *Highbrow/Lowbrow*, 115.

29. Levine, *Highbrow/Lowbrow*, 114–15.

30. John Tasker Howard, *Our American Music*, 3rd ed. (New York: Thomas Y. Cromwell, 1946), 595.

31. From *Dwight's Journal of Music*, October 9, 1869; cited in Owen, *The Organ in New England*, 264–65.

32. Ives began working as a substitute organist at an unknown Danbury church in August 1888; from February until October 1889 he worked at the Second Congregationalist Church; and from October 1889 until April 30, 1893 he worked at the Baptist Church. Ives, *Memos*, 325–26.

33. Information on composers and authors from *The Cyber Hymnal* (available at http://www.cyberhymnal.org/index.htm#lk; accessed January 15, 2006).

34. The following list of organ scores in Ives's collection published by 1894 was gathered from Perlis, Vivian, *Register to the Charles Ives Papers*, Mss. 14, Irving S. Gilmore Music Library, Yale University (New Haven: 1983), 188–89, 192 (available at http://webtext.library.yale.edu/xml2html/music.ives.nav.html; accessed December 19, 2007). The scores fall into five general categories:

1. original compositions by Europeans (Lemmens's Grand Fantasia in E minor [*The Storm*] of 1882; six Guilmant works published in 1876 including *Prayer, Two Amens, Funeral March, Melody,* and *Anthem,* as well as his First Sonata, and three complete and partial undated Bach collections: the Organ Works Vols. 2 and 3, and the Two and Three Part Inventions)

2. original compositions by Americans (Buck's *Variations on Scotch Air* from 1871; Shelley's "Twilight Picture" of 1887; two 1888 works by Chadwick, "O Day of Rest and Gladness" and "Brightest and Best"; and Paine's Concert Variations on the Austrian Hymn for the Organ, published by 1889)

3. arrangements of Beethoven symphonies by Batiste, by 1876 (the "Grand Sortie" of the Ninth Symphony; the Adagio from Fifth Symphony; and the Larghetto from Second Symphony)

4. arrangements for organ by Harry Rowe Shelley (Barnby's "The Soft Sabbath Calm" of 1888; Gluck's "Great Redeemer, Friend of Sinners" of 1890; Gounod's "Happy are We" of 1887; and Raff's March from *Leonora* of 1884) and Dudley Buck (Overture to *Stradella* by Flotow, 1868; Overture to *William Tell* by Rossini, 1868; *Home Sweet Home* by Bishop, 1890)

5. arrangements and compilations by other Americans (three Sousa marches arranged for piano, *The High School Cadets March* of 1890, *The Liberty Bell March* of 1893, and *The Directorate March* of 1894; Liszt's "The Sands of Time Are Sinking," arrangement by N. H. Allen, 1889; Guilmant's *Torchlight March,* arrangement by Warren, 1884; Rink's *Practical Organ School,* edited by W. T. Best; Dulcken's *Liszt Organ Method* (n.d.); Henselt's *Ave Maria,* arrangement by Bartlett, 1887; and Henselt's *Das Ferne Land,* arrangement by Leavitt, 1881)

35. Laurence David Wallach, "The New England Education of Charles Ives" (Ph.D. dissertation, Columbia University, 1973), 152.

36. Cited in Ochse, *History of the Organ,* 198.

37. From Wallach, "New England Education," 195: "The music of both [Buck and Shelley] had been sung in Baptist Church services. Shelley's 'Hark, my soul' appeared as the Offertory on Dec. 22, 1889 (morning service) and proved so effective that it was repeated the following Sunday. Buck's works were used in 1891 and his famous choral work *Light of Asia* was performed on March 23, 1892." Among the Buck works from 1891 that Wallach lists are "Sing Alleluia" on April 5; "My Pilgrimage" on May 17; and "I Will Call" on August 2.

38. See Sherwood, "'Buds the Infant Mind,'" 173–74, for more on the quartet choir. Kirkpatrick suggests that Ives's "Rock of Ages" was performed in April 1893 at the Danbury Baptist Church (after Ives had left that post), but the performance may have been of Buck's own composition instead (Sinclair, *Descriptive Catalogue,* 480–81).

39. Feder, *My Father's Song,* 123. Ives's post at St. Thomas's seems to have been an unhappy one, in the end. Part of the stress came from the choir director, Charles Bonney, whom Ives described as "a martinet." But part of Ives's trouble lay in figuring out the congregation's pointing chant. His inexperience with this style of liturgy, perhaps coupled with the lack of opportunity or encouragement to perform his own anthems and organ music, led Ives to seek another position the next year. See Sherwood, "The Choral Works of Charles Ives," 101–3.

40. Ives, *Memos,* 46–47.

41. See Sherwood, "The Choral Works of Charles Ives," 395–96, for transcriptions.

42. The *New York Times,* August 23, 1893, states that during Ives's visit fair attendance averaged between 120,000 and 150,000 even on ordinary "non-event" days.

43. In addition to Guilmant's three recitals, Walter Hall, a Canadian organist, gave a recital on August 23, and the nationally renowned Clarence Eddy performed on August 25. *Chicago Tribune,* August 23 and 25, 1893.

44. Cameron, *World's Fair,* 274.

45. For example, Levine, *Highbrow/Lowbrow,* 208. For a different opinion, see Robert Muccigrosso, *Celebrating the New World* (Chicago: Ivan R. Dee, 1993), 164.

46. Cited in the *New York Times,* July 2, 1893.

47. *Chicago Tribune,* August 22, 1893.

48. According to the *Chicago Tribune,* September 2, 1893, the noon program that day included the following: March "Heroique" (Massenet); Overture "Merry Wives of Windsor" (Nicolai); *Spring Song* (Mendelssohn); *Airs: Velaques,* for flute (Doppler); Waltz "Wine, Women, and Song" (Strauss); *Bal Costume,* No. 2 (Rubinstein); Overture "Massanielle" (Auber); Ballet "Faust" (Gounod); Aria "Qui lo voce," from "Il Puritani" [sic] (Bellini); Rhapsody No. 3 (Dvořák); Waltz "Seid umschlungen millionen" (Strauss); Suite "Algerienne" (Saint-Saëns).

49. Wallach, "New England Education," 235–36.

50. *Chicago Tribune,* September 1, 1893.

51. Orpha Ochse, *Organists and Organ Playing in Nineteenth-Century France and Belgium* (Bloomington: Indiana University Press, 1979), 112.

52. *Chicago Tribune,* September 3, 1893.

53. Charles Ives Papers, Mss. 14, Irving S. Gilmore Music Library, Yale University (New Haven), Box 33, Folder 1 (available at http://www.library.yale.edu/musiclib/archival.htm#ives; accessed December 19, 2007). Documentation of Shelley's January 1893 performance from Wallach, "New England Education," 70–71.

54. CEI to his mother, Mollie P. Ives, January 20, 1895, edited by Thomas Owens, in *Charles Ives and His World,* ed. J. Peter Burkholder (Princeton: Princeton University Press, 2002), 203.

55. Summarized from Ives's letters to his father in February and October 1894, ibid., 201, 202.

56. Levine, *Highbrow/Lowbrow,* 220.

57. Feder, *My Father's Song,* 128–29, suggests that George felt bitter at taking an office job to assist Charles and his brother in paying for college.

Chapter 2: Classes

1. "Chicago World's Fair," William K. Kearns, *Horatio Parker (1863–1919): His Life, Music, and Ideas* (Metuchen, N.J.: The Scarecrow Press, 1990), 82; and Wallach, "New England Education," 235–36; "critic Louis Elson," Kearns, *Horatio Parker (1863–1919): His Life, Music, and Ideas,* 38.

2. "'The major effort,'" Kearns, *Horatio Parker (1863–1919): His Life, Music, and Ideas,* 19; "'for the purpose,'" *New York Times,* December 20, 1893. General information about the Church Choral Society concerts from the *New York Times* on the fol-

lowing dates: May 4 and December 20, 1893; January 19, December 19, and December 21, 1894; February 22, 1895.

3. *New York Times,* December 20, 1893.

4. "'Inadequacy of the chorus,'" *New York Times,* May 4, 1893; "Handel and Haydn Society," Kearns, *Horatio Parker (1863–1919): His Life, Music, and Ideas,* 22.

5. Quoted in ibid., 20.

6. Ibid., 19 and 20.

7. Course descriptions reprinted from William K. Kearns, "Horatio Parker (1863–1919): A Study of His Life and Music" (Ph.D. dissertation, University of Illinois, Urbana–Champaign, 1965), 110–11, 119–20.

8. Isabella Parker Semler, *Horatio Parker: A Memoir for his Grandchildren* (New York: G. P. Putnam's Sons, 1942), 202.

9. Kearns, *Horatio Parker (1863–1919): His Life, Music, and Ideas,* 28.

10. Semler, *Horatio Parker,* 170–71.

11. Kearns, *Horatio Parker (1863–1919): His Life, Music, and Ideas,* 35–36.

12. Semler, *Horatio Parker,* 173–74.

13. Ibid., 174, quoting John C. Adams, a professor in Yale's English Department.

14. Quoted in ibid., 175.

15. For example, Schirmer's commission in the 1890s for a series of sacred cantatas.

16. Ives's later reference to "Prof. $5000," an imaginary figure who criticizes the *Concord Sonata,* could be at least a partial reference to Parker, since this amount would reflect Parker's shared paycheck for *Mona* (Ives, *Memos,* 189; see also 116 for discussion of Damrosch as "Prof. $5000"). In *Essays Before a Sonata,* Ives made a similar complaint about composers "trying to write . . . a ten-thousand-dollar prize opera"; apparently, Parker's success dug deep. *Essays Before a Sonata* (New York: Knickerbocker Press, 1920); reprinted in *Essays Before a Sonata, and Other Writings,* ed. Howard Boatwright (New York: W.W. Norton, 1962), 93.

17. Semler, *Horatio Parker,* 296.

18. Ives, *Memos,* 48. Ives's scholastic record was reconstructed and helpfully interpreted by Kirkpatrick; it is reproduced with commentary in Appendix 6 of *Memos* (180–84). Kirkpatrick suggested that a combination of audited courses and independent compositional study with Parker during the first two years at Yale supports Ives's "four years with Parker" (ibid., 183). But Solomon notes that in letters written to George in his first term at Yale, Ives mentions Parker only once, in a very distant context and not in conjunction with any coursework: "Mr. Parker gives an organ recital this evening" (letter of October 24, 1894, as quoted in Solomon, "Questions of Veracity," 462). If Ives had been studying with Parker in his first term at Yale, or even had any sustained one-on-one contact with Yale's foremost musician, it seems likely that he would have reported this information to his father.

19. Kearns states that Parker's music history course was intended as a public lecture series, with between forty and seventy students in attendance (*Horatio Parker*

(1863–1919): His Life, Music, and Ideas, 112). To qualify for the instrumentation and strict composition courses, Ives was required to either pass qualifying examinations in history and harmony, or audit these classes at Yale (Ann Besser Scott, "Medieval and Renaissance Techniques in the Music of Charles Ives: Horatio at the Bridge?," *Musical Quarterly* 78, no. 3 [Fall, 1994]: 461). The level of Ives's technical writing in 1894 probably would not have been considered adequate training by Parker's standards, so it is very unlikely that Ives would have passed out of the harmony course. Ives's auditing of certain music courses was completely consistent with the practice of the time. For example, the majority of extant pre-1900 assignments from the strict composition course are by students who did not register for any music courses, based on a comparison of Yale College record books (classes of 1896–1900) with the Yale School of Music archival registry. See Yale College Records in Manuscripts and Archives, Sterling Memorial Library, New Haven; and student assignments in Yale University School of Music Papers (Irving S. Gilmore Music Library, Yale University, New Haven), Mss. 3, Folder 1 (available at http://webtext.library.yale.edu/xml2html/music.ysm.nav.html; accessed December 19, 2007). And, as one former student recalled, Parker's harmony, counterpoint, and strict composition classes had, around the turn of the century, "about thirty or more students in a class"—a class size that represents several times the number of credit takers, which rarely exceeded ten students (Kearns, *Horatio Parker (1863–1919): His Life, Music, and Ideas,* 123–24). Student Edwin Arthur Kraft studied with Parker ca. 1899–1901. According to Kirkpatrick's record of the enrollment in each of Ives's registered music courses from 1894–98 (Ives, *Memos,* 182), the harmony class was the largest (up to thirteen registered students), while the free and strict composition and instrumentation classes had as few as one or two registered students.

20. Ives, *Memos,* 182.

21. Jerome Karabel, *The Chosen: The Hidden History of Admission and Exclusion at Harvard, Yale, and Princeton* (New York: Houghton Mifflin, 2005), 19, quoting from a Yale study of 1903. Karabel notes as well that "[s]cholarly performance . . . had been dropping regularly since 1896–97," Ives's junior year, and that between 1894 and 1903 the secret societies had tapped notably fewer valedictorians. Regarding the criteria of the secret societies, see 19–20.

22. Yale College Records, Yale Manuscripts and Archives, Sterling Memorial Library.

23. Although there is no direct evidence, there are some circumstantial clues that Ives took the free composition class. Several resettings of German and French lieder date from 1897–98 including "Feldeinsamkeit," "Qu'il mirait bien," "Die Lotusblume," "Chanson die Florian," "Ich Grolle nicht," and "Wie Melodien." Following the course description, these "smaller forms of . . . vocal music" were probably composed for the free composition class. Further student resettings may have included "Minnelied" and "Ein Ton." It is more likely that George Chadwick's visit to Ives's class in 1898 (recounted by Ives on the manuscript of "Feldeinsamkeit") occurred in conjunction with

the free composition class, rather than the strict composition class as suggested by Kirkpatrick (Ives, *Memos*, 183–84). In this context, a reference to the First Symphony on a later manuscript of the song "Abide With Me" is significant, as it reads "2nd theme for Symphony in Parker Free composition class." Kirkpatrick transcribed the memo as "2nd theme for Symphony in Parker Fres [i.e., Freshman] composition class . . ."; however, "Fres" is more likely "Free," as Ives did not take any Freshman composition class with Parker (ibid., 159). That Ives composed at least part of his First Symphony in the free composition class is again supported by the course description—"the student will be required to produce an extended work, probably in sonata form." Only the outline sketch and score-sketch of the first movement of the symphony appear to date from the Yale period (ca. 1898 handwriting, paper types dated between 1888 and 1899; patches supplementing the score-sketch, and sources for the remaining movements date from 1898–1902). In *Memos,* Ives relegated the work to the end of his Yale period, stating, "It was written . . . for a degree—that is, to complete my four years academic course at Yale" (87, 51). Parker's reported dislike of parts of the work might further explain Ives's lower mark in the second term of the course.

24. Ives's final assignment for strict composition also survives in the sketches and ink score of the Organ Fugue in E-flat. The Yale School of Music Archives preserves copies of three other student fugues (one dated "June 1898"), that are written on the same theme, though in C minor—rather than E-flat, the key of Ives's fugue. The fugues are by L.F. Graeber, Emma Spieske, and Ruth Wallace (who dated her work), and are found in the Yale School of Music Archives, Box 3, File 1. It is unclear whether this alteration was an intentional decision on Ives's part, or the result of a careless reading of the assigned theme in the wrong clef, mistaking a notation in the treble for one in the bass. The second hypothesis may better explain Ives's resentful notation on the extant pencil sketch—"a stupid fugue and a stupid subject."

25. Ives, *Memos,* 183; Elizabeth Goode, "David Stanley Smith and His Music" (Ph.D. dissertation, University of Cincinnati, 1978), 29.

26. Griggs's publications are listed in J. Peter Burkholder, *Charles Ives: The Ideas Behind the Music* (New Haven: Yale University Press, 1985), 157–58.

27. Ives, *Memos,* 254.

28. An advance notice of the lecture is printed on the program of Griggs's lecture of October 25, 1895. It lists music by the "Choir and Organist of Center Church, New Haven, assisted by . . . Professor Horatio W. Parker of Yale University." In Ives Papers, Box 50, Folder 1.

29. Ives Papers, Box 51, Folder 1.

30. Val Hicks, "Barbershop quartet singing," in Grove Music Online, ed. L. Macy (available at http://www.grovemusic.com; accessed November 24, 2007). For a general overview of the cultural background of the barbershop style, see Deac Martin, "The Evolution of Barbershop Harmony," *Music Journal Anthology Annual* (1965): 40–41, 106–7.

31. Sinclair, *Descriptive Catalogue*, 134. See Jonathan Elkus, *Charles Ives and the American Band Tradition: A Centennial Tribute*, American Arts Pamphlet 4 (Exeter: University of Exeter, 1974), 15, 17, 20, 22, and 26 for a discussion of this work.

32. Parker's choruses from the mid-1890s on blended elements of American barbershop with characteristics of German Lieder, Mannerchör, and cantata styles (Kearns, *Horatio Parker (1863–1919): His Life, Music, and Ideas*, 281–86). Most notable are the more elaborate accompaniment and extended length of works like *The Lamp in the West* from 1901. Parker's more formal European approach to secular choral music is clearly detectable in Ives's *The Bells of Yale* from 1898. This, Ives's most successful and elaborate part-song, may well have been written for his senior year free composition class that included the writing of "part-songs, glees for male and mixed voices." Understandably, *The Bells of Yale* offers the most obvious appropriation of Parker's style in its unparalleled length and sophistication. The work exists in multiple arrangements using combinations of men's chorus, solo baritone, chimes, piano, cello, and violin, which may indicate a new interest in instrumentation as a result of his courses with Parker. The work includes a motivically developed accompaniment in the Lied tradition and a baritone solo, features characteristic of Parker's secular choruses and that represent a fundamental shift in focus for Ives.

33. Ives, *Memos*, 51.

34. As has been well documented, Parker resisted the instruction of his own American teacher, George Chadwick, although the two men became great friends. George W. Chadwick recalls: "As my pupil he was far from docile. In fact, he was impatient of the restrictions of musical form and rather rebellious of the discipline of counterpoint and fugues. . . . His lessons usually ended with his swallowing his medicine, but with many a wry grimace. It was quite natural that before long our relation should develop from that of teacher and pupil into a warm and sincere friendship, as it ever afterward remained" (*Horatio Parker* [New Haven: Yale University Press, 1921], 8).

35. Lecture notes also survive from 1904 and 1915, and are extensions of the Columbia talk. The "Church Music" lectures are found in the Horatio Parker Papers, Mss. 32, Irving S. Gilmore Music Library, Yale University, (New Haven), Box 35, Folders 5–7 (available at http://webtext.library.yale.edu/xml2html/music.parker.nav.html; accessed December 19, 2007). The underlining in this excerpt is found in Parker's original notes.

36. Parker, "Church Music," 1897, 12–13, 17–19.

37. Horatio Parker, "Address before Guild of Organists," in "Addresses, Essays, Lectures," No. 2: quoted in Kearns, "Horatio Parker (1863–1919): A Study of His Life and Music," 601.

38. Parker, "Church Music," 1897, 11–12. An excerpt from "Elijah" had been performed as an example of appropriate solo quartet music in Griggs's lecture of October 25, 1895, again illustrating differences of opinion between the two. Program, Charles Ives Papers, Box 51, Folder 1.

39. Parker, "Church Music," 1904, 14–15.

40. Parker's attacks on Buck are particularly interesting given that Buck was George Chadwick's teacher and therefore a kind of compositional grandfather to Parker.

41. Key figures in the Oxford movement included Rev. John Kebles and Vicar (later Cardinal) John Henry Newman; the movement was founded in 1833 by several fellows of Oriel College, Oxford. As defined in their published tracts and lectures, this group advocated a "Counter-Reformation" to return the Church of England to its sixteenth-century condition. Kearns, *Horatio Parker (1863–1919): His Life, Music, and Ideas*, 573–77 and John Carrick, *Evangelicals and the Oxford Movement* (Bridgend, Mid Glamorgan: Evangelical Press of Wales on behalf of the Evangelical Library, London, 1984), 7–36. For the musical impact of the movement see Bernard Rainbow, *The Choral Revival in the Anglican Church (1839–1872), Studies in English Church Music Series* (London: Barrie and Jenkins, 1970), 6–14, 90–92.

42. Robert M. Stevenson, *Protestant Church Music in America* (New York: Norton, 1970), 106–9; and Kearns, *Horatio Parker (1863–1919): His Life, Music, and Ideas*, 575.

43. Ives, *Memos,* 131–32. Ives's criticisms of academia in general echoes Buck's comments on the "Mus.Doc." Kirkpatrick notes that, "Miss [Eva] O'Meara (Librarian Emerita of the Yale School of Music) thinks that this must be Parker himself, who was known to say: 'The hymn tune is the lowest form of musical life'" (ibid., 132n1); however Parker gave this description to the "rhythmically stiff and uncharming" Anglican chant. Parker, "Church Music," 1904, 12.

44. Ives, *Memos,* 93–94.

45. Feder, *My Father's Song,* 134–37.

46. Ives, *Memos,* 116. In the manuscript of *Memos,* earlier in this passage, Ives realized the misdating by crossing out the phrase "in Freshman year."

47. Ibid., 115. Regarding Molly, see Perlis, *Charles Ives Remembered,* 72, quoting Ives's nephew Brewster Ives: "Uncle Charlie was extremely fond of his mother, and there was a great bond between them. I hardly believe there was another mother that could have been prouder of her son than Grandmother Ives. She would constantly remind us all of his genius. She convinced herself that he was one, and she thought of her husband in the same way. She'd usually start talking about Grandfather Ives and tell us how he pioneered in music . . ."

48. Ives, *Memos,* 131.

49. Feder, *My Father's Song,* 84, 94, and passim discusses what Ives may have perceived as an economic and social imbalance between George Ives and his far wealthier and more powerful siblings.

50. Jeffrey Magee, "Ragtime and Early Jazz," in *The Cambridge History of American Music,* ed. David Nicholls (Cambridge: Cambridge University Press, 1998), 389.

51. Ives, *Memos,* 56.

52. Ives cites the pianist at Poli's Bijou Theater, George Felsburg, as having accompanied silent films and vaudeville shows, and that when Ives was at Yale "I used

to go down there and 'spell him' a little if he wanted to go out for five minutes and get a glass of beer, or a dozen glasses" (ibid.). It seems unlikely that Felsburg would have known piano ragtime repertoire, since instrumental ragtime was not part of a vaudeville show. More likely, Ives would have picked up the process of ragging rather than the repertory itself through vaudeville song performances.

53. Edward A. Berlin, *Ragtime: A Musical and Cultural History* (Berkeley: University of California Press, 1980), 76, quoting James Weldon Johnson.

54. Ibid., 69.

55. Karabel describes the population of the "Big Three" Ivy League schools (Yale, Princeton, and Harvard) as "overwhelmingly from well-to-do backgrounds" and "[a]lmost exclusively white . . . composed largely of graduates of elite private schools, the student body represented the most privileged strata of society. . . . [T]he Big Three were strikingly homogeneous, not only in race and class, but also in religion and ethnicity. . . . [T]he same relatively compact social group predominated at each school: old-stock, high-status Protestants, especially Episcopalians, Congregationalists, and Presbyterians" (*The Chosen,* 23). Ives fits this bill remarkably well, particularly in the "old-stock, high-status" realm—except that his father's religion was Baptist and Methodist.

56. Ives, *Memos,* 130.

57. The assignment from the end of the first term was either a two-voice canon for organ or, more rarely, a double fugue for string quartet. Three double fugues survive in Box 3, Folder 1 of the Yale School of Music Archives, Yale Music Library, Mss. 3, by E. S. Marsh, C. Edward Moulthrop, and Leslie Edward Vaughan (who dated his assignment "Jan. 22, 1897"). According to Yale College student records, these students were never officially registered for any music courses.

58. See Burkholder, *All Made of Tunes,* 89–102, for a discussion of the First Symphony's quotations.

59. Ibid., 101.

60. The following quotations are taken from Richard Taruskin, "Nationalism: 10. Tourist Nationalism, and 11. Colonialist Nationalism" in *New Grove Dictionary of Music and Musicians,* ed. Stanley Sadie and John Tyrell, 2nd ed. (New York: Oxford University Press, 2001).

61. Music and text reprinted in Burkholder, *All Made of Tunes,* 100–101.

62. William Gallo, "The Life and Church Music of Dudley Buck" (Ph.D. diss., Catholic University of America, 1968), 101. The cantatas included *Christ the Victor* (1896), *Coming of the King* (1895), *The Story of the Cross* (1892), and *The Triumph of David* (1892) (Howard, *Our American Music,* 594). See Sherwood, "'Buds the infant mind,'" 163–89, for an extended comparison of *The Celestial Country* with works by Buck and Parker.

63. Ives's choir at Central Presbyterian Church in New York included seventeen voices altogether in the chorus, plus a solo SATB quartet. The chorus was certainly amateur, since Ives's nonmusical roommates were recruited to sing in the choir on occasion.

64. Ives's cantata uses organ accompaniment in all movements except the fourth (for string quartet) and fifth (a capella double quartet). The only other instrumentation is the addition of two optional horns in the final movement. Even in his use of solo instruments Ives imitates Buck's technique. According to Howard, Buck's 1881 male chorus *King Olaf's Christmas* was accompanied by "piano obbligato, reed organ, and string quartet ad lib. The composer knew what was practical in the way of accompaniment in his day" (Howard, *Our American Music*, 594).

65. Burkholder, *Ideas Behind the Music*, 81–82; Feder, *My Father's Song*, 171–74.

66. Burkholder, *Charles Ives and His World*, 276.

67. Luther Noss, *A History of the Yale School of Music, 1855–1970* (New Haven: Yale School of Music, 1984), 84. There is little information on Haesche: this brief outline of his career is taken from Kirkpatrick's research, in Ives, *Memos*, 33n4.

68. *Yale Daily News* XXV, no. 151 (April 17, 1902).

69. Yale School of Music Papers, Box 1, Folder 3 (Correspondence, 1902).

70. Broyles, "Charles Ives and the American Democratic Tradition," 138.

71. Semler, *Horatio Parker*, 141, 161.

Chapter 3: On the Verge

1. Ives, *Memos*, 57, states that in May 1902 "I resigned as a nice organist and gave up music."

2. The following information is summarized from Katherine Snyder, "A Paradise of Bachelors: Remodeling Domesticity and Masculinity in the Turn-of-the-Century New York Bachelor Apartment," in *Prospects: An Annual of American Cultural Studies,* ed. Jack Salzman (New York: Cambridge University Press, 1998), vol. 23, 250–69. I am grateful to Amy Fuller for introducing me to Snyder's article.

3. For details on the inhabitants and locations of Poverty Flat, see Ives, *Memos,* 263–67.

4. Robert E. Wright and George David Smith, *Mutually Beneficial: The Guardian and Life Insurance in America* (New York: New York University Press, 2004), 41.

5. Ibid., 43.

6. Broyles, "Charles Ives and the American Democratic Tradition," 136, suggests that Brewster, who helped fund Ives's studies, continued to act as a role model for Ives after his graduation from Yale. Feder, *My Father's Song,* 180–81, suggests that Brewster's death was partially responsible for Ives's depression during this time.

7. Marquis James, *The Metropolitan Life: A Study in Business Growth* (New York: The Viking Press, 1947), 143–44.

8. Ives, *Memos,* 266.

9. The following paragraphs are summarized from these histories of the nursing profession: Philip Arthur Kalisch and Beatrice Kalisch, *The Changing Image of the Nurse* (Menlo Park, CA: Addison-Wesley, 1987), 30–31; Kalisch and Kalisch, *American Nursing: A History* (Philadelphia: Lippincott, Williams and Wilkins, 2004), 117–18,

123; Susan M. Reverby, *Ordered to Care: The Dilemma of American Nursing, 1850–1945* (New York: Cambridge University Press, 1987), 95, 97–98, 112–17.

10. Based on the following histories of public health nursing: Thelma M. Schorr and Maureen Shawn Kennedy, *100 Years of American Nursing: Celebrating a Century of Caring* (Philadelphia: Lippincott, Williams and Wilkins, 1999), 12; M. Louise Fitzpatrick, ed., *Prologue to Professionalism: A History of Nursing* (Bowie, Md.: R.J. Brady Co., 1983), 14–18; Kalisch and Kalisch, *American Nursing*, 162–72.

11. Fitzpatrick, *Prologue to Professionalism*, 16.

12. Ives, *Memos*, 275.

13. Sinclair, *Descriptive Catalogue*, 290–91.

14. Henry Cowell and Sidney Cowell, *The Music of Charles Ives* (New York: Oxford University Press, 1955), 76; Feder, *My Father's Song*, 286, which cites the 1931 medical reports; and Broyles, "Charles Ives and the American Democratic Tradition," 158n50, which reaffirms the absence of any mention of heart troubles in a 1909 medical report.

15. Amelia Ives Brewster to CEI, October 29, 1907; HTI to CEI, March 11 and February 6, 1908.

16. Editor's preface to George M. Beard, *A Practical Treatise on Nervous Exhaustion (Neurasthenia): Its Symptoms, Nature, Sequences, Treatment*, 3rd ed., ed. A. D. Rockwell (New York: E.B. Treat, 1896), 3.

17. "The Problem of Finding an Adequate Cure for Our National Malady," *New York Times*, September 1, 1907.

18. J. H. Kellogg, *Neurasthenia or Nervous Exhaustion*, 2nd ed. (Battle Creek, Mich.: Good Health Publishing, 1915), 15–16, 18.

19. Ibid., 17, 42.

20. Francis G. Gosling, *Before Freud: Neurasthenia and the American Medical Community, 1870–1910* (Urbana: University of Illinois Press, 1987), 86–87.

21. Savill, *Clinical Lectures on Neurasthenia*, 3rd ed. (New York: William Wood, 1907), 25, 67.

22. Kellogg, *Neurasthenia or Nervous Exhaustion*, 280–91, 272. Savill notes similar symptoms (*Clinical Lectures*, 34–37).

23. Marie Joseph Paul Hartenberg, *Treatment of Neurasthenia*, trans. Ernest Playfair (London: Henry Frowde and Hodder & Stoughton, 1914), 138, 220.

24. J. Mitchell Clarke, *Hysteria and Neurasthenia* (London and New York: John Lane) 199–200, 218, 220–21.

25. Albert Abrams, *The Blues (Splanchnic Neurasthenia): Causes and Cures*, 3rd ed. (New York: E.B. Treat, 1908), 84–85; and Edwin Ash, *The Problem of Nervous Breakdown* (New York: MacMillan, 1920), 192, 237. For more detail, see Sherwood, "Charles Ives and 'Our National Malady,'" 562n31.

26. Clarke, *Hysteria and Neurasthenia*, 270, 272–73, 275–77, 280, 284.

27. Robert W. Taylor, *A Practical Treatise on Sexual Disorders of the Male and Female*, 3rd ed. (New York: Lea Brothers, 1905), 371–72. Savill likewise suggests that "a

change to the seaside, or some bracing mountain district, with some friend or relative who is agreeable to the patient, may be sufficient." Savill, *Clinical Lectures,* 160.

28. Wright and Smith, *Mutually Beneficial,* 46.

29. Ibid., 46, 218. Broyles suggests that the Mutual office had already recognized Ives as an up-and-coming executive before his trip to Virginia, based on their involvement in diagnosing and treating Ives's illness, as well as asking Myrick to accompany Ives. Broyles subsequently concludes that Mutual's maneuvers involving the Raymond Agency, Washington Life, and Ives's two companies was part of a carefully constructed plan in which Ives's business career was never in danger ("Charles Ives and the American Democratic Tradition," 139–41).

30. Sidney Ratner, James H. Soltow, and Richard Sylla, *The Evolution of the American Economy: Growth, Welfare, and Decision Making,* 2nd ed. (New York: Macmillan, 1993), 340–41, 440–41.

31. "'Completely used up,'" quoted by Kirkpatrick in Ives, *Memos,* 276; "Later references," Joseph Twichell to HTI, July 27, 1913: "Here's a letter from Dave that will afford you the means of judging his condition and outlook. I am glad to think that in both respects the signs disclosed in it are favorable." As noted by Jan Swafford, David committed suicide on August 12, 1924, immediately after leaving Asheville (*Charles Ives: A Life with Music* [New York: W. W. Norton, 1996], 342).

32. For references, see Sherwood, "Charles Ives and 'Our National Malady,'" 568–69.

33. Reverby states, "Family demands that interrupted a nurse's career impinged on single nurses as well. . . . Families demanded such labors from their 'spinster' members as they had for generations. Given the trained nurse's obvious expertise, however, such demands were perhaps even more inevitable for her than for other single women" (*Ordered to Care,* 113).

34. From Sherwood, "Charles Ives and 'Our National Malady,'" 581.

35. Two later accounts of their marriage describe Harmony as Ives's nurse. Luemily Ryder, a neighbor in Redding, states that Harmony "kept him alive with her training and her concern," while Ives's son-in-law George Grayson Tyler observed that Ives "lived to be seventy-nine, and this was in large part due to the wonderful care that he received from Mrs. Ives who had been a registered nurse." Quoted in Perlis, *Charles Ives Remembered,* 98, 105. For more relevant excerpts from Harmony's correspondence and consideration of her role as a nurse, see Sherwood, "Charles Ives and 'Our National Malady,'" 568–72, 580–81.

36. Hartenberg, *Treatment of Neurasthenia,* 247.

37. Joyce Henri Robinson, "'Hi Honey, I'm Home': Weary (Neurasthenic) Businessmen and the Formulation of a Serenely Modern Aesthetic," in *Not At Home: The Suppression of Domesticity in Modern Art and Architecture,* ed. Christopher Reed (New York: Thames and Hudson, 1996), 102. On neurasthenia and gender roles, see also Tom Lutz, *American Nervousness, 1903: An Anecdotal History,* (Ithaca, N.Y.: Cornell University Press, 1991), 31–35 and passim.

38. HTI to CEI, October 27–28, 1907. Transcribed in Thomas Clarke Owens, ed., "Selected Correspondence," in Burkholder, *Charles Ives and His World*, 206. For alternate views of Harmony's support of Ives's compositional activities, see Feder, *My Father's Song*, 213–14 and passim; and Swafford, *A Life with Music*, 183–87, 225–27, 232–33, and passim.

39. Lutz, *American Nervousness*, 6, 19.

40. Ibid., 19.

41. Clarke, *Hysteria and Neurasthenia*, 176; Lutz, *American Nervousness*, 6.

42. Levine, *Highbrow/Lowbrow*, 176.

43. All quotations from T. J. Jackson Lears, *No Place of Grace: Antimodernism and the Transformation of American Culture, 1880–1920* (Chicago: University of Chicago Press, 1981), 48.

44. In his later writings, Ives rejected both the concept and label of "nationalism" as divisive and confining. However, I have chosen to use this word—in the absence of a clearer concept—since it does accurately describe Ives's use of quotations from diverse regions of the United States, and because the writings that reject nationalism date from after the composition of these works and the destructive power of nationalism had been tragically realized in the First World War. For a discussion of Ives and the concepts of "nationalism," "Americanness," and "Americanism," see Owens, "Images of 'Americanness,'" 16–17, 147–57, and passim.

45. Burkholder, *All Made of Tunes*, 134.

46. Ives's symphony resembles the *Symphonic Sketches* of George Chadwick in this amalgam as well: the comparison is particularly noticeable in that the main theme of the first movement of Chadwick's work, "Jubilee," resembles Foster's "Camptown Races." According to Victor Fell Yellin's biography of Chadwick, "Jubilee" was written in 1895—at the time that Ives was studying with Chadwick's student, Horatio Parker, at Yale (*Chadwick: Yankee Composer* [Washington, D.C.: Smithsonian Institution Press, 1990], 112). See also Ives, *Memos*, 183–84, for Ives's anecdote about Chadwick's visit to Parker's classroom in 1898.

Chapter 4: "A New Sweet World"

1. "Loving Cup for Damrosch," *New York Times*, March 16, 1910; "Concerts of the Week," *New York Times*, March 13, 1910; "Requiem to Prof. Sanford," *New York Times*, March 17, 1910.

2. Ives, *Memos*, 86–87. According to Parker's letters, he was in New York several times during that week and, in a letter of March 20, 1910, mentions seeing "Walter" at the Sanford memorial concert—the day after Damrosch's reading of Ives's symphony. Semler, *Horatio Parker*, 188.

3. "Samuel S. Sanford Dead," *New York Times*, January 7, 1910. I am grateful to Jonathan Elkus for suggesting the connections between Damrosch, Ives, Parker, and Sanford.

4. The parts may be connected to Edgar Stowell's reading of the Second Symphony in 1910 or 1911—see below.

5. Ives, *Memos,* 51.

6. Ibid., 189.

7. Mentioned in Kirkpatrick's editorial interpolation, ibid., 86. The page begins "'rehearsal.' The result of his playing it is referred to above. The first movement of this *First Symphony* was not shown to Wally . . ."

8. Ibid., 87. Kirkpatrick's insertion of Ives's later handwritten comments ("No" after each part of the statement, plus the mediating sentence, "The last time I played it, over a year or so ago, I felt more like it, I liked it well, and didn't feel the way I did once") obscures Ives's original, very harsh condemnation of "[t]his music, at least the last three movements."

9. Ibid., 261.

10. Julia Cushman Twichell to HTI, November 4, 1908. Vacation dates mentioned in Ives, *Memos,* 329.

11. John Kirkpatrick confirms Wooldridge's assumption in his review of *From the Steeples and the Mountains,* while simultaneously reinforcing his own role as the family's guardian. Kirkpatrick, "Review of *From the Steeples and the Mountains* by David Wooldridge," *High Fidelity/Musical America* 24, no. 9 (September 1974): 33–36; and Kirkpatrick and Wooldridge, "The New Ives Biography: A Disagreement," *High Fidelity/Musical America* 24, no. 12 (December 1974): 18–20.

12. Karen L. Michaelson states that "less than 5 percent of women delivered in hospitals in 1900" (*Childbirth in America: Anthropological Perspectives* (South Hadley, Mass.: Bergin & Garvey Publishers, 1988). According to Sylvia Rinker, early twentieth-century nurses often cared for both mother and infant "even in the rare event when a physician had been engaged to attend births," but did not arrive in time ("To Cultivate a Feeling of Confidence: The Nursing of Obstetric Patients, 1890–1940," in *Enduring Issues in American Nursing,* ed. Ellen D. Baer et al. [New York: Springer, 2001], 108–11).

13. Selected excerpts from *Our Book* are included in Kirkpatrick's notes to Ives, *Memos,* 87n8.

14. Perlis, *Charles Ives Remembered,* 98, quotes Luemily Ryder as saying that Harmony "was moderately active in our little church here, and I guess she participated a little in the New York church."

15. For an extensive comparison of Ives's music with that of Debussy, see John Gibbens, "Debussy's Impact on Ives: An Assessment," DMA thesis, University of Illinois, Urbana–Champaign, 1985.

16. See Burkholder, *All Made of Tunes,* 137–38, for a definition of cumulative form and cumulative setting based on Ives's works; and James Hepokoski, *Sibelius: Symphony No. 5,* Cambridge Music Handbooks, gen. ed. Julian Rushton (Cambridge: Cambridge University Press, 1993), 26–27, for a definition of the process as used in Sibelius', post-1912 compositions, as well as predecessors in the works of Richard Strauss and Mahler.

17. "Damrosch Pleads for American Opera," *New York Times,* March 13, 1910. Damrosch's ultranationalist ranting is, in some ways, echoed in Zangwill's novel, *The Melting Pot* of 1908, in which the idealistic young composer/violinist David Quixano attempts to write the ultimate American symphony by drawing on contemporary immigrant identities.

18. George Martin outlines Damrosch's troubles with both institutions between 1902 and 1904 (*The Damrosch Dynasty: America's First Family of Music* [Boston: Houghton Mifflin, 1983], 168–72).

19. Damrosch may have remembered being compared with Mahler in print two years earlier. According to an unsigned review of March 25, 1908, in the *Musical Courier,* Mahler's reading of the third *Leonora* overture was so superior to Damrosch's "chaotic conducting" that "there is no use going to New York concerts" lead by Damrosch. Cited in Zoltan Roman, *Gustav Mahler's American Years, 1907–1911: A Documentary History* (Stuyvesant, N.Y.: Pendragon Press, 1989), 108.

20. Ibid., 157–58, citing reports from *Musical America* of August and September 1908.

21. Walter Damrosch, *My Musical Life* (New York: C. Scribner's Sons, 1923), 329–31.

22. "Damrosch Pleads for American Opera," *New York Times,* March 13, 1910.

23. See Judith Tick, "Charles Ives and Gender Ideology," in *Musicology and Difference: Gender and Sexuality in Music Scholarship,* ed. Ruth Solie (Berkeley: University of California Press, 1993), 125–47; also Swafford, *A Life with Music,* 374–76; Rossiter, *Charles Ives and His America,* 35–36 and passim; and Feder, *My Father's Song,* 336–38.

24. Copies of Ives's letters to Damrosch concerning these symphonies are available in Ives Papers, Box 29, Folder 1 (December 14, 1911, for the Second Symphony and June 24, 1915, for the Third Symphony), and transcribed in Thomas Clarke Owens, ed., *Selected Correspondence of Charles Ives* (Berkeley: University of California Press, 2007), 54–55. Accounts differ as to whether Damrosch ever looked at the scores. Bernard Herrmann claimed that he and Damrosch found Ives's original score of the Second Symphony "in the same cupboard that he had put it in forty years before. [Damrosch] had never played it" (Perlis, *Charles Ives Remembered,* 156). Yet in the same collection, George F. Roberts (Ives's copyist beginning in the 1930s) claimed that Ives "told me about sending Walter Damrosch the score for the *Second Symphony.* Damrosch wanted to correct it for him. He thought it was just carelessly written" (ibid., 186), which suggests that Damrosch at least read over the score.

25. Ives claims that Mahler saw a copy of the Third Symphony being copied at the Tam's office and "asked to have a copy—he was quite interested in it," which has been taken to mean that Mahler obtained a score of the Third Symphony (*Memos,* 121). If so, the irony—that the European Mahler was more interested in the work than the American Damrosch—is apparent. David Wooldridge suggests that the lost score may be in a Munich archive, and reports a chance interview with an elderly musician named Messerkliner who remembered playing the work under Mahler's direction

in Munich in the summer of 1910 (*From the Steeples and the Mountains* [New York: Alfred A. Knopf, 1974], 150–51). Wooldridge's speculation on a possible European performance of the Third Symphony is, in fact, fairly balanced: he appears skeptical of the musician's memories, while suggesting how this unlikely reading could have occurred.

26. Cited in "New Immigration is Better Than Old," *New York Times*, June 16, 1912. Rudolph J. Vecoli outlines the various political, social, and cultural manifestations of what he terms the "self-conscious Anglo-American ethnonationalism" of the early twentieth century, particularly the national debate on immigration and the "American character." "Ethnicity and Immigration," in *Encyclopedia of the United States in the Twentieth Century*, vol. 1, The American People, ed. Stanley I. Kutler (New York: Scribner, 1996): 161–65.

27. "Organist Dudley Buck Dead," *New York Times*, October 7, 1909; "Apollo Club at Dudley Buck's Funeral," *New York Times*, October 10, 1909.

28. Swafford, *A Life with Music*, 197.

29. See Timothy A. Johnson, *Baseball and the Music of Charles Ives: A Proving Ground* (Lanham, Md.: Scarecrow Press, 2004), 87–132 and passim.

30. Discussed in Sherwood, "Choral Works of Charles Ives," 108; a notated example of the swipe is reproduced in V. Hicks, "Barbershop quartet singing."

31. David Nicholls, "*In Re Con Moto Et Al:* Experimentalism in the works of Charles Ives (1874–1954)," in *American Experimental Music, 1890–1940* (Cambridge: Cambridge University Press, 1990), 5–88 (especially 54–58, which discusses *Over the Pavements*); J. Philip Lambert, *The Music of Charles Ives*, Composers of the Twentieth Century (New Haven: Yale University Press, 1997), 128–30, and Sherwood, "Choral Works of Charles Ives," 168–69, 176–82, discuss *Psalm 24;* Sherwood, "Choral Works of Charles Ives," 192–99, and H. Wiley Hitchcock, *Ives: A Survey of the Music* I.S.A.M. Monographs, no. 19 (London and New York: Oxford University Press, 1977), 37–38, discuss the second *Harvest Home Chorale*. Lambert, *The Music of Charles Ives*, offers the most extensive investigation of Ives's experimental music: his identification and discussion of the "Ives Omnibus" (170–85), a means by which Ives combined several experimental approaches including interval and rhythmic cycles, wedge-shapes, and palindromes, is particularly valuable. See also Nachum Schoffman, "Serialism in the Works of Charles Ives," *Tempo* 138 (September 1981): 21–32.

32. See articles on individual composers in Grove Music Online, ed. L. Macy (available at http://www.grovemusic.com; accessed February 29, 2008). Hauer (1883–1959), who like Schoenberg lived in Vienna, developed his method of "tropes" derived from all twelve-tones during the summer of 1919. Roslavets (1881–1944) was born in Ukraine and took his inspiration from Scriabin: he was writing entirely twelve-tone works by 1913, after several years of experimenting with the concept.

33. Schoenberg's oft-cited claim appears originally in a 1921 or 1922 letter to his friend Josef Rufer: it is cited as an example of "covert nationalisms" by Richard Tar-

uskin, "Nationalism, 14: Musical Geopolitics," in Grove Music Online, ed. L. Macy (available at http://www.grovemusic.com; accessed February 29, 2008).

34. Lambert, *The Music of Charles Ives,* 132–33, discusses the integration of cyclic patterns and aggregate structures with quotation-based material in Ives's "Fourth of July" as "one of the best examples in [Ives's] work of an integration of compositional approaches" (133).

35. Sinclair, *Descriptive Catalogue,* 10, citing Ives, *Memos,* 87, refers to a performance of part of the first movement of the Second Symphony by "Edgar Stowell, a violinist and director of the Music Settlement School Orchestra in New York City" in 1910 or 1911 that probably used the extant copyist parts.

36. Biographical information from the online outline of the Max Smith Papers, Mss. 8, Irving S. Gilmore Music Library, Yale University, New Haven (available at http://webtext.library.yale.edu/xml2html/music.maxsmith.nav.html; accessed October 30, 2007).

37. Ives, *Memos,* 74, 98. Swafford, *A Life with Music,* 216, states that Ives would get together with friends to play his music and other chamber works during the teens, but does not cite a source for this information.

38. For example, Ives often appealed to parents to provide for their children through life insurance, or for young men facing college to put their father in contact with an insurance agent. See samples of Ives's insurance writings in Perlis, *Charles Ives Remembered,* 53–55, as well as the edition of Ives's insurance pamphlet "The Amount to Carry: Measuring the Prospect" in Howard Boatwright, ed., *Essays Before a Sonata, The Majority and Other Writings by Charles Ives* (New York: W.W. Norton, 1962), 235–40.

39. Perlis, *Charles Ives Remembered,* 54.

40. Ibid., 56, quoting George Hofmann. For a detailed consideration of Ives's insurance writings and the training of his agents in aggressive salesmanship, see Swafford, *A Life with Music,* 197–212.

41. Ives, *Memos,* 132–33.

42. Perlis, *Charles Ives Remembered,* 83. The visits took place between the Iveses' first summer in Redding in 1913, and Joseph Twichell's death in 1918.

43. Ives, *Memos,* 70.

44. "Franz Milcke," *New York Times,* January 22, 1944.

45. Bernard Herrmann's much later statement is intriguing in this light: "Ives really didn't get on with the establishment in his time, because the establishment were [sic] all Germans" (Perlis, *Charles Ives Remembered,* 162). Unfortunately, Herrmann did not elaborate on this idea.

46. For a contrasting interpretation of the relationship between European form and American hymn tunes, see Burkholder, *All Made of Tunes,* 161: "Through the process of development and gradual accumulation, [Ives's cumulative settings] raise the hymn tunes that he uses to the level of art music." Burkholder outlines the movements' formal structure; see 154–61, 174–77, 206–12.

Chapter 5: A Tragic Day

1. Henry Cowell and Sidney Cowell, *The Music of Charles Ives* (New York: Oxford University Press, 1955), 97.

2. "American Embassy as Neutral Centre," *New York Times*, August 1, 1914.

3. *New York Times*, August 2, 1914.

4. "Look to England to Keep Seas Clear," *New York Times*, August 4, 1914.

5. "Germany's Wars," *New York Times*, August 5, 1914.

6. "The German Propaganda in This Country," *New York Times*, February 1, 1915.

7. Ibid.

8. "The Law of the *Lusitania* Case," *New York Times*, May 9, 1915.

9. Ives, *Memos*, 92–94.

10. Burkholder, *All Made of Tunes*, 264. For an alternative interpretation of this work, see 262–66.

11. Perlis, *Charles Ives Remembered*, 76.

12. Ibid. According to James Thomas Flexner, who knew her as a young woman, Edith "was not a very happy young lady, and I think she was lonely. . . . [S]he confided that she was an adopted child. I got the impression that Edie was unfamiliar with her natural family, and that she had been told very little if anything about them" (ibid., 103).

13. Ives, *Memos*, 279.

14. Perlis, *Charles Ives Remembered*, 129, quoting Monique Schmitz Leduc, the daughter of family friend and musician E. Robert Schmitz. See also the quote from Flexner, above.

15. Perlis, *Charles Ives Remembered*, 129.

16. Ibid., 48.

17. Ibid., 116.

18. Ibid., 104.

19. The reality of their domestic life seems to have been less than the ideal represented in musical creations. In a letter of June 8, 1916, Harmony relates to Ives that Edith "wakes at 5—or before," leaving Harmony "used up and shaky." Harmony's expression of the sheer exhaustion of raising a child is revised (glowingly) in "To Edith," the text of which was written jointly by both parents, according to Harmony, and by Harmony alone according to Charles. Letter from HTI to CEI, Ives Papers, Correspondence Addendum. Transcribed in Owens, *Selected Correspondence of Charles Ives*, 97–98.

20. For a discussion of the song's similarities with Debussy, see Gibbens, "Debussy's Impact on Ives," 60–61. Sinclair maintains that "The Children's Hour" was written much earlier (1901), a suggestion supported, with alterations, by H. Wiley Hitchcock, who dates it between 1902 and 1907. Yet, Ives's apparent presentiment of his adopted child's name and hair color seems better explained by a later date of the

work. For a discussion of the date, see Gayle Sherwood Magee, "Review of Charles Ives, *129 Songs,* edited by H. Wiley Hitchcock," *Institute for Studies in American Music Newsletter* 34, no. 2 (Spring 2005).

21. Louise Berneri (nee Garbarino), Ives's secretary from 1921 to 1929, states that "he asked me to remember that anything he ever dictated was purely personal and was not to be discussed with anybody in the office. . . . His concern was about Edith. He was afraid of somebody who was trying to reach him about this child, and he had said to me that if anyone should ever ask, I was not to ever say anything about her. I got the impression that there had been trouble, and that this was his reason for asking me not to allow anyone in his office who was not connected with insurance, unless they were announced" (Perlis, *Charles Ives Remembered,* 64).

22. Hughes's "acceptance of the support of the German-American alliance [is] an insult to the American people," and the Republicans "are saying just the right things and then allying themselves with the persons whose alliance makes it impossible to do the right thing" ("Wilson Sees Foes in Plot to Control Banking System," *New York Times,* October 17, 1916; "Wisconsin Hinges on the Hyphen Vote" *New York Times,* October 26, 1916).

23. "The Changing Tide of Immigration," *New York Times,* November 5, 1916.

24. Quoted in ibid.

25. Frank Julian Warne, *The Tide of Immigration* (New York: D. Appleton, 1916).

26. For a perceptive survey of Ives's wartime compositions, see Glenn Watkins, *Proof Through the Night: Music and the Great War* (Berkeley: University of California Press, 2003), 345–54.

27. The paper dates of early stages of the sources are reliably dated through paper types, as described in Sinclair, *Descriptive Catalogue,* 39–40, which places the fragmentary pencil-and-ink sketches of "The 'St. Gaudens'" "no earlier than 1915;" the fragmentary pencil-and-ink sketches of the first version of "Putnam's Camp" "no earlier than 1914;" and the pencil score-sketch fragment of "The Housatonic" "no earlier than 1913."

28. Quoted in Feder, *My Father's Song,* 224.

29. Cooney, "The 'St. Gaudens' in Boston Common," 14, states: "At the same time the nation was wrestling with the consequences of its recently expanded international role, there was a growing public preoccupation with the Civil War. Observations of the centenary of Abraham Lincoln's birth in 1909 connected a past that was emotionally charged with a present searching for a renewed national identity. . . . Stories about the Civil War enjoyed a high profile over the next six years as the nation marked the fiftieth anniversaries of important victories and defeats associated with the conflict. The Civil War became a current event."

30. For a discussion of "The 'St. Gaudens'" as a memorial to George Ives, see Feder, *My Father's Song,* 236–37. Cooney connects several published literary accounts, memorials, poems, and book-length studies to Ives's own poem that accompanies his setting of "The 'St. Gaudens,'" suggesting that Ives placed "his works [i.e., both the

poem and the musical movement] within national artistic traditions." Cooney, "The 'St. Gaudens' in Boston Common," 45.

31. According to Sinclair, *Descriptive Catalogue*, "the surviving sketches [of Decoration Day] are on paper datable to no earlier than 1915" (24), while "the surviving score-sketch of "The Fourth of July" "is on paper datable to no earlier than 1917" (27). Sinclair suggests that the work as a whole may have been assembled around 1917 (21).

32. Feder, *My Father's Song*, 238–40.

33. This analysis is indebted to Robert Morgan's provocative ideas in his essay, "'The Things Our Fathers Loved': Charles Ives and the European Tradition," in *Ives Studies*, ed. J. Philip Lambert (Cambridge: Cambridge University Press, 1997), 3–26. However, the analysis offered here differs significantly from Morgan's work. See also Feder, *My Father's Song*, 253–55, who describes the work as "Ives's most concentrated work of nostalgia."

34. Hitchcock identifies this superscription as a paraphrase of a famous biblical passage: "And now faith, hope, and love abide, And the greatest of these is love" (I Corinthians 13:13). H. Wiley Hitchcock, ed., *Charles Ives: 129 Songs*, Music of the United States of America (MUSA) vol. 12 (Madison, Wis.: A-R Editions, 2004), 449.

35. Erik Kirschbaum, *The Eradication of German Culture in the United States: 1917–1918*, American-German Studies vol. 2 (Stuttgart: Hans-Dieter Heinz, 1986), 135.

36. Kirkpatrick reports a letter from Lanham stating that "Mr. Lewis and I worked . . . for countless weeks, really never making head or tail of [the song] . . . the dissonance was unbearable . . . however I was glad to attempt it for the sake of old and faithful friend Mike Myrick!" (Ives, *Memos*, 271). Rossiter cites a 1968 letter from Myrick to George A. Knutsen as support for his assertion that Myrick "got his friend McCall Lanham (an insurance man) to sing ["In Flanders Fields"] at a Mutual managers' luncheon at the Waldorf only days after the American declaration of war," and that it was Myrick who "suggested that Ives set the poem to music" in the first place (*Charles Ives and His America*, 154, 346n28). I am grateful to Jonathan Elkus for providing this reference.

37. "Life Insurance Men Discuss War Rates," *New York Times*, April 28, 1917.

38. For the clearest explanation of the likely dates of the sources, see Geoffrey Block, *Charles Ives: Concord Sonata* (Cambridge: Cambridge University Press, 1996), 20–27. The following paragraphs are summarized from this section of Block's book.

39. Ives, *Memos*, 163.

40. Burkholder, *Ideas Behind the Music*, 72–76.

41. Block, *Charles Ives: Concord Sonata*, 26–27. Ives could have continued working on the *Concord* after his breakdown in October 1918 (see below) until the engraving of the work at Schirmer began in fall 1919, but the extent of his work is unclear. Notes in the Iveses' diary (summarized in Ives, *Memos*, 82n) seem to indicate that Ives spent

his time in Asheville (January 16–March 18, 1919) writing the *Essays*, something that would seem to require the completion of the composition by then. However, an entry in Ives's own hand dated February 20, 1919, reads "Emerson, Alcotts & Thoreau all finished & copied—3 movements." If this refers to the musical movements rather than the prose, Ives's wording could indicate two discrete stages, first finishing the compositional work, then copying the movements.

42. See also Michael Broyles and Denise Von Glahn, "Later Manifestations of Concord: Charles Ives and the Transcendentalist Tradition," in *Transient and Permanent: The Transcendentalist Movement and its Contexts*, ed. Charles Capper and Conrad Edick Wright, Studies in American History and Culture, no. 5 (Boston: Massachusetts Historical Society, 1999), 574–604.

43. Discussed in detail in Owens, "Images of 'Americanness,'" 169–78 and passim. Owens maintains that "Ives consciously or unconsciously organized the *Essays* as a whole around implied comparisons between 'the American' and 'the European.'"

44. Charles Ives, *Essays Before a Sonata, and Other Writings*, ed. Howard Boatwright (New York: W.W. Norton, 1962), 51.

45. Block, *Charles Ives: Concord Sonata*, 26–27, notes that early, pre-1914 sketches of "the central 'human faith melody' . . . in contrast to its final form, lack the Beethoven's Fifth Symphony motive." The second quotation to appear in every movement is the hymn tune *Martyn* (Ibid., 61, and Sinclair, *Descriptive Catalogue*, 195).

46. Quoted in Geoffrey Block, "Ives and the 'Sounds That Beethoven Didn't Have,'" in Block and Burkholder, *Charles Ives and the Classical Tradition*, 40.

47. Block states that "the fleeting allusion to 'Stop That Knocking' (nearly identical rhythm and melodic contour for most of two measures) appears to be a plausible, if less certain source" than the extensive self-reference to Ives's own "He Is There" (Block, *Charles Ives: Concord Sonata*, 52).

48. It may be possible to read the *Concord Sonata* as another seasonal and human cycle (similar to the *Holidays Symphony*, as discussed above) on the model of Thoreau's *Walden*. In such a scenario, "Emerson" would represent the earliest life/winter; "Hawthorne" is the joy and folly of youth (through the ragtime gestures as well as "secular" elements such as the quotation from *Take-Off No. 3*)/spring; "The Alcotts" is maturity (perhaps implied by the quotation of the "Wedding March")/summer or fall; and "Thoreau" is death/winter ("Massa's in de Cold Ground"). The transposition of "Hawthorne" into the "Comedy" movement of the Fourth Symphony could suggest a similar interpretation for that work, since the dominant hymn in the finale—"Nearer, My God to Thee"—was often featured in New Year's Eve services, also called "Watch night" or "Watch" services. For example, see the listing of musical performances at "Watch night" services in New York in "Big New Year Fete at Time Square," *New York Times*, January 1, 1905, and "Quieter Throngs See 1914 Come In," *New York Times*, January 1, 1914.

49. See Block, *Charles Ives: Concord Sonata*, 32–37.

50. Ives, *Essays Before a Sonata, and Other Writings*, 47–48.

51. Ibid., 45, 47–48.

52. See Block, "Ives and the 'Sounds That Beethoven Didn't Have,'" 34–50 for a consideration of Ives's relationship to Beethoven's music.

53. It is tempting to identify this 1917 concert as that recalled by nephew Brewster Ives in Perlis, *Charles Ives Remembered*, 72–74, not the 1924 concert identified by Perlis. Brewster was born in 1903 and states that he couldn't have been "more than fifteen" when Ives took him to hear a performance of a violin sonata: if Brewster was in fact fourteen at the time, the dates would fit, while he would have been around twenty-one at the later concert. Either Brewster is misremembering that the concert took place at Aeolian Hall, or there could have been a second reading of this work after the Carnegie Hall invited performance.

54. Ives, *Memos*, 118.

55. Perlis, *Charles Ives Remembered*, 195.

56. Ibid., 123–24.

57. For a transcription of the letter, see the John Kirkpatrick Papers, Irving S. Gilmore Library, Yale University, Folder 87, no. 797.

58. Feder, *My Father's Song*, 285, 379n4 (chap. 19), cites a draft of a letter from Ives to "Tom," that originated in Asheville, North Carolina (i.e., after Ives's October 1 breakdown) as confirming that Ives "would serve for six months in France with the volunteer ambulance service of the YMCA." Swafford quotes Ives as saying that a doctor (presumably Dr. Bradshaw) had warned him against enlisting, stating that "if you have a heart attack, which you probably will . . . you will most likely send yourself to the next world, and also the wounded soldiers in your ambulance" (Swafford, *A Life with Music*, 283, 481n44). However, since Ives reported this significantly after the fact, the reliability of the report is questionable.

59. For an expansion of this interpretation, see Feder, *My Father's Song*, 283, 285.

60. Paul-Louis Hervier, *The American Volunteers with the Allies* (Paris: Éditions de La Nouvelle Revue, 1918), 228–80, recounts the activities of the American ambulance drivers in particularly heroic terms. Swafford makes the connection between Whittlesey and the Yale Club, presumably through the address on the extant September 4th letter. Swafford, *A Life with Music*, 283.

61. Ives, *Memos*, 11. Later reports consistently tie Ives's efforts to the Red Cross, not the YMCA, which is clearly identified in his own correspondence. This may again represent a revision in emphasis that helped obscure the real purpose for his enlistment. See Perlis, *Charles Ives Remembered*, 96, 161, where Will Ryder and Bernard Herrmann mention Ives's donation of $1,000 to the Red Cross for "two completely equipped ambulances." In fact, the Red Cross called for volunteers to drive ambulances in early September 1918, but they specifically wanted female drivers. "An emergency ambulance service for the transporting of sick and wounded . . . has been completely organized by the New York County Chapter of the American Red

Cross. . . . From among these corps and others, organized in other Red Cross divisions, the 300 women needed for motor service overseas will be recruited. A call for 300 women drivers recently was issued by the National Red Cross Headquarters." "Red Cross Starts Ambulance Service," *New York Times,* September 1, 1918.

62. Perlis, *Charles Ives Remembered,* 81.

63. "President Signs 18 to 45 Draft Bill," *New York Times,* September 1, 1918.

64. "Sets Draft Drawing Early in October," *New York Times,* September 6, 1918; "President Draws the First Number in the Draft, 322," *New York Times,* October 1, 1918.

65. Damrosch, *My Musical Life,* 264–65. Thus, Ives missed both incarnations of Damrosch's school—that is, the 1918 military music school and Fountainebleau.

66. "Better Band Music to Inspire Troops," *New York Times,* August 24, 1918. Damrosch's school opened on October 1, 1918 (Damrosch, *My Musical Life,* 252, 262).

67. According to his autobiography, Walter Damrosch acquired a personal letter from former president Theodore Roosevelt when he enlisted; that Roosevelt might have been involved with Ives's October 1 breakdown illustrates the strangely overlapping ties between the three men (ibid., 223).

68. The following paragraphs are summarized from Sherwood, "Charles Ives and 'Our National Malady'," 564–66.

69. See ibid., 565. The explanation provided by his cousin, Amelia Van Wyck, for Ives's breakdown is that Ives had a heart attack after a fierce argument with Franklin Delano Roosevelt over issuing fifty-dollar bonds (Perlis, *Charles Ives Remembered,* 12). As Perlis notes, Roosevelt would not have been at any meeting with Ives on October 1, 1918, since he was recovering from his own bout with influenza (not pneumonia, as stated by Perlis)—and it is hard to imagine the Secretary of the Navy being assigned to sell bonds during wartime in any case. A more obvious problem with Van Wyck's explanation is that the decision to sell fifty-dollar bonds had been announced the week before, apparently without the help of Ives's strenuous argument. "[A] larger portion of $50 bonds had been printed this time than ever before, and . . . loan committees had been included to make strong efforts to sell these 'baby bonds' to persons of very small means, who were inclined not to participate in the loan" ("Intend to Push $50 Bonds," *New York Times,* September 26, 1918).

70. Owens, "Images of 'Americanness,'" 216–17. For a discussion of one of the clearest examples of the German/American dichotomy (which I would suggest is a direct result of the First World War) in the *Essays,* see ibid., 236–37.

Chapter 6: Revising a Life

1. A. Maerz, "Assails 'Broadcast' Ban," *New York Times,* April 22, 1928; "Baritone in Songs by Americans," *New York Times,* November 29, 1922; "George S. Madden, Baritone, Heard," *New York Times,* June 2, 1927. See also "Another Month for Orchestras," *New York Times,* February 24, 1924.

2. Sinclair notes, "The White Gulls" was actually premiered in a concert in Danbury on June 8, 1922, by singer Mary B. Holley and a pianist, according to a preview article "by Robina C. Clark, Danbury Evening News (June 6, 1927 [recte 1922])" (Sinclair, *Descriptive Catalogue*, 391).

3. "A Night Thought" is Ives's adaptation of his earlier "In My Beloved's Eyes," originally dated 1895 but probably written in 1897–98 as part of his coursework for Parker. Sinclair, *Descriptive Catalogue*, 412, 451; Hitchcock, *129 Songs*, 413.

4. Sinclair, *Descriptive Catalogue*, 391.

5. Block, *Charles Ives: Concord Sonata*, 28–29.

6. See Owens, "Images of 'Americanness,'" 180–84.

7. For an outline of the reception of the work, see Block, *Charles Ives: Concord Sonata*, 11–19.

8. Carol J. Oja describes Ornstein as having "transplanted the star magnetism of a nineteenth-century keyboard virtuoso into a modernist context" (*Making Music Modern: New York in the 1920s* [New York: Oxford University Press, 2002], 14), while Hicks connects Cowell's constant early performances of his keyboard works to a larger approach advocated by Charles Seeger, that, "having devised new techniques, he had to write pieces to illustrate those techniques and then perform them himself." Michael Hicks, *Henry Cowell, Bohemian* (Urbana: University of Illinois Press, 2002), 100.

9. Cited in Burkholder, *Charles Ives and His World*, 374. Earlier notices of Ives as a Parker student—information that was provided by Ives, as at the premiere of *The Celestial Country*—appeared in several reviews and biographical articles, the earliest of which are two 1921 reviews of the *Concord Sonata* by Bellamann in *The Double Dealer* (ibid., 281) and by Edwin J. Stringham in the *Rocky Mountain News* (ibid., 285–86).

10. A. Walter Kramer, "A Pseudo-Literary Sonata!!!" *Musical America* 33, no. 23 (April 2, 1921): 36; reprinted in Burkholder, *Charles Ives and His World*, 278.

11. Edwin J. Stringham, "Ives Puzzles Critics with His Cubistic Sonata and 'Essays,'" *Rocky Mountain News* (Denver, July 31, 1921); reprinted in Burkholder, *Charles Ives and His World*, 285–86.

12. Unsigned review, "Ives," *Musical Courier* 85, no. 12 (September 21, 1922): 20; reprinted in Burkholder, *Charles Ives and His World*, 288.

13. Ernest Walker, "Review of *Second Pianoforte Sonata, 'Concord, Mass., 1840–1860'* and *Essays Before a Sonata*, by Charles E. Ives," *Music & Letters* 2, no. 3 (1921): 287–88; reprinted in Burkholder, *Charles Ives and His World*, 287–88.

14. Sinclair, *Descriptive Catalogue*, 194.

15. Ives, *Memos*, 192n12 and 192n13 includes excerpts from such letters.

16. H. Wiley Hitchcock, "Ives's *114* [+15] Songs and What He Thought of Them," *Journal of the American Musicological Society* 52, no. 1 (Spring 1999): 109, mentions that the collection titled *50 Songs* (which actually includes fifty-two songs) was pre-

pared from the plates of the *114 Songs* to offer "songs of more general interest" than the larger collection.

17. Quoted in an unsigned review in the *New York Herald Tribune,* reprinted in Burkholder, *Charles Ives and His World,* 291. See also Burkholder, *Ideas Behind the Music,* 5–7, 20–32, and passim for an extended discussion of this issue.

18. Oja, *Making Music Modern,* 179–81.

19. For Carpenter, see the online registry of the E. Robert Schmitz Papers, Mss. 54, Irving S. Gilmore Music Library, Yale University, New Haven (available at http:// webtext.library.yale.edu/xml2html/music.schmitz.nav.html; accessed October 31, 2007); and "Festival Days Afield," *New York Times,* June 10, 1923. For Griffes, see Richard Aldrich, "Music," *New York Times,* March 6, 1923.

20. For an overview of Schmitz's musical and personal relationship with Ives that does not critique the serendipity of this meeting, see Ronald V. Wiecki, "Two Musical Idealists—Charles Ives and E. Robert Schmitz: A Friendship Reconsidered," *American Music* 10, no. 1 (Spring 1992): 1–19.

21. Ives, *Memos,* 11; and Perlis, *Charles Ives Remembered,* 125.

22. Perlis, *Charles Ives Remembered,* 50.

23. The most likely connection would have been through *Musical Courier,* which the previous fall had equated Ives with Satie, a modern French composer and influence on Schmitz's friends Honegger and Milhaud. Unsigned review, "Ives," *Musical Courier* 85, no. 12 (September 21, 1922): 20; reprinted in Burkholder, *Charles Ives and His World,* 288–89.

24. Perlis, *Charles Ives Remembered,* 128–29.

25. Ibid., 128. Sinclair, *Descriptive Catalogue,* 233, lists the possibly incomplete two-piano work *Burlesque Storm* and a partial arrangement of the second *Ragtime Dance* as the only other works for multiple keyboards. Gibbens, "Debussy's Impact on Ives," 53–54, notes that the quotation from the *Marseillaise* in the quarter-tone "Chorale" parallels a similar quotation by Debussy in the prelude *Feux d'artifice,* and that the quote "may be an interpolation in honor of the sponsor," that is, Schmitz and his organization.

26. For an interpretation linking "On the Antipodes" with Ives's own early cantata *The Celestial Country,* see Sherwood, "'Buds the Infant Mind,'" 163–65.

27. Sinclair, *Descriptive Catalogue,* 464–65.

28. Perlis, *Charles Ives Remembered,* 125.

29. Programs for the 1925 and 1927 concerts reproduced in ibid., 126; program for the 1928 concert reconstructed from Oja, *Making Music Modern,* 371, 386, 391, 396, 399, 401. Schmitz's premieres of Ives's works seem less like a "daring stroke" than an accommodation, in light of Ives's role as financial sponsor of the society (ibid., 181).

30. Lou Harrison stated, "Ives sent half of the Pulitzer Award to me. He was a wonderfully generous man. He assigned to me quite a large number of royalties. Beginning about five years ago [ca. 1965], the checks got to be quite large. I am un-

der the impression that Mr. Ives told me that these were meant to help in my own music, or for general musical purposes. I don't know how many people are recipients of the assigned royalties, but I know that I'm not the only one. I devote the money to musical purposes in every instance, and not entirely for my own music, either." Perlis, *Charles Ives Remembered,* 203.

31. Olin Downes, "Franco-American Musical Society," *New York Times,* February 15, 1925; and "Music: Pro-Musica Society," *New York Times,* January 30, 1927; both reprinted in Burkholder, *Charles Ives and His World,* 293–95.

32. Lawrence Gilman, "Music: A New Opera, a New Symphony, and a New Debussy Fragment," *New York Herald Tribune,* January 31, 1927; reprinted in Burkholder, *Charles Ives and His World,* 296.

33. Oja, *Making Music Modern,* 221–27 and passim, discusses the connection between musical modernism and masculinity.

34. Ibid., 178–79, 181, 185, 287–88.

35. Ibid., 113.

36. Ibid., 384, 395.

37. As Oja suggests, anti-Semitism may have played a role in the battle between the ICG and League as well. Ibid., 186, 217–18. See also Rossiter, *Charles Ives and His America,* 217–19, 259–64. I am grateful to Jonathan Elkus for suggesting this citation.

38. Of the performances of the ICG in 1923, Schoenberg fumed to Varèse, "no single German among 27 composers performed!" Cited in Oja, *Making Music Modern,* 289.

39. Ibid., 194.

40. M. Hicks, *Henry Cowell, Bohemian,* 109, quoting Seeger.

41. Ibid., 121.

42. Henry Cowell, "Charles E. Ives," in *American Composers on American Music,* ed. Henry Cowell (Stanford, Calif.: Stanford University Press, 1933: reprinted with a new introduction by the editor, New York: Frederick Ungar Publishing, 1962), 128–45; Cowell, "American Composers. IX. Charles Ives," *Modern Music* 10 (1932–33): 24–33; Cowell, "Charles E. Ives," *Disques* (November 1932): 374–75; reprinted in Burkholder, *Charles Ives and His World,* 368–72.

43. Ives dates this work from 1910–16 in his worklist (cited in Ives, *Memos,* 164), but Sinclair, *Descriptive Catalogue,* 18, states that the first two movements of the work were revised between around 1917 and 1926, and "the earliest surviving score of mvt iv . . . was completed c1923." Swafford, *A Life with Music,* 342–45, strenuously defends Ives's misdating of his work on the Fourth Symphony (from its actual date in the 1920s to the 1916 completion date) as an intentional lie, stating that Ives "did not want the office to know how much time he was giving to writing and promoting his music after 1918, because he did a lot of it on company time."

44. For an extensive discussion of the relationships between the "Comedy," the "Hawthorne" movement, and the *Hawthorne Piano Concerto,* see Thomas M. Brod-

head, "Ives's *Celestial Railroad* and his Fourth Symphony," *American Music* 12 (Winter 1994): 389–424.

45. Swafford, *A Life with Music,* 356.

46. Quotations from John Kirkpatrick, "Preface," in Charles E. Ives, Symphony No. 4, (New York: Associated Music Publishers), viii. The description of the third movement comes from Henry Bellamann, "Program Notes to Ives's Fourth Symphony," *Pro Musica Program* (January 29, 1927), while Ives provided the more expansive description of the finale in "The Fourth Symphony for Large Orchestra" [Second Movement of Symphony No. 4.], *New Music* 2, no. 2 (January 1929).

47. For an extended analysis of borrowings in the Fourth Symphony, see Burkholder, *All Made of Tunes,* 389–410.

48. Transcription from Sinclair, *Descriptive Catalogue,* 37; I have altered Sinclair's suggested punctuation.

49. See Lambert, *Music of Charles Ives,* 186–206.

50. M. Hicks, *Henry Cowell, Bohemian,* 80–81.

51. Perlis, *Charles Ives Remembered,* 138.

52. For discussions of Ives's failing health after 1918, see Feder, *My Father's Song,* 286–87; 319–20; 323–24 and passim. For more on Harmony's role as Ives's scribe, see below as well as Owens, "Selected Correspondence 1881–1954," 227–28.

53. Harmony's comment is cited in the editors' notes in Charles Ives, *Psalm 90,* ed. John Kirkpatrick and Gregg Smith (Bryn Mawr: Merion Music, 1970), 3.

54. Sinclair, *Descriptive Catalogue,* 576. Interestingly, Ives's impulse to set this tune comes only a few years after James Weldon Johnson and J. Rosamond Johnson published their art-song arrangements in *The Book of American Negro Spirituals* (James Weldon Johnson, ed., with J. Rosamond Johnson and Lawrence Brown [New York: Viking Press, 1925]).

Epilogue: Beyond Advocacy

1. Jane Smiley, *Horse Heaven* (New York: Alfred W. Knopf, 2000), 86.

2. M. Hicks, *Henry Cowell, Bohemian,* 20, states that "Harry was a distant yet intermittently intrusive figure in Henry's life, one whose influence Henry never lost and whose absence he never overcame."

3. Oja, *Making Music Modern,* 363–64; M. Hicks, *Henry Cowell, Bohemian,* 123–24; Rossiter, *Charles Ives and His America,* 244–55.

4. M. Hicks, *Henry Cowell, Bohemian,* 124, quoting Henry Cowell, "Kept Music," *Panorama* 2 (December 1934), 6.

5. Ives, *Memos,* 28. For a thorough discussion of engendered rhetoric in Ives's writings, see Tick, "Charles Ives and Gender Ideology."

6. Ives, *Memos,* 30.

7. Oja, *Making Music Modern,* 201–27. Oja remarks that "women patrons and activists, in short, came to symbolize far more than the sum of their monetary con-

tributions or number of hours volunteered, and they were easy targets for the frustrations of modernists and their critics. Social discourse at the time permitted gendered bigotry" (227).

8. M. Hicks, *Henry Cowell, Bohemian,* 80–81. Ives's own acquaintance with Ornstein is unknown, but there is one clue that he at least knew the name. A letter to Ives from someone named Walter Goldstein described *Concord Sonata* as "in the Schoenberg-Scriabin-Ornstein idiom." Ives's sketched but unsent response reads, "Ain't never heard nor seen any of the music—not even a god damn note—of Schoenberg-Scriabin—Or Ornstein" (transcribed in Swafford, *A Life with Music,* 318–19). Ives's separation of Ornstein from the other composers suggests that he at least knew the name. Moreover, Lincoln Ballard suggested that Ives's knowledge of Scriabin was far more extensive than previously thought. ("Charles Ives and Scriabin: An Unanswered Question?" paper given at the Society for American Music National Meeting, Eugene, Ore., February 17, 2005.)

9. M. Hicks, *Henry Cowell, Bohemian,* 134–40; Michael Hicks, "The Imprisonment of Henry Cowell," *Journal of the American Musicological Society* 44 (Spring 1991): 92–119.

10. For "mediated correspondence," see Owens, "Selected Correspondence, 1881–1954," 227; see also Owens, *Selected Correspondence of Charles Ives,* 1–5. Harmony's letters to Charlotte Ruggles are quoted in Swafford, *A Life with Music,* 405, which includes extensive excerpts from Harmony's correspondence on the issue.

11. Perlis, *Charles Ives Remembered,* 131–33, 214.

12. Kirkpatrick's statement, "I never called him Charlie. I didn't get to know him quite that well" (ibid., 225), is surprising considering everything that Kirkpatrick did for Ives, even before his death. Yet this protective isolation was carefully planned and executed. As Owens suggests, in his later years Ives used his wife and daughter as scribes who copied letters sketched behind "the veil of the third person," thereby creating "a buffer personality" that "seclude[d] Ives within his correspondence just as the remoteness of his West Redding farm distanced him from the turmoil of his New York City business life" (Owens, "Images of 'Americanness,'" 131).

13. Gilman's review for the *New York Herald Tribune* of the concert of January 20, 1939, is reprinted in Burkholder, *Charles Ives and His World,* 316–17.

14. Ibid., 317, 320.

15. The actual text of *Memos* occupies less than 120 pages (including copious footnotes and cross-references) of the book's 337 pages, not including the index. In fact, John Kirkpatrick's extensive annotations both within and after the main text use a smaller font than Ives's main text; otherwise, the total page count would be significantly higher, and Ives's writings would occupy an even smaller proportion. I am grateful to Jonathan Elkus for this observation.

16. See, for example, Charles Ives, *Turn Ye, Turn Ye,* ed. John Kirkpatrick (Bryn Mawr: Mercury Music Corp, 1973).

17. For a parallel discussion of accessible modernism by Copland, see Jennifer DeLapp, "Speaking to Whom? Modernism, Middlebrow, and Copland's *Short Symphony*," in *Copland Connotations,* ed. Peter Dickinson and H. Wiley Hitchcock (London: Boydell Press, 2004).

18. For a discussion of the growth of the American concert audience after 1919, see Joseph Horowitz, *Classical Music in America: A History of Its Rise and Fall* (New York: Norton, 2005), 397–432 and passim.

19. Matthew Frye Jacobson, *Whiteness of a Different Color* (Cambridge: Harvard University Press, 1998), 246–73, traces the emergence of "whiteness"—and the ideological dichotomy of "white" versus "black" American identity—during the late 1930s and through the 1940s as, among other things, a reaction against the growing Civil Rights movement.

20. Horowitz, *Classical Music in America,* 516.

21. Sinclair, *Descriptive Catalogue,* 21.

22. WPA concerts, see Sherwood, "Choral Works of Charles Ives," 263–67; for Cowell, see George Boziwick, "Henry Cowell at the New York Public Library: A Whole World of Music," *Notes* 57, no. 1 (September 2000), 52; and Amy Beal, "The Army, the Airwaves, and the Avant-Garde: American Classical Music in Postwar West Germany," *American Music* 21, no. 4 (Winter 2003), 503–5; regarding the oral history project, see Perlis, *Charles Ives Remembered,* xix. Government support of Ives's music has continued into a new century through the NEH funding of the Music in the United States of America (MUSA) project, which financed the publication of Hitchcock's 2004 edition of Ives's songs. Cited in Hitchcock, *129 Songs,* xi.

23. *Run Lola Run (Lola rennt),* directed by Tom Tykwer. Sony Pictures Classics, 1999; *The Thin Red Line,* directed by Terrence Malick, 20th Century Fox, 1998. I am grateful to Professor Bernard Bopp of The University of Toledo for telling me about these films.

24. *Frasier,* episode 23, season 4: "Ask Me No Questions," trans. Nick Hartley (first aired May 21, 1997).

25. *USA Today,* March 18, 2003; the clue is number 37 across.

26. For a comparison of Adams's *On the Transmigration of Souls* (a "memory piece" based on the September 11, 2001, terrorist attacks) and Ives's "From Hanover Square North," see David Schiff, "Memory Spaces," *Atlantic Monthly,* April 2003. For a biographical portrait of Thomas, see the San Francisco Symphony's Web site: http://www.sfsymphony.org/templates/mttInfo.asp?nodeid=60&callid=59.

27. News release of the work's premiere from Boosey and Hawkes (April 2003).

Works Cited

Abrams, Albert. 1908. *The Blues (Splanchnic Neurasthenia): Causes and Cures.* 3rd ed. New York: E.B. Treat.

Ash, Edwin. 1920. *The Problem of Nervous Breakdown.* New York: MacMillan.

Badger, Reid. 1979. *The Great American Fair: The World's Columbian Exposition and American Culture.* Chicago: Nelson Hall.

Baer, Ellen D. et al. 2001. In *Enduring Issues in American Nursing.* New York: Springer.

Bailey, James. 1896. *A History of Danbury.* Danbury, Conn.: Burr Printing House.

Ballard, Lincoln. 2005. "Charles Ives and Scriabin: An Unanswered Question?" Paper given at the Society for American Music National Meeting, Eugene, Ore., February 17, 2005.

Baron, Carol K. 1992. "George Ives's Essay in Musical Theory: An Introduction and Annotated Edition." *American Music* 10, no. 3 (Fall): 429–47.

———. 1990. "Dating Charles Ives's Music: Facts and Fictions." *Perspectives of New Music* 28, no. 1 (Winter): 20–56.

Beal, Amy. 2003. "The Army, the Airwaves, and the Avant-Garde: American Classical Music in Postwar West Germany." *American Music* 21, no. 4 (Winter): 474–513.

Beard, George M. 1896. *A Practical Treatise on Nervous Exhaustion (Neurasthenia): Its Symptoms, Nature, Sequences, Treatment.* 3rd ed. Edited by A. D. Rockwell. New York: E.B. Treat.

Bellamann, Henry. 1927. "Program Notes to Ives's Fourth Symphony." *Pro Musica Program,* January 29.

Berlin, Edward A. 1980. *Ragtime: A Musical and Cultural History.* Berkeley: University of California Press.

Block, Geoffrey. 1996. *Charles Ives: Concord Sonata.* Cambridge: Cambridge University Press.

————. 1988. *Charles Ives: A Bio-Bibliography.* Bio-Bibliographies in Music, No. 14. Westport, Conn.: Greenwood.

Block, Geoffrey, and J. Peter Burkholder, eds. 1996. *Charles Ives and the Classical Tradition.* New Haven: Yale University Press.

Boatwright, Howard, ed. 1962. *Essays Before a Sonata, The Majority and Other Writings by Charles Ives.* New York: W.W. Norton.

Bolotin, Norman and Christine Laing. 2002. *The World's Columbian Exposition: The Chicago World's Fair of 1893.* Urbana: University of Illinois Press.

Boosey and Hawkes. 2003. Press release (April). Available at http://www.boosey.com/downloads/Adams%20IVES%20-%20FP.pdf. Accessed March 7, 2006.

Boziwick, George. 2000. "Henry Cowell at the New York Public Library: A Whole World of Music." *Notes* 57, no. 1 (September): 46–58.

Brodhead, Thomas M. 1994. "Ives's *Celestial Railroad* and his Fourth Symphony." *American Music* 12 (Winter): 389–424.

Broyles, Michael. 1996. "Charles Ives and the American Democratic Tradition." In *Charles Ives and His World,* 118–60. Edited by J. Peter Burkholder. Princeton: Princeton University Press.

Broyles, Michael, and Denise Von Glahn. 1999. "Later Manifestations of Concord: Charles Ives and the Transcendentalist Tradition." In *Transient and Permanent: The Transcendentalist Movement and its Contexts,* 574–604. Edited by Charles Capper and Conrad Edick Wright. Studies in American History and Culture, No. 5. Boston: Massachusetts Historical Society.

Burkholder, J. Peter. 2002. "The Organist in Ives." *Journal of the American Musicological Society* 55, no. 2 (Spring): 255–310.

————. 1999. "Ives and Yale: The Enduring Influence of a College Experience." *College Music Symposium* 39: 27–42.

————. 1995. *All Made of Tunes: Charles Ives and the Uses of Musical Borrowing.* New Haven: Yale University Press.

————. 1988. "Charles Ives and His Fathers: A Response to Maynard Solomon." *Institute for Studies in American Music [ISAM] Newsletter* 18, no. 1 (Fall): 8–11.

————. 1985. *Charles Ives: The Ideas Behind the Music.* New Haven: Yale University Press.

————. 1983. "The Evolution of Charles Ives's Music: Aesthetics, Quotation, Technique." Ph.D. diss., University of Chicago.

Burkholder, J. Peter, ed. 2002. *Charles Ives and His World.* Princeton: Princeton University Press.

Burkholder, J. Peter, James B. Sinclair, and Gayle Sherwood. "Charles Ives: Works." In Grove Music Online. Ed. Laura Macy. Available at www.grovemusic.com. Accessed November 24, 2007.

Cameron, William E. 1893. *The World's Fair.* Philadelphia: National Publishing Co.

Carrick, John. 1984. *Evangelicals and the Oxford Movement.* Bridgend, Mid Glamorgan: Evangelical Press of Wales on behalf of the Evangelical Library, London.

Chadwick, George W. 1921. *Horatio Parker.* New Haven: Yale University Press.

Chadwick, George W., and Victor Herbert, ed. 1909. *Heart Songs.* Boston: Chapple Publishing Company.

"The Charles Ives Society, Inc." Available at http://www.charlesives.org/. Accessed October 25, 2007.

Chmaj, Betty. 1983. "Fry versus Dwight: American Music's Debate over Nationality." *American Music* 3: 63–84.

Clarke, J. Michell. 1905. *Hysteria and Neurasthenia.* London and New York: John Lane.

Columbian Art Company. 1891. *Artistic Guide to Chicago and the World's Columbian Exposition.* Chicago: R. S. Peale.

Cooney, Denise Von Glahn: *see also* Von Glahn, Denise.

Cooney, Denise Von Glahn. 1997. "New Sources for The 'St. Gaudens' in Boston Common (Colonel Robert Gould Shaw and His Colored Regiment)." *Musical Quarterly* 81, no. 1 (Spring): 13–50.

———. 1996. "A Sense of Place: Charles Ives and 'Putnam's Camp, Redding Connecticut.'" *American Music* 14, no. 3 (Fall): 276–312.

———. 1995. "Reconciliations: Time, Space and American Place in the Music of Charles Ives." Ph.D. diss., University of Washington.

Cowell, Henry. 1934. "Kept Music." *Panorama* 2 (December): 6.

———. 1932–33. "American Composers. IX. Charles Ives." *Modern Music* 10: 24–33.

———. 1932. "Charles E. Ives." *Disques* (November): 374–75.

Cowell, Henry, ed. [1933] 1962. *American Composers on American Music.* Stanford, Calif.: Stanford University Press. Reprinted with a new introduction. New York: Frederick Ungar Publishing.

Cowell, Henry, and Sidney Cowell. 1955. *The Music of Charles Ives.* New York: Oxford University Press.

The Cyber Hymnal. Available at http://www.cyberhymnal.org/index.htm#lk. Accessed January 15, 2006.

Damrosch, Walter. 1923. *My Musical Life.* New York: C. Scribner's Sons.

Danbury Museum and Historical Society. "Danbury Fair." Available at http://danburyhistorical.org/DanburyFair.html. Accessed September 6, 2004.

DeLapp, Jennifer. 2004. "Speaking to Whom? Modernism, Middlebrow, and Copland's *Short Symphony.*" In *Copland Connotations.* Edited by Peter Dickinson and H. Wiley Hitchcock. London: Boydell Press.

Dickinson, Peter, and H. Wiley Hitchcock, ed. 2004. *Copland Connotations.* London: Boydell Press.

Drummond, R. Paul. 1989. *A Portion for the Singers.* Atwood, Tenn.: Christian Baptist Library & Publishing Co.

Elkus, Jonathan. 1974. *Charles Ives and the American Band Tradition: A Centennial Tribute.* American Arts Pamphlet 4. Exeter: University of Exeter.

Feder, Stuart. 1992. *Charles Ives: My Father's Song.* New Haven: Yale University Press.

Fields, Armond, and L. Marc Fields. 1993. *From the Bowery to Broadway*. New York: Oxford University Press.

Fitzpatrick, M. Louise, ed. 1983. *Prologue to Professionalism: A History of Nursing*. Bowie, Md.: R. J. Brady Co.

Frasier. Episode 23, season 4. "Ask Me No Questions." Transcribed by Nick Hartley. First aired May 21, 1997. Available at http://www.geocities.com/Hollywood/ Derby/3267/423.html. Accessed March 6, 2006.

Gallo, William. 1968. "The Life and Church Music of Dudley Buck." Ph.D. diss., Catholic University of America.

Gibbens, John. 1985. "Debussy's Impact on Ives: An Assessment." DMA thesis, University of Illinois at Urbana–Champaign.

Goode, Elizabeth. 1978. "David Stanley Smith and His Music." Ph.D. diss., University of Cincinnati.

Gosling, Francis G. 1987. *Before Freud: Neurasthenia and the American Medical Community, 1870–1910*. Urbana: University of Illinois Press.

Hartenberg, Marie Joseph Paul. 1914. *Treatment of Neurasthenia*. Translated by Ernest Playfair. London: Henry Frowde and Hodder & Stoughton.

Henahan, Donal. 1990. "The Polysided Views of Ives's Polytonality." *New York Times*. June 10.

Hepokoski, James. 1993. *Sibelius: Symphony No. 5*. Cambridge Music Handbooks, Julian Rushton, General Editor. Cambridge: Cambridge University Press.

Hervier, Paul-Louis. 1918. *The American Volunteers with the Allies*. Paris: Éditions de La Nouvelle Revue.

Hicks, Michael. 2002. *Henry Cowell, Bohemian*. Urbana: University of Illinois Press.

———. 1991. "The Imprisonment of Henry Cowell." *Journal of the American Musicological Society* 44, no. 1 (Spring): 92–119.

Hicks, Val. 2001. "Barbershop quartet singing." In Grove Music Online. Ed. Laura Macy. Available at www.grovemusic.com. Accessed November 24, 2007.

Hitchcock, H. Wiley. 1999. "Ives's 114 [+15] Songs and What He Thought of Them." *Journal of the American Musicological Society* 52, no. 1 (Spring): 97–144.

———. 1977. *Ives: A Survey of the Music*. I.S.A.M. Monographs, no. 19. London and New York: Oxford University Press.

Hitchcock, H. Wiley, ed. 2004. *Charles Ives: 129 Songs*. Music of the United States of America, Vol. 12. Middleton, Wis.: A-R Editions.

Hitchcock, H. Wiley, and Vivian Perlis, eds. 1977. *An Ives Celebration: Papers and Panels of the Charles Ives Centennial Festival-Conference*. Urbana: University of Illinois Press.

Horowitz, Joseph. 2005. *Classical Music in America: A History of Its Rise and Fall*. New York: Norton.

Howard, John Tasker. 1946. *Our American Music*. 3rd edition. New York: Thomas Y. Cromwell.

Ives, Charles. 1973. *Turn Ye, Turn Ye.* Edited by John Kirkpatrick. Bryn Mawr: Mercury Music Corp.

———. 1972. *Memos.* Edited by John Kirkpatrick. New York: Norton.

———. 1970. *Psalm 90.* Edited by John Kirkpatrick and Gregg Smith. Bryn Mawr: Merion Music.

———. 1929. "The Fourth Symphony for Large Orchestra." [Second Movement of Symphony No. 4.] *New Music* 2, no. 2 (January).

———. 1920. *Essays Before a Sonata.* New York: Knickerbocker Press. Reprinted 1962, in *Essays Before a Sonata, and Other Writings.* Edited by Howard Boatwright. New York: W.W. Norton.

Ives, Charles. Papers. Mss. 14. Irving S. Gilmore Music Library, Yale University. New Haven. Available at http://www.library.yale.edu/musiclib/archival.htm#ives. Accessed December 19, 2007.

Jackson, William Henry. 1894. *The White City.* Chicago: White City Art Co.

Jacobson, Matthew Frye. 1998. *Whiteness of a Different Color.* Cambridge: Harvard University Press.

James, Marquis. 1947. *The Metropolitan Life: A Study in Business Growth.* New York: The Viking Press.

Johnson, Frances Hall. [1931] 1970. *Musical Memories of Hartford.* Hartford: n.p. Reprint, New York: AMS Press.

Johnson, James Weldon, ed. 1925. *The Book of American Negro Spirituals.* With J. Rosamond Johnson and Lawrence Brown. New York: Viking Press.

Johnson, Timothy A. 2004. *Baseball and the Music of Charles Ives: A Proving Ground.* Lanham, Md.: Scarecrow Press.

Kalisch, Philip Arthur, and Beatrice Kalisch. 2004. *American Nursing: A History.* Philadelphia: Lippincott, Williams and Wilkins.

———. 1987. *The Changing Image of the Nurse.* Menlo Park, Calif.: Addison-Wesley.

Karabel, Jerome. 2005. *The Chosen: The Hidden History of Admission and Exclusion at Harvard, Yale, and Princeton.* New York: Houghton Mifflin.

Kearns, William K. 1990. *Horatio Parker (1863–1919): His Life, Music, and Ideas.* Metuchen, N.J.: The Scarecrow Press.

———. 1965. "Horatio Parker (1863–1919): A Study of His Life and Music." Ph.D. diss., University of Illinois at Urbana–Champaign.

Kellogg, J. H. 1915. *Neurasthenia or Nervous Exhaustion.* 2nd ed. Battle Creek, Mich.: Good Health Publishing.

Kirkpatrick, John. 1974. "Review of *From the Steeples and the Mountains* by David Wooldridge." In *High Fidelity/Musical America* 24, no. 9 (September): 33–36.

———. 1965. "Preface." In Charles E. Ives, Symphony No. 4, vii–x. New York: Associated Music Publishers.

———. 1960. *A Temporary Mimeographed Catalogue of the Music Manuscripts and Related Materials of Charles Edward Ives, 1874–1954.* New Haven: Yale University Music Library.

Kirkpatrick, John, and David Wooldridge. 1974. "The New Ives Biography: A Disagreement." In *High Fidelity/Musical America* 24, no. 12 (December): 18–20.

Kirkpatrick, John. Papers. Mss. 56. Irving S. Gilmore Music Library, Yale University. New Haven. Available at http://webtext.library.yale.edu/xml2html/music .Kirkpatrick.nav.html. Accessed December 19, 2007.

Kirschbaum, Erik. 1986. *The Eradication of German Culture in the United States: 1917–1918.* American-German Studies Vol. 2. Stuttgart: Hans-Dieter Heinz.

Kramer, A. Walter. 1921. "A Pseudo-Literary Sonata!!!" *Musical America* 33, no. 23 (April 2): 36.

Lahee, Henry. 1902. *The Organ and Its Masters.* Boston: L. C. Page & Co.

Lambert, J. Philip. 1997. *The Music of Charles Ives.* Composers of the Twentieth Century. New Haven: Yale University Press.

———. 1989. "Communications." *Journal of the American Musicological Society* 42, no. 1 (Spring): 204–9.

Lambert, J. Philip, ed. 1997. *Ives Studies.* Cambridge: Cambridge University Press.

Lears, T. J. Jackson. 1981. *No Place of Grace: Antimodernism and the Transformation of American Culture, 1880–1920.* Chicago: University of Chicago Press.

Levine, Laurence. 1988. *Highbrow/Lowbrow: The Emergence of Cultural Hierarchy in America.* Cambridge: Harvard University Press.

Lutz, Tom. 1991. *American Nervousness, 1903: An Anecdotal History.* Ithaca, N.Y.: Cornell University Press.

Magee, Gayle Sherwood: *see also* Sherwood, Gayle.

Magee, Gayle Sherwood. 2005. "Review of Charles Ives, *129 Songs,* edited by H. Wiley Hitchcock." *Institute for Studies in American Music Newsletter* 34, no. 2 (Spring): 11, 15. Available at http://depthome.brooklyn.cuny.edu/isam/NewsletS05/Magee .htm. Accessed January 15, 2006.

Magee, Jeffrey. 1998. "Ragtime and Early Jazz." In *The Cambridge History of American Music.* Edited by David Nicholls. Cambridge: Cambridge University Press.

Malick, Terrence, dir. 1998. *The Thin Red Line.* 20th Century Fox.

Martin, Deac. 1965. "The Evolution of Barbershop Harmony." *Music Journal Anthology Annual:* 40–41, 106–7.

Martin, George. 1983. *The Damrosch Dynasty: America's First Family of Music.* Boston: Houghton Mifflin.

Michaelson, Karen L. et al. 1988. *Childbirth in America: Anthropological Perspectives.* South Hadley, Mass.: Bergin & Garvey Publishers.

Morgan, Robert P. 1997. "'The Things Our Fathers Loved': Charles Ives and the European Tradition." In *Ives Studies,* 3–26. Edited by J. Philip Lambert. Cambridge: Cambridge University Press.

———. 1978. "Ives and Mahler: Mutual Responses at the End of an Era." *19th Century Music* 2 (July): 72–81.

———. 1973. "Rewriting Music History: Second Thoughts on Ives and Varèse." *Musical Newsletter* 3, no. 1 (January 1973): 3–12.

———. 1973. "Rewriting Music History: Second Thoughts on Ives and Varèse." *Musical Newsletter* 3, no. 2 (April 1973): 15–23.

Muccigrosso, Robert. 1993. *Celebrating the New World.* Chicago: Ivan R. Dee.

Nicholls, David. 1990. *American Experimental Music, 1890–1940.* Cambridge: Cambridge University Press.

Noss, Luther. 1984. *A History of the Yale School of Music, 1855–1970.* New Haven: Yale School of Music.

Ochse, Orpha. 1979. *Organists and Organ Playing in Nineteenth-Century France and Belgium.* Bloomington: Indiana University Press.

———. 1975. *The History of the Organ in the United States.* Bloomington: Indiana University Press.

Oja, Carol J. 2002. *Making Music Modern: New York in the 1920s.* New York: Oxford University Press.

Owen, Barbara. 1979. *The Organ in New England.* Raleigh, N.C.: The Sunbury Press.

Owens, Thomas Clarke. 1999. "Charles Ives and His American Context: Images of 'Americanness' in the Arts." Ph.D. diss., Yale University.

Owens, Thomas Clarke, ed. 2007. *Selected Correspondence of Charles Ives.* Berkeley, University of California Press.

———. 1996. "Selected Correspondence, 1881–1954." In *Charles Ives and His World,* 199–270. Edited by J. Peter Burkholder. 2002. Princeton: Princeton University Press.

Parker, Horatio. Papers. Mss. 32. Irving S. Gilmore Music Library, Yale University. New Haven. Available at http://webtext.library.yale.edu/xml2html/music.parker.nav.html. Accessed December 19, 2007.

Penn, W. E., W. H. Morris, and E. A. Hoffman. 1900. *New harvest bells for Sunday schools, revivals, and all religious meetings; containing selections from the most popular song writers of the day, together with the unpublished songs of the late W. E. Penn.* Eureka Springs, Ark.: Mrs. W. E. Penn.

Perlis, Vivian. [1974] 2002. *Charles Ives Remembered: An Oral History.* New Haven: Yale University Press. Reprinted with a foreword by J. Peter Burkholder. Urbana: University of Illinois Press.

Perlis, Vivian, compiler. 1983. *Register to the Charles Ives Papers.* Mss. 14. Irving S. Gilmore Music Library, Yale University. New Haven. Available at http://webtext.library.yale.edu/xml2html/music.ives.nav.html. Accessed December 19, 2007.

Rainbow, Bernard. 1970. *The Choral Revival in the Anglican Church (1839–1872), Studies in English Church Music.* London: Barrie and Jenkins.

Ratner, Sidney, James H. Soltow, and Richard Sylla. 1993. *The Evolution of the American Economy: Growth, Welfare, and Decision Making,* 2nd ed. New York: Macmillan.

Reverby, Susan M. 1987. *Ordered to Care: The Dilemma of American Nursing, 1850–1945.* New York: Cambridge University Press.

Rinker, Sylvia. 2001. "To Cultivate a Feeling of Confidence: The Nursing of Obstetric Patients, 1890–1940." In *Enduring Issues in American Nursing.* Edited by Ellen D. Baer et al. New York: Springer.

Robinson, Joyce Henri. 1996. "'Hi Honey, I'm Home': Weary (Neurasthenic) Businessmen and the Formulation of a Serenely Modern Aesthetic." In *Not At Home: The Suppression of Domesticity in Modern Art and Architecture.* Edited by Christopher Reed. New York: Thames and Hudson.

Roman, Zoltan. 1989. *Gustav Mahler's American Years, 1907–1911: A Documentary History.* Stuyvesant, N.Y.: Pendragon Press.

Ross, Alex. 2004. "Pandemonium: Charles Ives." *New Yorker* (June 7, 2004). Available at http://www.therestisnoise.com/2004/05/charles_ives.html; accessed January 6, 2006.

———. 1996. "Vindicating Ives on Dates and Music." *New York Times.* August 20.

Rossiter, Frank R. 1975. *Charles Ives and His America.* New York: Liveright.

San Francisco Symphony Orchestra. "Michael Tilson Thomas, Music Director: Biography." Available at http://www.sfsymphony.org/templates/mttInfo .asp?nodeid=60&callid=59. Accessed March 7, 2006.

Savill, Thomas D. 1907. *Clinical Lectures on Neurasthenia.* 3rd ed. New York: William Wood.

Schiff, David. 2003. "Memory Spaces." *Atlantic Monthly* (April): 127–30. Available at http://www.theatlantic.com/issues/2003/04/schiff.htm. Accessed March 7, 2006.

———. 1997. "The Many Faces of Ives." *Atlantic Monthly* 279, no. 1 (January): 84–87. Available at http://www.theatlantic.com/issues/97/jan/ives/ives.htm. Accessed May 14, 2001.

Schmitz, E. Robert. Papers. Mss. 54. Irving S. Gilmore Music Library, Yale University. New Haven. Available at http://webtext.library.yale.edu/xml2html/music.schmitz .nav.html. Accessed October 31, 2007.

Schoffman, Nachum. 1981. "Serialism in the Works of Charles Ives." *Tempo* 138 (September): 21–32.

Schorr, Thelma M., and Maureen Shawn Kennedy. 1999. *100 Years of American Nursing: Celebrating a Century of Caring.* Philadelphia: Lippincott, Williams and Wilkins.

Scott, Ann Besser. 1994. "Medieval and Renaissance Techniques in the Music of Charles Ives: Horatio at the Bridge?" *Musical Quarterly* 78, no. 3 (Fall): 448–78.

Semler, Isabella Parker. 1942. *Horatio Parker: A Memoir for His Grandchildren.* New York: G. P. Putnam & Sons.

Sherwood, Gayle: *see also* Magee, Gayle Sherwood.

Sherwood, Gayle. 2001. "Charles Ives and 'Our National Malady.'" *Journal of the American Musicological Society* 54, no. 3 (Fall): 555–84.

———. 1999. "'Buds the Infant Mind': Charles Ives's *The Celestial Country* and American Protestant Choral Traditions." *19th Century Music* 23, no. 2 (Fall): 163–89.

———. 1995. "The Choral Works of Charles Ives: Chronology, Style, Reception." Ph.D. diss., Yale University.

———. 1989. "Questions and Veracities: Reassessing the Chronology of Ives's Choral Works." *Musical Quarterly* 42, no. 1: 209–18.

Sinclair, James B. 1999. *A Descriptive Catalogue of the Music of Charles Ives.* New Haven: Yale University Press.

Smiley, Jane. 2000. *Horse Heaven.* New York: Alfred W. Knopf.

Smith, Max. Papers. Mss. 8. Irving S. Gilmore Music Library, Yale University. New Haven. Available at http://webtext.library.yale.edu/xml2html/music.maxsmith .nav.html. Accessed October 30, 2007.

Snyder, Katherine. 1999. "A Paradise of Bachelors: Remodeling Domesticity and Masculinity in the Turn-of-the-Century New York Bachelor Apartment." In *Prospects: An Annual of American Cultural Studies.* Vol. 23: 250–69. Edited by Jack Salzman. New York: Cambridge University Press.

Solie, Ruth, ed. 1993. *Musicology and Difference: Gender and Sexuality in Music Scholarship.* Berkeley: University of California Press.

Solomon, Maynard. 1987. "Charles Ives: Some Questions of Veracity." *Journal of the American Musicological Society* 40, no. 3 (Fall): 443–70.

Starr, Larry. 1992. *A Union of Diversities: Style in the Music of Charles Ives.* New York: Schirmer Books.

Stevenson, Robert M. 1970. *Protestant Church Music in America.* New York: Norton.

Stringham, Edwin J. 1921. "Ives Puzzles Critics with His Cubistic Sonata and 'Essays.'" *Rocky Mountain News,* Denver (July 31): 1, 17.

Swafford, Jan. 1996. *Charles Ives: A Life with Music.* New York: W.W. Norton.

———. n.d. "Charles Edward Ives." Available at http://www.charlesives.org/02bio .htm. Accessed December 8, 2005.

Taruskin, Richard. 2001. "Nationalism: 10. Tourist Nationalism; 11. Colonialist Nationalism; 14. Musical Geopolitics." In Grove Music Online. Ed. Laura Macy. Available at www.grovemusic.com. Accessed November 24, 2007.

Taylor, Robert W. 1905. *A Practical Treatise on Sexual Disorders of the Male and Female.* 3rd ed. New York: Lea Brothers.

Thomson, Virgil. [1970, 1971] 1981. "The Ives Case." *New York Review of Books* 14, no. 10 (May 21, 1970): 9–11. Reprinted in *American Music Since 1910.* New York: Rinehart and Winston, 1971, 22–30; and in *A Virgil Thomson Reader.* Boston: Houghton Mifflin, 1981, 460–67.

Tick, Judith. 1993. "Charles Ives and Gender Ideology." In *Musicology and Difference: Gender and Sexuality in Music Scholarship,* 125–47. Edited by Ruth Solie. Berkeley: University of California Press.

Tykwer, Tom, dir. 1999. *Run Lola Run (Lola rennt).* Sony Pictures Classics.

Vecoli, Rudolph J. 1996. "Ethnicity and Immigration." In *Encyclopedia of the United*

States in the Twentieth Century. Vol. 1: The American People, 161–65. Edited by Stanley I. Kutler. New York: Scribner.

Von Glahn, Denise: *see also* Cooney, Denise Von Glahn.

Von Glahn, Denise. 2003. *The Sounds of Place: Music and the American Cultural Landscape.* Boston: Northeastern University Press.

Walker, Ernest. 1921. "Review of *Second Pianoforte Sonata, 'Concord, Mass., 1840–1860'* and *Essays Before a Sonata,* by Charles Ives." *Music & Letters* 2, no. 3: 287–88.

Wallach, Laurence David. 1973. "The New England Education of Charles Ives." Ph.D. diss., Columbia University.

Warne, Frank Julian. 1916. *The Tide of Immigration.* New York: D. Appleton.

Watkins, Glenn. 2003. *Proof Through the Night: Music and the Great War.* Berkeley: University of California Press.

Wiecki, Ronald V. 1992. "Two Musical Idealists—Charles Ives and E. Robert Schmitz: A Friendship Reconsidered." *American Music* 10, no. 1 (Spring): 1–19.

Wooldridge, David. 1974. *From the Steeples and the Mountains.* New York: Alfred A. Knopf.

———. 1974. "The New Ives Biography: A Disagreement." In *High Fidelity/Musical America* 24, no. 12 (December): 18–20.

Wright, Robert E., and George David Smith. 2004. *Mutually Beneficial: The Guardian and Life Insurance in America.* New York: New York University Press.

Yale College Records, 1896–1900. Sterling Memorial Library Manuscripts and Archives, Yale University. New Haven.

Yale University School of Music Papers. Mss. 3. Irving S. Gilmore Music Library, Yale University. New Haven. Available at http://webtext.library.yale.edu/xml2html/music.ysm.nav.html. Accessed December 19, 2007.

Yellin, Victor Fell. 1990. *Chadwick: Yankee Composer.* Washington, D.C.: Smithsonian Institution Press.

Zangwill, Israel. 1908. *The Melting Pot: A Drama in Four Acts.* New York: Macmillan.

Index

GAYLE SHERWOOD MAGEE is an assistant professor of musicology at the University of Illinois at Urbana-Champaign. She is author of *Charles Ives: A Guide to Research.*

"Susanna," "Jeanie," and "The Old Folks at Home": The Songs of Stephen C. Foster from His Time to Ours (2d ed.)   *William W. Austin*

Songprints: The Musical Experience of Five Shoshone Women   *Judith Vander*

"Happy in the Service of the Lord": Afro-American Gospel Quartets in Memphis   *Kip Lornell*

Paul Hindemith in the United States   *Luther Noss*

"My Song Is My Weapon": People's Songs, American Communism, and the Politics of Culture, 1930–50   *Robbie Lieberman*

Chosen Voices: The Story of the American Cantorate   *Mark Slobin*

Theodore Thomas: America's Conductor and Builder of Orchestras, 1835–1905   *Ezra Schabas*

"The Whorehouse Bells Were Ringing" and Other Songs Cowboys Sing   *Guy Logsdon*

Crazeology: The Autobiography of a Chicago Jazzman   *Bud Freeman, as Told to Robert Wolf*

Discoursing Sweet Music: Brass Bands and Community Life in Turn-of-the-Century Pennsylvania   *Kenneth Kreitner*

Mormonism and Music: A History   *Michael Hicks*

Voices of the Jazz Age: Profiles of Eight Vintage Jazzmen   *Chip Deffaa*

Pickin' on Peachtree: A History of Country Music in Atlanta, Georgia   *Wayne W. Daniel*

Bitter Music: Collected Journals, Essays, Introductions, and Librettos   *Harry Partch; edited by Thomas McGeary*

Ethnic Music on Records: A Discography of Ethnic Recordings Produced in the United States, 1893 to 1942   *Richard K. Spottswood*

Downhome Blues Lyrics: An Anthology from the Post-World War II Era   *Jeff Todd Titon*

Ellington: The Early Years   *Mark Tucker*

Chicago Soul   *Robert Pruter*

That Half-Barbaric Twang: The Banjo in American Popular Culture   *Karen Linn*

Hot Man: The Life of Art Hodes   *Art Hodes and Chadwick Hansen*

The Erotic Muse: American Bawdy Songs (2d ed.)   *Ed Cray*

Barrio Rhythm: Mexican American Music in Los Angeles   *Steven Loza*

The Creation of Jazz: Music, Race, and Culture in Urban America   *Burton W. Peretti*

Charles Martin Loeffler: A Life Apart in Music   *Ellen Knight*

Club Date Musicians: Playing the New York Party Circuit   *Bruce A. MacLeod*

Opera on the Road: Traveling Opera Troupes in the United States, 1825–60   *Katherine K. Preston*

The Stonemans: An Appalachian Family and the Music That Shaped Their Lives   *Ivan M. Tribe*

Transforming Tradition: Folk Music Revivals Examined   *Edited by Neil V. Rosenberg*

The Crooked Stovepipe: Athapaskan Fiddle Music and Square Dancing in Northeast Alaska and Northwest Canada   *Craig Mishler*

Traveling the High Way Home: Ralph Stanley and the World of Traditional Bluegrass Music   *John Wright*